World Financial Orders

In *World Financial Orders*, Langley challenges the predominance of neo-liberalism as a mode of knowledge about contemporary world finance, and claims that it neglects the social and political bases as well as the malign consequences of change. He looks to the field of International Political Economy (IPE) to construct an alternative mode of knowledge, one that critically restores society and politics. An 'historical' approach to IPE is advanced that accounts for modern world finance since the seventeenth century as a succession of structurally distinct hierarchical social orders.

Comparative historical inquiry across modern world finance reveals the unique character of the contemporary order. This order combines new forms of credit practices, decentralised and de-territorial spatiality, change in the very nature of financial power, unprecedented multilateral governance arrangements and contradictions that threaten its own future.

This book will be of interest to those working in the field of IPE and to those scholars, researchers and students from across the social sciences who seek to challenge the common-sense, neo-liberal explanation of contemporary world finance.

Paul Langley is lecturer in International Politics at the University of Northumbria at Newcastle, UK. His research interests are in the field of International Political Economy with particular reference to globalisation, finance and the environment. His work has been published in a variety of journals including *New Political Economy* and *Review of International Political Economy*.

Routledge/RIPE Series in Global Political Economy

Series editors: Otto Holman, Marianne Marchand (*Research Centre for International Political Economy, University of Amsterdam*), Henk Overbeek (*Free University, Amsterdam*) and Marianne Franklin (*University of Amsterdam*)

This series, published in association with the *Review of International Political Economy*, provides a forum for current debates in International Political Economy. The series aims to cover all the central topics in IPE and to present innovative analyses of emerging topics. The titles in the series seek to transcend a state-centred discourse and focus on three broad themes:

- the nature of the forces driving globalisation forward
- resistance to globalisation
- the transformation of the world order.

The series comprises two strands:

The *RIPE Series in Global Political Economy* aims to address the needs of students and teachers, and the titles will be published in hardback and paperback. Titles include:

Transnational Classes and International Relations
Kees van der Pijl

Gender and Global Restructuring
Sightings, sites and resistances
Edited by Marianne H. Marchand and Anne Sisson Runyan

Global Political Economy
Contemporary theories
Edited by Ronen Palan

Ideologies of Globalization
Contending visions of a new world order
Mark Rupert

The Clash Within Civilisations
Coming to terms with cultural conflicts
Dieter Senghaas

Routledge/RIPE Studies in Global Political Economy is a forum for innovative new research intended for a high-level specialist readership, and the titles will be available in hardback only. Titles include:

1. Globalization and Governance*
Edited by Aseem Prakash and Jeffrey A. Hart

2. Nation-States and Money
The past, present and future of national currencies
Edited by Emily Gilbert and Eric Helleiner

3. The Global Political Economy of Intellectual Property Rights
The new enclosures?
Christopher May

4. Integrating Central Europe
EU expansion and Poland, Hungary and the Czech Republic
Otto Holman

5. Capitalist Restructuring, Globalisation and the Third Way
Lessons from the Swedish model
J. Magnus Ryner

6. Transnational Capitalism and the Struggle over European Integration
Bastiaan van Apeldoorn

7. World Financial Orders
An Historical International Political Economy
Paul Langley

* Also available in paperback

World Financial Orders

An Historical International Political Economy

Paul Langley

London and New York

First published 2002
by Routledge
11 New Fetter Lane, London EC4P 4EE

Simultaneously published in the USA and Canada
by Routledge
29 West 35th Street, New York, NY 10001

Routledge is an imprint of the Taylor & Francis Group

Typeset in Baskerville by M Rules
Printed and bound in Great Britain by
Biddles Ltd, Guildford and King's Lynn

British Library Cataloguing in Publication Data
A catalogue record for this book is available from the British Library

Library of Congress Cataloging in Publication Data
A catalog record for this book has been requested

ISBN 0–415–25574–0

Contents

Series editors' preface

In a world where political and economic well-being is more or less gauged by the vagaries of the Dow Jones Index (as shown on peak-time television news broadcasts), and political decision-making is increasingly inter-locked with breathless decisions made in world financial centres such as London, New York and Tokyo, Paul Langley's book, *World Financial Orders: An Historical International Political Economy* is appearing not a moment too soon. This exciting new research monograph in the *RIPE Series in Global Political Economy* builds on previous titles in the series such as Emily Gilbert and Eric Helleiner's edited volume, *Nation-States and Money*, and Christopher May's *Global Political Economy Intellectual Property Rights*. Like these, it takes a broad historical and critical perspective to the specific subject matter (national currencies and property rights as historically contestable).

This study of the rise and fall of the Dutch, British and American World Financial Orders and their respective World Financial Centres (Amsterdam, London, New York) over the last four hundred years is, in Langley's words, a 'call to history' in a century that has seen the demise of the post-Second World War 'American' Financial Order and the emergence of a more diffuse, albeit powerful, 'Global' Financial Order based in London, New York and, now, Tokyo. Langley's call to history allows for a fresh look at not only the continuities in the structures and mechanics (credit movements, financial regulation and liberalisation, multilateral governance agreements such as Bretton Woods) of past world financial orders but also at how and why the contemporary neo-liberal economic order differs from those of the past. Langley develops a distinct approach in which he combines the best of world-systems theory work in this area (Wallerstein and in particular Arrighi), the unique approaches of Susan Strange and of Saskia Sassen, and the work on world order by Robert Cox and like-minded scholars.

Thus, in *World Financial Orders* Langley plots how neo-liberal notions of what constitutes governance of financial markets, domestic and international monetary policies, and social relations are *historically embedded*. They are thereby contested and contestable as opposed to unquestionable. In this way, Langley's study of the rise and fall of these three discrete historical moments in the *longue durée* of western capitalism, as a 'world system' (broadly speaking) firmly demystifies the neo-liberal catch-cry of the 1980s that there is (and was) 'no alternative' but to liberalise financial markets and thereby disengage political and social forces and institutions from the 'big business' of where and how credit flows in and through different economies. But Langley also argues that the upshot, a neo-liberal World Financial Order that lurches from one financial crisis and its international repercussions (Mexico in the 1980s) to another (the Asian Crisis of the 1990s) has been underpinned by 'orthodox' (Liberal and Realist) International Political Economy frameworks that divorce political questions from economic ones, and social issues and power relations from both. Through a careful historical and theoretical reconstruction of the key issue areas of International Political Economy (states, markets, trade and finance and how to govern all these interactions), Langley shows that whilst today's World Financial Order may boast relative stability (where current credit practices are legitimated and London, New York and Tokyo share – rather then compete for – prominence) it is also 'crisis-ridden'. The reasons for this are not, in Langley's analysis, simply due to the rise and fall of US financial hegemony in the last part of the twentieth century. Far from it. Instead of offering a satisfactory framework for 'explaining why' these complexities occur, such 'orthodox IPE' frameworks perpetuate a 'problem-solving' approach that does not question basic assumptions. This leads to both an over-statement of the inevitability of market liberalisation and an under-estimation of possibilities for structural change in the world order and political organisation in national contexts. In this respect, Langley's concluding chapter is a particularly welcome addition to critical analyses of the contemporary world financial order to date, many of which are often resigned to its boom and bust dynamics and rely on crisis-management rather than a concerted effort to ensure long-term change.

For students of burgeoning IPE courses, especially those who are increasingly aware of the many methodological and philosophical differences *within* this (sub)discipline and how these relate to the classic meta-theoretical debates in International Relations theory, Paul Langley's study is a valuable contribution to understanding these differences as both historical events and intellectual 'meaning-making'. His ability to integrate a broad historical sweep (1600s to present-day) with the details of contemporary credit movements, changes in banking regulations, and the geographic and social particulars of the Netherlands, Britain and the USA in a sophisticated analysis of 'stability, crisis and governance in the contemporary world financial order' will appeal to both specialists and non-specialists alike. Along with his practical policy and regulatory suggestions, this book certainly lives up to Langley's project to show exactly why the understanding of 'the contemporary financial order does not lie in a simple focus on the . . . US state, but rather on changes in the very nature of financial power and developments in the wider world order'.

Otto Holman
Marianne Marchand
Henk Overbeek
Marianne Franklin

Acknowledgements

This book began its life in 1995 as a successful application for a UK Economic and Social Research Council research studentship. I have no doubt that the doctoral thesis upon which the book is based would not have been completed without this financial assistance, for which I am very grateful. I would also like to express my thanks to the University of Northumbria at Newcastle (UNN) for providing financial support for the revision and updating of the original thesis into its book form.

Several individuals and groups of people have assisted me in the realisation of *World Financial Orders*. The Department of Politics, University of Newcastle provided an enabling environment for doctoral study between 1995 and 1998. I would like to thank Ronen Palan, James Babb and, in particular, Randall Germain for their supervisory help. Randall's sharp wit, friendship and intellectual enthusiasm proved a constant source of strength. I would like to acknowledge the contribution of the members of Newcastle International Political Economy Working Group, especially Louise Amoore, Richard Dodgson, Barry Gills, Don Marshall and Iain Watson, to the formation of some of the ideas that find their expression in the following pages. The comments of Craig Murphy and Barry Gills during the examination of my doctoral thesis provided some very important insights for the subsequent development of *World Financial Orders*.

All the staff at the Sustainable Cities Research Institute, UNN encouraged me to maintain my interest in world finance during 1999 and 2000. Particular thanks are due to Mark Mawhinney and Mary Mellor for allowing me to pursue my research even though it did not necessarily sit well with the Institute's purpose. Judith Parks patiently assisted in formatting the final text and compiling the index.

Away from Newcastle, I am very grateful to the many bankers, economists and regulators from institutions in Frankfurt and the City of London who gave up their time during 1997 and 1998 to answer the questions of a political economist who often saw the world through very different eyes. Unfortunately, their wishes to remain anonymous prevent me from thanking them by name. I would also like to show appreciation to those participants at the British International Studies Association Annual Conferences in 1997 and 1998 and the International Studies Association Annual Convention in 1999 who commented on papers that I presented. While none of the papers are presented here in their original form, the comments made by Tim Sinclair and Robert O'Brien proved particularly useful.

More recently, the perceptive observations of two anonymous reviewers and the editorial team of the RIPE Series have been of considerable assistance. I would also like to thank Heidi Bagtazo, Grace McInnes, Craig Fowlie and Jennifer Lovel at Routledge for their guidance.

My gratitude to Louise Amoore, my partner in life, for her love, encouragement, patience and intellectual support during the completion of this book will always remain immeasurable.

Abbreviations

AMF	Asian Monetary Fund
BCCI	Bank of Credit and Commerce International
BIS	Bank of International Settlements
CD	certificate of deposit
CHIPS	Clearing House Interbank Payments System
COB	Commission des Bourses
COM	European Commission
CRP	City Research Project
ECB	European Central Bank
EPU	European Payments Union
EU	European Union
FDI	foreign direct investment
FSA	Financial Services Authority
FSF	Financial Stability Forum
GATS	General Agreement on Trade in Services
HIPCs	heavily indebted poor countries
HST	hegemonic stability theory
IBF	International Banking Facility
IET	Interest Equalisation Tax
IMF	International Monetary Fund
IOSCO	International Organisation of Securities Commissions
IPE	International Political Economy
IR	International Relations
ISI	Import Substitution Industrialisation
LETS	Local Economic Trading Systems
LSE	London Stock Exchange
LTCM	Long Term Capital Management
MCP	Mandatory Control Program
MNC	multinational corporation
MOUs	Memoranda of Understanding
NAFTA	North American Free Trade Agreement
NASDAQ	National Association of Securities Dealers' Automated Quotation System

NGO	non-governmental organisation
NYSE	New York Stock Exchange
OECD	Organisation for Economic Co-operation and Development
OEEC	Organisation for European Economic Co-operation
OFC	offshore financial centre
PIER	politics of international economic relations
ROSC	Report on the Observance of Standards and Codes
SEAQ	Stock Exchange Automated Quotation
SEC	Securities and Exchange Commission
T-bond	United States Treasury bond
TOM	Tokyo Offshore Market
TSE	Tokyo Stock Exchange
VCRP	Voluntary Credit Restraint Program
WFC	world financial centre
WTO	World Trade Organisation

Introduction

Apprehending world finance

> The Stock Exchange is chiefly attended by persons who are unremittingly attentive to their business, and are well acquainted with its details; but there are very few in number who have much knowledge of political economy, and consequently they pay little attention to finance, as a subject of science. They consider more, the immediate effect of passing events, rather than their distant consequences.
>
> (David Ricardo 1814, in Kynaston 1994: 18)

World finance today, as with the London Stock Exchange of David Ricardo's time, is dominated by financiers whose nervous physical energies are focused upon daily events. News of profit warnings, changing credit ratings, share offers, mergers and acquisitions is reflected in the fluctuating market price of one financial instrument or another with 'immediate effect'. Yet, as the wave of financial chaos that spread from Asia through Latin America and Eastern Europe during the last years of the 1990s once again starkly illustrated, world finance can have wide-reaching social consequences that are far from benign. Ephemeral preoccupations with daily events clearly become inadequate when world finance has 'distant consequences' of such magnitude. Knowledge of world finance from 'political economy' becomes indispensable if we are to understand its social and political significance and move towards some form of progressive action to address its deleterious consequences.

Ricardo's call for a political economy of world finance is not, however, as straightforward as it might appear. We live in a period characterised not only by volatile daily shifts in market prices but by a structural transformation in world finance. As with so many other areas of social life, this structural change is often captured under the rubric of 'globalisation'. International organisations, national governments and the financial press all tend to suggest that contemporary world financial restructuring is marked by the unprecedented emergence of a genuinely integrated, twenty-four hour global marketplace – that is, so-called 'global finance'. Meanwhile, academic interventions have either reinforced or cast doubt upon the accuracy of this reading of change. For instance, challenges have been made to the assumptions that markets for all wholesale financial instruments are genuinely global and that today's world financial markets have become more integrated than those of the late nineteenth century (Hirst and Thompson 1996; Watson 1999). In developing a political economy of contemporary world finance, then, it is necessary to confront the uncertain structural transformation that may be leading to a reworking of the social and political significance of world finance.

The construction of a political economy of contemporary world finance encounters an additional problematic alongside the need to address restructuring. The preoccupation of financiers with daily events is no accident, but at once reflects and contributes to neo-liberal political economy as the prevailing mode of knowledge of world finance.[1] Our attempts to comprehend contemporary world finance are, by and large, strait-jacketed by neo-liberal political economy. At its roots, neo-liberalism combines the classical liberal assumption that economy is a distinct set of market relations separable from politics and society with the neo-classical liberal belief that the economic behaviour of *Homo economicus* is rational and utility maximising. 'Economy' and 'market' tend to be equated and used interchangeably in common-sense parlance, and the combination of economy as separable realm with economy as mode of behaviour is mutually reinforcing (Langley and Mellor, 2002). Perhaps most significantly, the market economy takes on a naturalised, trans-historical and universal quality, pushing inexorably across space and enduring throughout time (Williams 1999). Empiricist epistemology and positivist methodology provide the meta-theoretical underpinnings that legitimate neo-liberal political economy,[2] enabling the exclusionary production of knowledge about economy that serves to 'fix' the common sense.[3] In particular, ontological assumptions of economy as a rational mode of behaviour are both predicated on and reinforced by the individualist methodology of positivism (Murphy and Tooze 1991b). Such is the heady, circularly reinforcing combination of ontology, epistemology and methodology in neo-liberal political economy that Hodgson (1994) and Fine (1999) see contemporary economics as 'colonising' other branches of the social sciences. Not only does economy as a mode of rational behaviour become applied to the study of socio-economic life but, with the development of rational choice theory, it tends to come to frame analysis of all aspects of social and political life. The primacy of rational economic motives is seen as taking precedence over other conflicting and transient motivations such as emotions, attachments and desires. In terms of world finance, market relations are viewed as ensuring that rational responses to daily events become expressed as price fluctuations.

Once the contemporary ascendancy of neo-liberal political economy in the framing of understandings of world finance is recognised, the ideological connotations of globalisation begin to be revealed. Neo-liberalism's trans-historical and teleological reading of restructuring is extended through the use of globalisation as an arresting metaphor for change (Amoore *et al.* 1997). The emergence of a twenty-four hour global marketplace for finance is effectively naturalised, cast as the benign and inevitable result of the expansionary rational logic of the market mechanism and carried forward by breakthroughs in information and telecommunications technologies. The structural transformation of world finance to realise 'global finance' is taken as a given. The practices and policies of financiers, economists, politicians and societies begin from the assumption that 'globalisation is . . .', undertaking rational responses to the new reality. Under the predominant neo-liberal mode of knowledge, shifting our concerns away from 'the immediate effect of passing events' is problematic as the legitimate consideration of the social and political dynamics of world finance is rendered fractious.

It is against this background of an uncertain structural transformation in world finance and the predominance of a restrictive and exclusionary mode of knowledge of transformation that the purpose of this book should be seen. Practices and policies informed by explanations of world finance that naturalise change, reify the market and fail to address the damaging consequences of contemporary world finance will continue to predominate unless alternative modes of knowledge are articulated. Once in place, alternative modes of knowledge may lead to contests over the concepts used to account for contemporary world finance. Such 'conceptual contestation' (Rosow 1994: 472) may (re)socialise and (re)politicise the practices, structures and institutions of world finance. The neo-liberal façade of globalisation is questioned once world finance is recognised to be historically constructed and resting on hierarchical social and power relations. In turn, the emancipatory and transformative potential of an alternative mode of knowledge is closely related to its capacity to highlight the dialectical possibilities present in restructuring, that is, the way in which transformation generates contradictions and new configurations of social and political forces capable of mounting effective movements for progressive change. In moving beyond a preoccupation with daily events and prices to a political economy of world finance that works towards forestalling the worst eventualities of restructuring, alternatives to the neo-liberal mode of knowledge are an essential starting point.

IPE and world finance

Dissatisfaction with the course taken by contemporary world financial restructuring and the neo-liberal mode of knowledge that has framed explanations of restructuring is reasonably well spread. What is less apparent, however, is on what basis an alternative mode of knowledge of world finance may be constructed. Clearly, we must look beyond the mainstream neo-liberal economists, financiers and journalists who currently act as the 'gatekeepers' (Cox 1992a/1996: 178) of knowledge of world finance. The mode of knowledge developed here is at once broadly situated within, and built upon an engagement with, International Political Economy (IPE). IPE is 'an area of investigation, a particular range of questions, and a series of assumptions about the nature of the international "system" and how we understand this "system"' (Tooze 1984: 2). The roots of the rebirth of interest in IPE as a field of inquiry lie in the crisis of the discipline of International Relations (IR) in the early 1970s.[4] The breakdown of the world economy during this period could not be accounted for within IR's research agenda, which was locked into Cold War security concerns. At the same time, international economists continued to pay little attention to international politics in their efforts to explain the world economy's predicament. IPE re-emerged to 'fill the gap' (Krasner 1996: 109) that resulted from this situation of 'mutual neglect' (Strange 1970) in international studies.

Given that the collapse of the Bretton Woods fixed-exchange arrangements between 1971 and 1973 was a key feature of the breakdown of the world economy, IPE has become established as a central avenue for inquiry into contemporary world money and finance. In practical terms IPE offers the fertile soil of an existing body of scholarship from which to begin to account for contemporary world finance. Furthermore, ontological, epistemological and theoretical debates within IPE are particularly informative as we seek to construct an alternative mode of knowledge of world finance from robust foundations. The roots of these debates lie in the belief shared by some scholars that a re-emergent IPE should do more than simply address the situation of mutual neglect between IR and international economics, instead striving for a mode of knowledge capable of casting light on 'a realistic strategy for gaining some control over the process of structural transformation' (Cox 1981: 64). While IPE is widely accepted as a field of inquiry and set of questions, such debates create considerable disagreement among IPE scholars as to what questions should be posed and what assumptions should be made. These debates, in turn, have resonated across inquiry in IPE into world finance. For our purposes, the struggle of what has been labelled 'new IPE' to establish itself in the face of the predominant 'orthodox IPE' is particularly informative (Murphy and Tooze 1991a; Payne and Gamble 1996: 3–10; Hay and Marsh 1999; Palan 2000). It is the way that ontology, epistemology and theory come together for each of these loose groupings that gives orthodox and new IPE their respective standings as conflicting modes of knowledge within the field. Given that orthodox IPE shares much of its ontology and epistemology with neo-liberal political economy, the critique of these features of orthodox IPE offered by new IPE supplies a starting point from which to begin to generate an alternative mode of knowledge capable of apprehending world finance.

Orthodox IPE and world finance

The ontology of orthodox IPE is derived from neo-liberal political economy. This suggests that the international economy is the cumulative product of exchange between national communities made up of rational individuals. When combined with the state-centric and formalist understanding of politics received from the theories of realism and liberalism ascendant within IR, the ontology of orthodox IPE tends to be expressed as the 'politics of international economic relations' (PIER) (Spero 1977; Strange 1988: 12). The central object for inquiry becomes the manner in which the rise and fall of state power, the politics of national economic policy-making and international economic agreements impinge upon the exchange (i.e. trade) relations between national economies (cf. Cohen 1990). Although they are considered together, politics and economics or states and markets remain largely opposed forms of social organisation (Gilpin 1987: 4). In short, orthodox

IPE is a science of and for the state in the context of the international exchange economy.

In epistemological terms, orthodox IPE tends to share with neo-liberalism a combination of empiricist epistemology and positivist methodology. The legitimacy of the knowledge created by orthodox IPE is 'primarily and initially derived from mainstream economics' (Murphy and Tooze 1991b: 17). Subject and object are separated in inquiry so that the truth of a theoretical statement is determined by how well it corresponds to an objective material reality (Krasner 1996: 108–9). Orthodox IPE has not, of course, remained isolated from epistemological debates taking place across the social sciences. However, even when confronted by the importance of subjective ideas as suggested in the hugely influential work of Kuhn (1962/1970), orthodox IPE tends to place ideas purely in the subjective realm and divorced from objective reality (Murphy and Tooze 1991b: 22–3). The result is endless debates between variants of realism and liberalism as the main theories that cannot be held to be wrong other than in terms of their capacity to reveal 'truth' through testable hypotheses. Under the individualism of positivist methodology and informed by neo-liberal assumptions of utility maximisation, the object of inquiry is explained in terms of the rational and egoistic action and interaction of 'individual' agents (Krasner 1994: 14). Where agents are recognised as acting in a structural context, for instance research that has built on the prominent work of Waltz (1979), structures become theoretically posited unchanging laws. Framed by the theories of orthodox IPE, the 'individual' agents considered are usually either states, in line with realism, or a wide range of institutional actors, in line with liberal institutionalism.

Following from its ontological and epistemological foundations, orthodox IPE has yielded a fairly distinct mode of knowledge of world money and finance. The principal concern for orthodox IPE has been with understanding the creation and maintenance of stable international monetary relations (Block 1977; Cohen 1977; Calleo 1982; Eichengreen 1990). The interest in international monetary relations follows from the neo-liberal privileging of exchange, as monetary arrangements are defined as 'the sum of all the devices by which nations organize their international economic relations' (Block 1977: 1). In this sense, 'international money matters' because stable international monetary relations form 'the critical nexus' which facilitates international exchange relations (Gilpin 1987: 118). Informed by a positivist search for observable laws and by neo-classical economics, international monetary stability tends to be held by orthodox IPE to hinge upon the provision of certain key prerequisites as 'public goods'. These include a supply of adequate liquidity for balance-of-payments financing, an adjustment mechanism with appropriate levels of capital mobility to resolve national balance-of-payments disequilibria, and confidence in the reserve currency or currencies.

In order to explain the availability or otherwise of international monetary stability, orthodox IPE has been dominated by the theory of hegemonic stability theory (HST). The roots of HST clearly lie in the seminal analysis of the Great Depression of the 1930s by economist Charles Kindleberger (1973). Kindleberger argued that only a hegemonic state, dominant in terms of relative wealth and power, could provide the public goods necessary for international monetary stability. The monetary instability of the Depression reflected, on the one hand, the decline of British hegemony, and on the other, the unwillingness of the rising US state to take the lead in the provision of the key prerequisites for the smooth functioning of international monetary arrangements. Both liberal and realist versions of orthodox IPE have subsequently converged around HST, arriving at the same set of conclusions. Liberal orthodox IPE, informed by neo-classical economics, has posited the necessity of the hegemonic state as a consequence of the inherent failure of the market to provide public goods (cf. Snidal 1985; Caporaso 1987). Realist orthodox IPE has, meanwhile, posited the necessity of the hegemonic state as a consequence of the disruption to international monetary relations caused by the anarchical international system of states (cf. Walter 1993). For both liberal and realist orthodox IPE the instability of contemporary international monetary relations results from the decline of US hegemony. Increased international co-operation and co-ordination of national monetary policies becomes essential in bringing about greater stability (Goodman 1992; Webb 1995).

In our terms, the utility of orthodox IPE lies in the raising of questions as to the hierarchical patterns of domination and subordination in world finance. Under the influence of HST, however, the questioning of how these patterns are reflected in the authority and roles of actors in the organisation of world finance is limited by state-centricism. Orthodox IPE continues to see politics and economics (read states and markets) as opposed forms of social organisation in world money and finance, regardless of historical context. The broader utility of orthodox IPE for our purposes is also seriously flawed in other ways.

First, the neo-liberal ontology of orthodox IPE prompts both a particular conception of money and finance and a privileging of international monetary concerns at the expense of world finance. Where world finance is considered by orthodox IPE scholars, the object of inquiry is also framed in neo-liberal terms. As such, the focus becomes international capital flows that function 'to transfer accumulated capital to where the marginal rate of return is highest' (Gilpin 1987: 306) and the implications of these for state policy-makers and associated domestic interest groups (e.g. Goodman and Pauly 1993; Andrews 1994; Kapstein 1994; Cohen 1996; Dombrowski 1998). The wide range of work from across the social sciences that casts serious doubt on neo-liberal conceptions of money and finance is left to one side by orthodox IPE.

Second, for realist orthodox IPE in particular, instability in world money and finance is assumed to result from disruptions generated by the conflicting interests of rational utility maximising states. While orthodox IPE has drawn on Kindleberger's *The World in Depression* in order to develop HST, it has largely failed to take seriously his other observations about the inherent instability and crisis tendencies of finance (Kindleberger 1978). Indeed, orthodox IPE has neglected to engage with a whole body of work by economists that, from the margins of their discipline, highlights the centrality of irrational collective expectations to inherent financial instability (cf. Heisler 1994; Krugman 1995; Chancellor 2000; Saber 1999).

Finally, given its deep roots in empiricist epistemology and positivist methodology, orthodox IPE inquiry into world finance is guided by what Robert Cox (1981/1996) terms a 'problem-solving' orientation. The general aim of inquiry is to make existing 'relationships and institutions work smoothly by dealing with particular sources of trouble', contrasting sharply with 'critical theory' that 'is directed toward an appraisal of the very framework for action, or problematic, which problem-solving theory accepts as its parameters' (Cox 1981/1996: 88).[5] In short, orthodox IPE seeks to 'explain how . . .' rather than 'understand why . . .' in world finance (cf. Hollis and Smith 1990). At worst, an orthodox IPE of contemporary world finance acts as an adjunct to the predominant neo-liberal mode of knowledge, suggesting that instability can be 'solved' by increased international co-operation in the absence of a single hegemonic state.

New IPE and world finance

Accounts of world finance in the so-called new IPE claim to have been built upon alternative ontological, epistemological and theoretical foundations. In ontological terms, new IPE rejects neo-liberal understandings of its subject matter. For new IPE, the central subject matter of IPE is social, and both greater than its national parts and subject to considerable change over time. New IPE has expressed this variously through concerns with, for instance, 'global political economy' (Gill and Law 1988; Palan 2000), 'world-economy' (Germain 1997) and 'world orders' (Cox 1987). While remaining diverse in the concepts used, new IPE scholars are, in the main, ontologically united by a belief in the significance of the transnational nature of the enterprises, social movements, social forces, institutions and markets that they wish to study (Strange 1988: 21). As such, new IPE is also distinguished from comparative political economy within the tradition of political economy. Broadly defined, while comparative political economy is concerned with change 'within' state-societies that is largely separate from the 'outside' world, new IPE asserts the interconnectedness of domestic and international alongside that of politics and economics (Tooze 1984).

In epistemological terms, new IPE has embraced a wide range of post-positivist epistemologies that are all willing to recognise the essential subjectivity of the social sciences and enable critical theory to impinge on inquiry (Murphy and Tooze 1991a: 6). As Payne and Gamble (1996: 6–7) note, the work of Robert Cox (1981/1996) proved especially significant in liberating new IPE from the confines of empiricist epistemology and positivist methodology. As a consequence, there is an acceptance among new IPE scholars that inquiry is open to claims and counter-claims, and that such debate is part of the collective processes of knowledge construction that have important political implications for society at large. By extension, and in opposition to the individualism of positivist methodology, new IPE has sought to engage with debates across the social sciences that have addressed the inseparability of structure-agency (e.g. Cerny 1990; Jones 1995). Here, structures become recognised as changing constraints and opportunities expressed through agency. This has, in turn, led new IPE to question the rationality of actors in the course of social change (Palan 2000). Stability and order are not simply explained in terms of utility maximising actors, but by structurally contingent forms of alliances and identities.

In terms of apprehending world finance, the ontologies of new IPE have informed alternatives to orthodox IPE at four interrelated levels. The pioneering work of the late Susan Strange (1986, 1988, 1990, 1998a) has proved particularly influential in this regard. First, built upon an engagement with work across the social sciences that has challenged neo-liberal conceptions of money and finance, new IPE has stressed that the consequences of the organisation of world money and finance are felt far beyond the international exchange economy. Second, new IPE accounts of world finance have tended to assert that contemporary international monetary relations can only be apprehended in the context of world finance in which transnational relationships predominate (Cerny 1993a; Underhill 1997a). In short, 'structural change' in world finance realises 'paradigmatic muddle' for orthodox IPE (Cerny 1994a; cf. Cohen 1996: 295–6). Third, given that 'separate national currencies themselves are increasingly inextricably locked into wider financial trends and structures' (Cerny 1994a: 591), it follows that the focus for inquiry should not be on 'international money' narrowly defined as the determination of currency values and the system used to exchange currencies. Instead, the first-order focus of new IPE accounts has been upon 'the field of finance', that is, 'the system by which credit is created, bought and sold and by which the direction and use of capital is determined' (Strange 1990: 259). Fourth, some new IPE scholars have critiqued the explanatory power of orthodox IPE in apprehending world finance prior to the contemporary era (Walter 1993; Germain 1997). The organisation of world money and finance is comparable to 'two trains running on parallel historical tracks . . . the progress of neither can be understood without the other' (Strange 1994: 49–50). World financial relationships have existed and impinged upon international monetary relations for centuries and, therefore, the mode of knowledge represented by orthodox IPE is rejected for apprehending both past and present.

In theoretical terms, new IPE has sought to challenge the theoretical closure that results from retaining close links to IR and mainstream neo-liberal political economy. As with its ontological and epistemological bases, new IPE seeks to retain an essential 'openness' to cross-disciplinary theoretical insights (Strange 1984). Such is this openness that new IPE has also been labelled 'heterodox IPE' (RIPE Editors 1994). New IPE remains, however, united in its commitment to what could be termed 'truly integrated political-economy' (Palan 2000: 3). New IPE shares with orthodox IPE a belief in the inseparability of politics and economics, but nevertheless rejects the assumption of orthodox IPE that politics and economics are necessarily opposed forms of social organisation. New IPE recognises politics and economics to be united as part of the same processes of social and historical change. This has been enabled by recourse to Marxist and institutionalist traditions of political economy in particular, but also to feminist and constructivist approaches. For new IPE, then, 'politics' is not limited to the formal politics of state institutions, and 'economics' is not limited to the marketised relationships of exchange.

Stemming from a theoretical commitment to a truly integrated political economy, new IPE accounts of world finance have been largely shaped by concerns with the restructuring of interrelationships between states and markets in the organisation of world finance. While rejecting HST, states and markets approaches have tended to concur with the orthodox IPE view that the foundations of contemporary world finance are largely a formal political creation. Market and technological forces of change are held as significant, but states, as the principal aggregations of political power, constitute the 'bottom line' in determining the nature of market structures (Strange 1986; Helleiner 1994). The key distinction from orthodox IPE is, however, that states and markets are recognised as necessarily socially and politically embedded (Underhill 1991). As such, while debate in orthodox IPE centres on 'the role of markets versus the role of governments in the management of international capital' (Cohen 1996: 280), for new IPE 'markets and politics are not opposing principles' in world finance (Underhill 1997a: 3). Instability in world finance tends to be held to result from the inability of existing political arrangements both to prevent inherent speculative excess in financial markets and to ensure that the credit needs of society are met in a satisfactory manner (Strange 1986).

Against this theoretical backdrop, research has focused on the coexistence and changing balance of relative state and market authority in contemporary world finance. New governance arrangements have been identified that incorporate a range of state, inter-state and non-state institutions in a complex melding of state and market authority (Porter 1993; Sinclair 1994a; Underhill 1997b; Germain 2000). Furthermore, some new IPE scholars have begun to disaggregate 'states' and 'markets' as analytical categories to reveal their various and changing social and institutional bases. Focuses for inquiry become the actual practices of credit creation themselves and the public and private institutions of finance through which they are organised. For instance, Porter (1993) has linked contemporary changes in the organisation of credit practices through market institutions to changes in regulatory practices organised through civil, state, inter-state and transnational institutions. Not dissimilarly, Germain (1997) has focused on the changing roles of public and private monetary agents within institutionalised credit networks. For Germain (1997), it is these credit networks, and in particular the way in which they come together in principal financial centres, which form the basis of the international organisation of credit. Disaggregating states and markets in this way means that the social and power relations which underlie the organisation of world finance can be shown to take a wide range of institutional forms across different periods, and be related to the changing nature of credit practices themselves.

Outline of the book

The prospects of new IPE as a foundation from which to build a robust alternative to the predominant neo-liberal mode of knowledge of contemporary world finance appear good. This is largely a consequence of new IPE scholars' efforts to delineate their inquiries from orthodox IPE and, in the process, to reject the ontological and epistemological bases that orthodox IPE shares with neo-liberalism. To this end, new IPE has benefited greatly from its openness to debates underway across the social sciences. However, the openness of new IPE has itself led to important ontological, epistemological and theoretical variations across the work of new IPE scholars. As a consequence, the development of a new IPE of world finance requires a degree of self-reflection to justify the approach taken in the course of inquiry. This book, then, has a secondary but important purpose – to move in support of a recent historical turn in new IPE to develop what is termed an 'Historical International Political Economy'.

Part I comprises two short chapters that, taken together, outline an Historical IPE approach and develop this approach in order to facilitate inquiry into world finance. Chapter 1 argues that new IPE should look to history as an anchor from which to construct knowledge of the international political economy. Starting from an ontology of historicity and recognising its epistemological and methodological implications, an Historical IPE approach is characterised by a concern with structured social practices, social change, social space, social time and social orders as the principal categories for inquiry. Each category is rounded out theoretically with reference to the work of new IPE scholars and social scientists more broadly. Chapter 2 develops the principal categories of an Historical IPE approach for the study of world finance. The focus for inquiry becomes the changing organisation of modern world credit practices since the seventeenth century in the context of the structures of power and governance of successive social orders, that is, world financial orders. While grounded in an awareness of the continuities of modern world finance, comparative historical study of successive financial orders stresses structural change from one order to another. World financial centres are cast as the key social spaces in world finance, where world credit practices, power and governance are centralised. Patterns of centralisation and decentralisation across world financial centres that reflect the shifting fortunes of ascendant and descendent social forces are posited to be decisive in the making and reproduction of world financial orders.

Part II commences our concrete study of modern world finance, beginning in Chapter 3 with the Amsterdam-centred Dutch financial order (1600–1815) and the London-centred British financial order (1815–1931). During both orders, world credit practices displayed a uni-polar spatiality, firmly centralised in Amsterdam and then London as the world financial centres of their day. The social forces of Amsterdam and London, largely as a consequence of favourable power relations but also due to structures in the wider world order that were conducive to their interests, were pivotal to the making of the Dutch and British financial orders. The growing power of London's social forces was also critical to the unravelling of the Dutch financial order. Furthermore, both Amsterdam and London were the key complexes of governance in their respective orders, forging the organisational principles and providing the formal institutionalised authority necessary for relative stability and reproduction. However, an important structural discontinuity marked the transition from the Dutch to the British financial order. The rise of London rested on the consolidation of the British national economy and ensured an increasing role for public institutions in the governance of world credit practices.

Chapter 4 addresses the unravelling of the British financial order and the associated rise of the New York-centred American financial order (1931–1974). Just as the ascent of London formed an essential dynamic in the unravelling of the Dutch order, the rise of New York in the wake of the Great War ruptured the authority of London's social forces in the reproduction of the post-1918 British order. Relative stability and broad-based agreement over the organisational principles that governed the American order was slow to emerge, only becoming established after the Marshall Plan of 1947. The American financial order was subsequently characterised by three principal structural differences from the orders that had preceded it. First, the significance of New York-centred world credit practices was diluted by the preponderance of long-term inter-governmental and corporate capital outflows emanating from the US political economy. Second, in terms of the making of the order, New York's social forces occupied a secondary position as accord was forged by industrialists, organised labour and state managers around organisational principles that promoted free trade and exchange rate stability at the expense of financial interests. Third, as national economies became consolidated further, US state institutions and US-dominated inter-state institutions played the vital roles in the formal governance and reproduction of the order. New York's standing as a complex of governance was subordinated amid a state-based structure of financial governance.

Informed by the historical inquiry of Part II, Part III moves to reflect upon the contemporary world financial order (1974 to the present). Chapter 5 begins with an account of the unravelling of the American financial order. As with the unravelling of the Dutch and British orders, the gradual demise of the New York-centred American order was associated with decentralisation and, in particular, the rise of London. What marked the unravelling of the American order, however, is that the ascending world financial centre was not underpinned by a prominent geographical shift in power relations. Rather, with the acquiescence of US and British state managers and support from New York's social forces, the rise of London rested on its reinvention as an offshore space.

In the wake of the unravelling of the American order, contemporary world credit practices have undergone a structural transformation that is usually captured under the notion of 'global finance'. While rejecting the efficacy of the global finance explanation, Chapter 5 emphasises the conjunctural distinctiveness of contemporary practices in terms of the credit instruments employed, patterns of institutionalisation, speculative excess and spatiality. The distinguishing spatiality of contemporary practices is shown to combine two elements. First, the asymmetrical decentralisation of practices between New York, London and Tokyo as a 'triad' of world financial centres appears, for the first time in modern world finance, as more than a temporary arrangement associated with the unravelling of one order and the rise of another. Second, the consolidation of offshore as a space of world credit practices contributes to the distortion of the centralisation–decentralisation–(re)centralisation dynamic that, prior to the current era, has characterised modern world finance.

Chapter 6 accounts for the distinctive organisation of today's world credit practices in terms of the power relations that have framed the making of the contemporary world financial order. Several important aspects of structural discontinuity in the making of the contemporary financial order are highlighted. Unlike previous world financial orders, the ascending social forces of a newly emergent world financial centre have not been to the fore in shaping the contours of the contemporary order. Rather, reflecting asymmetrical power relations and conditions in the wider world order, the social forces of long-established New York and London and not those of recently ascendant Tokyo have been at the forefront in framing the possible organisation of credit practices. Underlying this structural discontinuity is a change in the very nature of power relations in world finance. The emergence of offshore space has transformed the patterns of material power that previously found expression in the successive rise of national financial centres to world status. As contemporary power relations become less hierarchical, world credit practices become more decentralised. Furthermore, a US-initiated competitive liberalisation and deregulation dynamic has been crucial to the changing form of contemporary credit practices and their institutionalisation. In the wider world order, the politics of economic slowdown, inter-state struggles for market shares and the continued importance of the US to world security and consumption have intensified competitive pressures and severely constrained the ability of states and social forces to resist this dynamic.

As with our inquiry into the Dutch, British and American financial orders, Chapter 7 asks whether the contemporary financial order is characterised by relative social and political stability and, if so, attempts to identify those organisational principles and institutions that serve to govern and reproduce the order. While no single world financial centre stands as a complex of governance as has been the case in previous world financial orders, this has not significantly hampered the forging of relative stability in the contemporary order. Based upon neo-liberal organisational principles of governance, the social forces of New York and London have been pivotal in forging acceptance of power relations and the organisation of credit practices in which they are manifest as legitimate. Their epistemic authority in this regard has resulted largely from the perceived competitive success of Anglo-American market institutions and the associated malaise of Japanese market networks. Relative stability in the contemporary financial order does, however, remain narrow in terms of the coalition of state and societal forces involved. Stability extends in a limited fashion across a transnational financial community of interests.

The forging of relative stability around the neo-liberal discourse of governance has, not surprisingly, entailed an explanation of the major financial crises that have plagued the contemporary financial order. Under this orthodoxy, crises are cast as resulting not from inherent features of world finance, but from misguided domestic economic policy choices and institutional arrangements that do not follow from the rationality of world credit practices. By contrast, Chapter 7 puts forward an understanding of these major crises that grounds them in speculative shifts in subjective market sentiment that are a structural feature of contemporary world finance.

In terms of the institutions of contemporary financial governance, attention is drawn to the historically unparalleled developments that are termed 'transnational multilateralism'. A fragmentation in the formal governance of world credit practices that might have been expected to accompany decentralisation between the triad of London, New York and Tokyo has been offset by the transnationalisation of hierarchical market institutional networks. Interdependent with this transnationalisation have been complex multilateral initiatives in regulation and crisis management, initiatives recently further entrenched by efforts to further the so-called 'new international financial architecture'. Contemporary complex multilateralism is broader in scope and institutionalised to a greater extent than the *ad hoc* inter-state co-operation that contributed to the governance of previous marketised world financial orders. Overall it is suggested that, as currently constituted, the contemporary financial order is fragile and beset with contradictions and tensions that the existing structure of governance serves only to perpetuate.

In the Conclusion, the book returns full-circle to the purposes of inquiry that have been laid out in this Introduction. Rather than 'closing out' inquiry by returning to the main chapters and repeating the arguments made, the Conclusion reflects upon the 'opening up' of political possibilities in the contemporary financial order. In line with the understanding of change in world finance that has been developed throughout, consideration is given to the prospects of progressive collective action that seeks to address the far from benign social consequences of contemporary world finance.

Notes

1 The notion of different 'modes of knowledge' is taken from Cox (1985/1996: 51). The existence of different modes of knowledge is a recognition that different understandings are built upon different ontological, epistemological and theoretical grounds.
2 Following Smith (1996: 14–18), 'positivism' is recognised as having three main chronological variants. First, that developed by Auguste Comte in the early nineteenth century as a project of applying the methods of the natural sciences to society in the search for causal laws to explain phenomena. Second, that of 'logical positivism', which emerged in the 1920s as the starkest form of positivism and denied all knowledge that was not scientifically observable. Third, the form of positivism that has been dominant in the social sciences over the last fifty years. Associated with the work of Hempel and Popper, it combines deductive logic, empirical verification to find the truth, the separation of theory and observation, and the belief that causation is the result of relationships between observed events. As such, positivism becomes understood as 'a methodological view that combines naturalism (in either its strong (ontological and methodological) or its weak (methodological) sense), and a belief in regularities. It is licensed by a strict empiricist epistemology itself committed to an objectivism about the relationship between theory and evidence . . . which grounds our knowledge of the world in justification by (ultimately brute) experience and thereby licensing methodology and ontology in so far as they are empirically warranted' (Smith 1996: 17).
3 On the exclusionary dynamics of epistemology in the sense of determining what exists as knowable, see Tooze and Murphy (1996) and MacLean (2000).
4 Clearly, however, the intellectual and historical roots of IPE stretch back to the seventeenth and eighteenth centuries, to the debates over national development and wealth creation, the division of labour and comparative advantage initiated by the mercantilists and carried through by Adam Smith, Karl Marx and Friedrich List among others.

5 Problem-solving and critical theory are not mutually exclusive, but can lend themselves to addressing different concerns within the overall process of critical inquiry. Problem-solving theory lends itself to limited spheres of action 'which are amenable to relatively close and precise examination' (Cox 1981/1996: 88). Critical theory leads to consideration of 'a larger picture of the whole of which the initially contemplated part is just one component, and seeks to understand the processes of change in which both parts and whole are involved' (Cox 1981/1996: 89).

Part I

World finance

Towards an Historical International Political Economy

1 An Historical International Political Economy

Any attempt to apprehend contemporary world finance encounters not only significant structural changes that cannot easily be captured, but also the predominance of neo-liberal political economy in framing our knowledge of world finance. Alternatives to the neo-liberal mode of knowledge of world finance are a necessary first step towards forestalling the worst eventualities of the current structural transformation. In the Introduction it was suggested that the field of IPE offered a promising avenue for inquiry in the light of this problematic. IPE offers the practical benefit of a strong body of existing scholarship concerned with world finance. Furthermore, given the close association of orthodox IPE with neo-liberal political economy, the critique of orthodox IPE by the new IPE provides a valuable starting point from which to begin to construct an alternative mode of knowledge of world finance. Given considerable debates among new IPE scholars as to the ontological, epistemological and theoretical bases of inquiry, this chapter argues that the new IPE should look to history as an anchor capable of providing the field with robust foundations.

IPE and the 'call to history'

The Historical IPE approach outlined here supports an existing 'call to history' among new IPE scholars. Two related threads of this appeal to take history seriously in IPE are distinguishable. First, a call has been made to historicise the field of IPE. Here, 'Historicizing IPE means seeing the present as a set of social practices situated in time and space', creating an IPE which is 'deeply sensitive to the influences of context on issues examined' (Amin and Palan 1996: 212). 'Historicism' in this sense reflects Mandelbaum's classic description of historicism as:

> the belief that an adequate understanding of the nature of any phenomenon and an adequate assessment of its value are to be gained by considering it in terms of the place it occupied and the role which it played within a process of development.
>
> (Mandelbaum 1971, in Ankersmit 1995: 143–4)[1]

The concerns of this thread of the call to history in new IPE tend to be shared by historical sociologists, who have sought to 'bring history back in' to IR (Hall 1996: 24–9; Hobson 1997: 19–20).

Second, the call to history in the work of Cox (1976/1996, 1981/1996, 1985/1996), Gill (1991, 1997) and Germain (1996a, 1997) is more ambitious. It constitutes one form of broadly critical reasoning that challenges the claims of orthodox IPE as to the focus of inquiry and the knowledge that it accepts as legitimate.[2] The key to the so-called 'historical mode of thought' (Cox 1981/1996: 91; Germain 1997: 174) is an ontology of historicity. This extends not only to the reflective agents that are the object of inquiry, but simultaneously to the historian or social scientist. Both human agents and the historian are necessarily reflective, as 'historicity' is not only being situated historically but also the awareness of that situation (Stanford 1994: 50–1). As such, while the first thread of the call to history in IPE addresses largely methodological concerns, the second thread combines these with the epistemological issues raised by the participation of reflective agents in history and their unique position to understand and communicate its contours. It is through and in support of this second thread specifically that the Historical IPE approach outlined here is developed. As I have argued elsewhere in conjunction with others (Amoore *et al.* 2000), an 'historical turn' in IPE must also be a reflective turn.

An historical mode of thought

It is clearly appropriate at the outset to question the reasons for grounding IPE inquiry in history. In a simple sense, the call to history is supportive of new IPE's aspirations as an open and interdisciplinary field of inquiry (cf. Strange 1984). Following Braudel (1980: 26), history can be seen as uniquely placed among the social sciences to seek 'an explanation of society in all its reality'. More significantly, history offers one avenue through which it is possible to construct an alternative to the predominant mode of knowledge of the international realm that rests upon a combination of empiricist epistemology and positivist methodology (cf. Smith 1996). This predominance has implications not only for questions of epistemology and methodology, but also necessarily shapes what can be studied as it determines what exists as knowable.

It is through reflection upon E.H. Carr's (1964) prescient question 'what is history?' that history becomes 'a *way* of knowing, or a mode of knowledge' (Stanford 1994: 112). Carr's (1964) purpose was to question what it is about the past that makes it knowable to historians. This led him to recognise the dual meaning of history as both the past and the study of the past in the present. Carr's analysis itself draws on a long lineage of work by historians who have engaged with the philosophy of history. For instance, elaborating on Croce's famous dictum that 'all history is contemporary history', Collingwood (1946: 2) holds that history 'is neither the past by itself . . . nor the historians thought about it by itself . . . but the two things in mutual relation'. Accounts of the past become an expression of the historian's pre-occupations in the present (Jenkins 1991). In short, by posing the question 'what is history?', the utility of an historical mode of thought for legitimating a different kind of knowledge claim in IPE to that which is legitimated by an empiricist epistemology begins to be revealed.

Rooted in an ontology of historicity, an historical mode of thought provides the epistemological and methodological warrant for the construction of a certain kind of knowledge. Following Collingwood (1946: 218), this can be termed 'historical knowledge'. Historical knowledge contrasts with knowledge generated on the basis of empiricism and positivism in six key related senses. First, an historical mode of thought repudiates the separation of subject and object that lies at the heart of empiricism. Objects of inquiry in the social sciences are inherently different to objects of inquiry in the natural sciences, such that subject and object are inseparable and reciprocally related in the social sciences. Second, once the inseparability of subject and object is accepted, the empiricist distinction between fact and value also unravels. Historical knowledge is not objective knowledge because 'fact' and 'value' are intertwined. As such, the creation of historical knowledge should not be confused with the work of historians who have effectively sought to eradicate the intrusion of subjective values by appealing to methodological rigour in an attempt to reveal the 'facts' (e.g. Marwick 1970). Third, the individualism of positivism in both its ontological and methodological forms is rejected. A 'science of human nature' cannot be undertaken once the historicity of human thought and action is accepted (Collingwood 1946: 205–9). Fourth, the positivist approach to causation that centres upon the relationships between events is also rejected. The construction of historical knowledge seeks an understanding of the meaning of historical change, not the explanation of causation. Fifth, and by implication, the positivist search for universal laws based upon the identification of regularities among events as observable phenomena becomes misguided. Finally, rather than employing a comparative methodology to facilitate the search for universal laws, a comparative historical method is utilised to assist in arriving at an understanding of the meaning of historical change. Comparison between the past and the present and the present and the past generates historical knowledge that can illuminate the 'development potential' of the present (Cox 1985/1996: 53), thereby informing future social action.

In methodological terms, the creation of historical knowledge takes the form of 'a reflective three-way dialogue' (Germain 1997: 175) between the meanings and understandings attached to social practices by human agents themselves, the evidence pertaining to the focus of inquiry, and the commitments and perspective of the historian or social scientist. It is the self-referential nature of this methodology that ensures consistency with an ontology of historicity in the creation of historical knowledge. In epistemological terms, the attempt to construct historical knowledge is part of a wider effort to foster a 'human self-knowledge' (Collingwood 1946: 10) that is capable of informing those conscious subjects who can actually affect the future. As Carr (1964: 27) asserts, 'Knowledge is knowledge for some purpose. The validity of knowledge depends upon the validity of purpose'. It is in these normative terms that the value of historical knowledge is to be judged. In particular, the explicit recognition of the connection between human action, knowledge and reflection by an historical mode of thought opens the potential for a politically motivated, transformative form of knowledge. Such transformative historical knowledge can translate an emancipatory commitment by the historian, which itself emerges out of their 'moral involvement' (Carr 1964: 125) in history, into a challenge to dominant modes of knowledge that legitimate existing social power relations. At the same time, transformative historical knowledge must remain sensitive to the historicity of the present and not be utopian in form.

Dimensions of Historical IPE inquiry

Following from an ontology of historicity and aside from the epistemological and methodological implications addressed above, five principal interrelated categories are held here as guiding the focus for inquiry of an Historical IPE: structured social practices, social change, social space, social time and social orders.

Structured social practices

As Collingwood (1946: 9) emphasises, history is, in the first instance, the 'science of *res gestae*, the attempt to answer questions about human actions done in the past'. An historical mode of thought identifies the historicity of reflective human actions that are necessarily concretely situated in time and space. An Historical IPE, therefore, is concerned with the changing relationships between social actions and the societies within which they take place. Such changing relationships have usually been expressed in the social sciences as a concern with the agency-structure problematic. As others and I have argued elsewhere (Amoore *et al.* 2000: 60–5), the recognition of the essential historicity of social actions and thought by the historical mode of thought is suggestive of a particular approach to the agency-structure problematic in IPE. In sum, agency and structure are acknowledged as inseparable in order to reveal the ways in which social structures, as real and perceived constraints and opportunities, are constructed and reconstructed by social thought and actions. Structures are recognisable as the appreciation of relative constraints and opportunities by reflective agents themselves within a particular context. Attention to the processes whereby agents reflect upon their structural circumstances is also held to throw open promising avenues for consideration of the individual and collective nature of agency.

History as the science of *res gestae* leads an Historical IPE to focus inquiry, in the first instance, upon structured social practices. In this sense, the field of IPE becomes revealed across time as human experience, which itself is understood through the actual historical subjects who are constituted through collectively imbricated structured social practices (Giddens 1979: 5). A focus for IPE inquiry upon structured social practices raises the question as to which practices, if any, are to be privileged. Contrary to the privileging of the practices of security and trade by IR and orthodox IPE scholars, constructivists (Burch and Denemark 1997), Habermasian critical theorists (Linklater 1996: 284–90) and feminists (Tickner 1991) effectively remind us that the privileging of certain sets of social practices risks marginalising experiences that tend to be excluded by the major ontologies of IR and IPE.

While seeking to further a spirit of openness in the consideration of sets of social practices, two points of qualification mark an Historical IPE. First, reflective agents' appreciation of the relative constraints and opportunities that confront them is necessarily shaped by competing modes of knowledge (cf. May 1996). Second, the study of a set of structured social practices, akin to what Cox (1981/1996: 100) terms a 'historical structure', is an 'initial subdivision of reality' which should not be treated as 'separated objects of knowledge' (Cox 1981/1996: 85). Rather, the study of a set of structured social practices is a starting point from which it is possible to construct a dynamic view of a larger whole. An Historical IPE seeks, in the first instance, to reveal the sets of structured social practices that are characteristic of particular eras.

Social change

While specific social structures frame human experience as social practices, the 'social' is 'in constant process of creation and transformation by man himself' (Carr 1964: 138). The changeable relationships between social practices and structures are, therefore, both part of and contributors to the processes of historical change. It is in this sense that an Historical IPE is concerned with historical change, understood in the first instance as social change (Carr 1964: 55; Hobsbawm 1997: 72–5). A concern with social change resonates clearly with the attempts of new IPE scholars to get 'beyond' IR and orthodox IPE. Indeed, the emergence of new IPE has been necessarily intertwined with seeking understanding of contemporary social change (Scholte 1993; Gill and Mittelman 1997). A few IR writers have themselves also been critical of their peers' denial of structural change in the international system (Buzan and Jones 1981; Ruggie 1985; Little 1994). As such, the conceptualisation of the subject matter of IPE offered by orthodox approaches has been recognised as largely incompatible with the study of social change. By contrast, the alternative ontologies of new IPE scholars, for instance world orders (Cox 1987) or world-economies (Germain 1996a), have the benefit of casting the subject matter of IPE as a transient social entity on a global scale.

An Historical IPE account of change within a set of structured social practices should, therefore, relate change to the dialectics of restructuring at a world-scale. Following Cox (1987), this is facilitated by an ontology of 'historical structures' and 'world orders'. Existing historical structures have inherent contradictions and give rise to social conflicts that are central to their transformation (Cox 1976/1996: 77–8). Attempts to resolve these antagonisms are bound by wider social and power relations in the prevailing world order.

Social space

An historical mode of thought insists on the historicity of social thought and action in time and space. The spatial dimension of historicity has, however, tended to be overlooked by new IPE scholars. While new IPE has offered a variety of ontologies that effectively define the subject matter of IPE as a world-scale social phenomenon, the space of social relations tends to be assumed rather than viewed as constituted through social and political processes (Drainville 1995). Recent cross-disciplinary debates illustrate that an explicit conception of space forms an indispensable part of any social theory (Simonsen 1996). IPE, however, tends to implicitly adopt what Agnew (1994) has termed 'the territorial assumptions of IR', whereby space is equated with territory. Such a state-centric conceptualisation of space sits awkwardly with new IPE ontologies that go beyond the states system in their definition of their subject matter. Different world orders necessarily involve different spatialities of social and power relations and, therefore, can be distinguished by their geographies. Such geographies are rendered invisible by ahistorical, territorial assumptions. As Agnew and Corbridge (1995) argue, the division of the world into discrete territories has been a matter for social and political construction.[3]

For an Historical IPE, space is not understood in the sense of the geographical environment which conditions social actions. Such a conceptualisation of space presents it as both passive and trans-historical, as the things and substances used in social actions regardless of context. Instead, following the philosopher and sociologist Henri Lefebvre (1991), space is understood as 'social space'. That is, space is recognised as fashioned, shaped and invested with social thought and action, inseparable from it and, as such, only understandable in its historically concrete existence as social space.

Social space is a generic term encompassing the uncountable sets of social space generated by different sets of social practices (Lefebvre 1991: 86). Within each set of social practices and their associated social space, key interconnected 'social spaces' emerge as the 'social locus' for practices (Lefebvre 1991: 87). The primacy of these social spaces is likely to be reinforced by those representations of space that form the dominant conceptualisation of space with regard to the set of social practices concerned. For instance, the territorial basis of state sovereignty is inseparable from the discourse of sovereignty. Key social spaces cannot, however, be considered in isolation from the wider social space of which they are part. As Lefebvre (1991: 86–7) asserts, 'Social spaces interpenetrate one another and/or superimpose themselves upon one another'. As Porter (1990), Krugman (1993) and the other contributors to 'new geographical economics' (Martin 1999a) serve to highlight, the key social spaces for sets of structured social practices may not – contrary to the assumptions of IR, orthodox IPE and neo-liberalism – simply correspond to the boundaries of territorial states.

Social time

In the course of social change, structures are both transformed and preserved. As Carr (1964: 62–6) observes, the processes of social change contain continuities as well as discontinuities, the general and the unique. Among historians, Braudel's (1980: 27–33) notion of the plurality of social time facilitates understanding of the complex interplay of continuity and discontinuity. While several IPE scholars have highlighted the problems of thinking about continuity and the extent or otherwise of change (e.g. Jones 1999), few have noted the potential utility of considering social time. Braudel distinguished between three speeds of the experience of social time. First, '*l'histoire évenmentielle*', that is, the 'short-time span, proportionate to individuals, to daily life, to our illusions, to our hasty awareness' (Braudel 1980: 28). Second, 'conjunctural' time, that is, cycles, movements and perceptible rhythms that tend to span between ten and fifty years. Third, the '*longue durée*', that is, those routinised patterns of action and thought which establish the 'limits of the possible' of social life across centuries. What clearly interested Braudel was the way in which the structures of the *longue durée* interacted with the more immediate and flexible constraints and opportunities of the medium- and short-time spans. In our terms, over the *longue durée* social practices are likely to display considerable continuities, while also exhibiting considerable conjunctural discontinuities.

Following Braudel, an Historical IPE considers social change over the time span of the *longue durée*. In this sense, an Historical IPE shares a time frame for inquiry with world-systems analysis (Wallerstein 1974; Chase-Dunn 1989). The notion of *durée* itself signifies lived experience, the speed of social time over which it is fitting to consider sets of structured social practices (Cox 1996a: 150, 1996b: 25). Considered over the *longue durée*, social practices retain a distinctive sense of continuity represented by the enduring features of what Braudel termed the *mentalité*, that is, 'the mental framework which guides the way human collectivities exploit their natural and social circumstances' (Germain 1996a: 206). As such, and in contrast to world-systems analysis, for an Historical IPE the length of the *longue durée* corresponds in the first instance to the set(s) of social practices upon which inquiry is focused.

Capturing change in sets of structured social practices is assisted by Braudel's notion of the conjuncture. As the neo-structuralist approach to IPE stresses by elevating the concept of the 'historical conjuncture' (Gills and Palan 1994: 7), a set of social practices over the *longue durée* displays variations in the meanings and values that informs and shapes it. For an Historical IPE, conjunctural time corresponds to the irregular span of those historical structures which together comprise a world order. Conjunctural time is, therefore, effectively re-conceptualised not simply in Braudelian terms as the ten to fifty year span of an economic cycle, but as a 'stage of development' (Overbeek 1990: 22–3) or the discrete span of a configuration of social and power relations, which is much less predictable in duration. Conjunctural inquiry into a set of social practices as an historical structure within a wider world order proceeds along two dimensions. As Sinclair (1996: 8) has noted, the notion of historical structures is designed to incorporate and integrate both the static or synchronic, and dynamic or diachronic. The synchronous corresponds to *l'histoire évenmentielle*, the simultaneous realm of events and individuals. In this sense, synchronic inquiry into an historical structure involves explanation within its own, day-to-day terms of the thought and action of social practices. The diachronous dimension is that of recurring social patterns, the exact form of which remains historically specific. In this sense, diachronic inquiry into an historical structure relates day-to-day practices to the development potential of the structure.

Diachronic understanding focuses upon potential and actual structural change and those social and power relations that underpin and shape social change (Cox 1996a: 150). Such diachronic understanding is likely to be facilitated by comparative historical inquiry between successive historical structures over the *longue durée*.

Social orders

A diachronic understanding of historical structures requires not only that dialectical transformation is related to the corresponding wider world order, but that sets of practices themselves are recognised as framed by a conjunctural complex of social and power relations which contribute to directing change. In short, in diachronic terms, an historical structure can be seen as a hierarchical social order. Such a concern with historical structures as social orders is clearly rooted in an historical mode of thought. In particular, an historical mode of thought is aware that social practices are informed by collectively held assumptions and procedures which are themselves forged in the context of the social and power relations of a social order (Collingwood 1946: 223).

Social and power relations surround the manner in which sets of social practices come to be organised. Taken together, material, social and political power relations constitute a basic 'structure of power' that emerges within a social order. This holds an 'enforcement potential' (Cox 1981/1996: 99) that ensures the domination of the strong over the weak in framing the possible organisation of social practices. However, a social order characterised by domination alone is likely to be rendered relatively unstable by social conflict. The hierarchical pattern of social forces, and the organisation of social practices in which this pattern is manifest, needs to be accepted as legitimate if a social order is to be marked by relative stability. As Maier (1987: 154) asserts, relative stability is not simply a matter of societal inertia but has to be produced and reproduced. It is for this reason that, following Gramsci, Cox (1981/1996: 99–100) seeks to distinguish between hegemonic and non-hegemonic historical structures, where a hegemonic structure is marked by the consensual integration of social forces and widespread acceptance of prevailing social and power relations as legitimate.

Alongside inquiry into the making and unravelling of social orders, an Historical IPE is concerned with the more continuous tendency for relative stability in social orders to be reproduced. Drawing upon Moore's (1987: 2) assertion that arriving at an explanation of the reproduction of relative stability requires an understanding of 'social relationships of authority', an Historical IPE develops the notion of 'structures of governance'. Power relations are always present in a social order, but tend to be visible as the binding authority relations that constitute a structure of governance during periods of relative stability. A structure of governance embodies intertwined but analytically separate 'formal' and 'informal' faces (Moore 1987: 14–15).[4] It is the way that the formal and informal come together in different periods that determines the structure of governance in a social order. Formal authority is exercised through those socially legitimated state, civil and market institutions that frame the organisation of social practices (Cutler *et al.* 1999). Informal or 'epistemic authority' is found in the various social mechanisms that mould the social convictions that frame social practices around prevailing norms, values and meanings as 'organizational principles' (Hewson and Sinclair 1999: 4, 10). The formal and informal faces of governance are contested and do not, therefore, emerge in a functional or technicist manner as a consequence of a structure of power (Latham 1999: 31–7; O'Brien *et al.* 2000). Rather, 'It is the means of world order realization that is the substance of global governance' (Sinclair 1999: 162). An explanation of a structure of governance within a social order requires that both the formal and informal faces of authority are considered, as concern lies with how the reproduction of relative stability manifests itself in the organisation of social practices.

Conclusions

In sum, by arguing for a new IPE that is anchored in history, we have begun to lay the groundwork for our critical inquiry into contemporary world finance. An Historical IPE approach takes as its starting point an ontology of historicity that forms the key plank of an historical mode of thought. Following from the historicity of social thought and action, an Historical IPE is guided by structured social practices, social change, social space, social time and social orders as the principal categories along which inquiry is pursued. As such, an Historical IPE proceeds, in the first instance, by focusing over the *longue durée* upon sets of social practices as historical structures that span irregular conjunctures. Social practices also necessarily assume and entail social space, which itself is constituted through social processes. In diachronic terms, a set of social practices comes to be organised in the context of both the shifting complex of hierarchical power relations that forms the corresponding social order, and the dialectics of the wider world order. In this sense, inquiry is concerned with the making and unravelling of social orders. Furthermore, attention is also given to periods of relative stability in social orders, marked by the broad-based acceptance of hierarchical power relations and the organisation of social practices in which they are manifest as legitimate. Informal and formal authority come together in a structure of governance that, by virtue of the acceptance of a role for its various elements in the management of social practices, serves to reproduce relative stability in a social order.

The historical knowledge produced by an Historical IPE rests on an alternative epistemological and methodological warrant to that which underpins the knowledge claims of neo-liberalism and orthodox IPE. An ontology of historicity leads to a critique of empiricism and positivism that, in particular, posits the reciprocity of subject and object and the subjective dimension of all social knowledge. The value of historical knowledge lies in its contribution to human self-knowledge, the appropriation of the past to inform the possibility of progressive transformation in the present and for the future.

Notes

1 Such an understanding of historicism is in contrast to that of Popper (1957/1960). Popper critiques historicism as the belief that prediction is the main aim of history and the social sciences, and that the so-called speculative philosophies of Hegel, Marx or Spengler offer such predictions.

2 As Germain (1996a: 202, 221) has observed, by seeking a mode of knowledge in IR and IPE that rests on a commitment to accept the epistemological and methodological consequences of the historicity of thought and action, this thread of the call to history is complementary with applications of both Habermasian critical theory (e.g. Linklater 1996) and reflectivist forms of constructivism (e.g. Burch and Denemark 1997). On the distinction between rationalist and reflectivist IPE, see Palan (2000).

3 In this sense, the concern of an Historical IPE with social space may open up potential linkages with scholars engaged critically in re-interpreting IR in a rapidly changing world. For these scholars, overcoming the territorial assumptions of IR is a key problematic (cf. Walker 1993; Ruggie 1993).

4 The identification of the formal and informal dimensions of governance is built upon a recognition that the scope of authority extends across both 'action and belief'. As Friedman (1990: 57) asserts, 'a person may be said to "have authority" in two distinct senses. For one, he may be said to be "in authority", meaning that he occupies some office, position, or status which entitles him to make decisions about how other people should behave. But, secondly, a person may be said to be "an authority" on something, meaning that his views or utterances are entitled to be believed (including, to complicate matters, beliefs about the right and wrong way of doing things)'.

2 An Historical International Political Economy of world finance

Following from the ontological significance attached to the historicity of social thought and actions, Historical IPE inquiry is guided by five principal interrelated dimensions: structured social practices, social change, social space, social time and social orders. With particular reference to the development of these categories of investigation, this chapter elaborates an Historical IPE framework for the understanding of world finance.

From finance to world credit practices

An Historical IPE approach suggests that inquiry into world finance should begin by identifying those structured social practices that comprise world finance. An initial focus on structured social practices contrasts with conceptualisations of money and finance put forward by neo-liberal political economy. Neo-liberals begin from the assumption that money is just another good that provides its holders with liquidity to facilitate exchange. Money, therefore, has four main functions – as a medium of exchange, a means of payment, a unit of account and a store of value. Finance becomes the automatic use of holdings of money as a store of value in order to facilitate investment and further exchange, equating saving and investment at a market-clearing rate of interest and maintaining macroeconomic equilibrium (cf. Guttmann 1994: 28). Contrary to neo-liberal political economy, however, research in sociology highlights that finance, in the form of credit, is not a commodity. Rather, given the centrality of debt relations to the creation, allocation, buying and selling of promises to pay, finance as credit is constituted by social relations that, in turn, may enable productive and exchange relations (Ingham 1996). Credit is not a commodity that emerges automatically in a functional manner as a consequence of the rational actions of individuals, but as a set of practices framed by institutions, norms and values is socially constructed specific to different times and different places (Dodd 1994; Mizruchi and Brewster Stearns 1994).

Despite the egalitarian potential of credit (Galbraith 1975: 70–1), sharp inequalities tend to characterise both access to credit instruments and the power to determine their creation and allocation. In addition, following Marx and the development of his work by geographer David Harvey (1982: 262–70), the social and economic significance of the structured social practices of credit can be seen as extending well beyond their contribution to exchange. Credit creation mobilises capital that would otherwise lie idle for both production and consumption, reduces the time and cost of the circulation of commodities, and includes the creation of 'fictitious capital', whereby capital usually made available for investment is extended indefinitely (typically through share issues). Credit creation itself may, in addition, come to provide an important means for the accumulation of capital.

Drawing upon the above, 'finance' can be seen as unequally distributed sets of structured social practices that create, allocate, buy and sell credit instruments (promises to pay) that come to be organised and made possible in the context of the historically specific social relations that constitute credit. Consideration of the relationships of finance to the international economy of commodity exchange, to the world economy of production, and to state-societies enables the identification of those world-scale credit practices that are the focus of inquiry here.[1] Five principal sets of world credit practices become discernible: commercial credit practices, the practices of international clearance, money-market practices, corporate credit practices and sovereign credit practices.

Commercial credit practices are those that, given the delay between the production and consumption of commodities traded over long distances and the resulting lag in payment, assist in the mediation of international trade. While usually regarded as contributing to international monetary arrangements in the sense that they act to organise payments, the practices of international clearance are also essential to the realisation of the claims and obligations arising from credit practices (Kindleberger 1984/1993: 19; Germain 1997: 12). The division of the world into state-societies from the seventeenth century and the related denomination of credit instruments in different national currencies has ensured a close relationship between clearance practices and those associated with foreign exchange. Meanwhile, the holding of short-term working balances of capital in order to clear outstanding obligations by all parties involved in credit relations has stimulated money-market practices. Money-market or inter-bank practices put otherwise idle working balances to use, supporting long-term credit creation through the continuous manipulation of short-term capital (Bagehot 1873/1991: 8–10). Corporate credit practices provide long-term capital for large-scale productive investment. While usually organised on a national scale as part and parcel of patterns of industrialisation and the consolidation of state-societies, corporate credit practices have been undertaken on a world scale largely in support of the expansionary strategies of multinational corporations (MNCs). Finally, for state-societies, the making of war and the construction of human (education, health, welfare and law and order) and physical (transportation and communication) infrastructures, alongside insufficient taxation revenues from their respective societies, has necessitated, at different times and to differing extents, recourse to long-term sovereign credit. Sovereign credit practices have also provided short-term credit for balance-of-payments deficits.

Modern world credit practices

The concern of an Historical IPE with social time suggests that the sets of world credit practices identified should be considered over the *longue durée*. De Goede's (1998) analysis of world finance as a discourse is particularly informative as to the formation of the *mentalité* that frames contemporary world credit practices. De Goede holds that the concepts and values that continue today to frame both the organisation of credit practices and understandings of the purposes to which credit is put first emerged in the specific setting of seventeenth and eighteenth century Europe. This is not to deny that credit practices were not undertaken prior to this period, or that the subsequent creation of credit became somehow divorced from the 'subjective and inherently volatile assessments of its participants' (Guttmann 1994: 21). Equally, it is recognised that world credit practices have taken contrasting conjunctural forms over the last three centuries, with different credit instruments (e.g. loans, bills, bonds, stocks etc.) and patterns of institutionalisation predominant during different periods. However, with the collapse of medievalism, world credit practices became subject to the modern assertions of rationality and reason (Neal 1990). The appeal to rationality and reason emerged to play a defining role in the legitimation of modern credit practices, a role that continues in the contemporary era. Rationality and reason, enabled by the first systematic information networks (Smith 1984), facilitated the invention of risk as a calculable entity (Leyshon and Thrift 1997: 294). The professional financier who dealt in risk and, therefore, legitimately sought to accumulate capital as a result of his credit practices became distinct from the gambler who sought to benefit from his dealings with uncertainty.

Capital, information, and technology

Throughout modern world finance, accumulated capital in its monetary form has been the basic material resource by which credit practices are framed and upon which they must draw. For every bank loan there must to a greater or lesser extent be savings, and for every share offer there must be holders of capital who are willing to buy. Across successive conjunctures, the availability or otherwise of capital for modern world credit practices has important spatial and temporal dimensions. The vast inequalities in rates of wealth creation across the world economy that Storper and Walker (1989) term 'the inconstant geography of capitalism' ensure that the capital upon which world credit practices rest tends to be concentrated in different localities at different times. World-systems writers have linked these spatial dynamics of capital accumulation with temporal dynamics as part and parcel of their overlapping three-step cyclical theory of consecutive state hegemonies. Wallerstein (1980: 38) provides a concise summary:

> The pattern of hegemony seems marvellously simple. Marked superiority in agro-industrial productive efficiency leads to dominance in the sphere of commercial distribution of world trade, with correlative profits accruing both

> from being the entrepôt of much world trade and from controlling the 'invisibles' – transport, communications, and insurance. Commercial primacy leads in turn to control of the financial sectors of banking (exchange, deposit and credit) and of investment (direct and portfolio). These superiorities are successive, but they overlap in time.

For world-systems writers, periods characterised by 'financial expansion' (Arrighi 1994: 87) or a 'financialization of capital' (Amin 1996) rest upon capital accumulated previously through production and commerce, and tend to coincide with stagnation or slow growth in production and trade.[2] The value of credit instruments created during such periods expands due to the speculative accumulation of capital through world credit practices themselves. While world credit practices are inherently subject to sporadic bouts of speculation in the search for extraordinary returns, during a financial expansion speculative accumulation becomes a structural feature of modern world finance. Following Amin (1996: 238–44), an Historical IPE emphasises the regularity and specificities of periods of financialisation rather than their cyclical and predictable nature. As Chancellor (2000: xiv) contends, 'speculation can only be understood within a social context'. When considering the spatial-temporal dimensions of the relationship of capital to credit there is a need to identify qualitative differences across different periods.

While the availability or otherwise of capital is likely to establish the material baseline for modern world credit practices, information is also a key material resource. Information allows credit practices to take place, facilitating the assessment of the risks inherent to the creation, allocation, buying and selling of credit as promises to pay (Strange 1990). Information networks hold necessary but imperfect information for credit practices that, in the era of modern world finance, tends to be interpreted through 'narrow assumptions about market efficiency' (Sinclair 1994a: 143). Meanwhile, technology constitutes potentially the most dynamic material resource that frames credit practices. The significance of technological change is not limited to the contemporary period, where scholars have identified close linkages between changes in world credit practices and the emergence of a global information and telecommunications infrastructure based around telematics (e.g. Strange 1998a: 22–42). In terms of modern world credit practices, innovations in information and communications technologies have, in particular, facilitated the movement of funds (both capital and credit), the creation and communication of information, the development of new and complex credit instruments, and increases in the speed and volume of credit practices.

Shared meanings

The material capabilities that frame world credit practices and upon which they draw cannot be separated from the ideational forces of world finance. The shared meanings of the *mentalité* of modern world finance effectively frame the terrain for world credit practices, establishing widely held understandings of practice. Modern attitudes to and understandings of credit have tended to assume the rational economic calculation of the creation and allocation of credit and associated concerns with risk, obligation and rates of interest. This is reflected in the complex mathematical models and hedging practices to calculate and manage risk employed in contemporary financial institutions. Yet rational calculation is not actual, but a deeply entrenched and continuous '*a priori* assumption' (Kindleberger 1978: 26) in the *mentalité* of modern world credit practices. This obscures the significance of changeable and shared meanings to the framing of daily practices.

Although risk is understood as subject to rational calculation in world credit practices, such abstraction remains impossible as perceptions of risk are grounded in changing subjective expectations as to the future market developments and the capacity of borrowers to fulfil their outstanding obligations (Eatwell and Taylor 2000). Expectations are collectively forged under the influence of so-called 'market sentiment'. Such is the importance of shared meanings to the daily ebb and flow of world credit practices that changes in market sentiment are widely held to lie at the roots of a particularly notable dynamic endemic to modern credit practices, that is, their crisis tendencies (Kindleberger 1978; Eichengreen and Portes 1987; Galbraith 1993). Following the 'historical economics' approach of Charles Kindleberger (1978: 7, 1984/1993: 4), financial crises can be seen to be sporadic but broadly and commonly characterised by four stages. First, shared perceptions of a new investment opportunity in one type of asset or another develop into a 'mania' or 'speculative excess' that is fuelled by credit expansion and reflected in the rising price of the asset concerned. This speculative excess is itself enabled by the very fungibility of capital in its monetary form. Periods of financialisation are likely to be crisis-ridden, as speculative excess moves from one type of financial asset to another. Second, a period of 'distress' ensues as market sentiment undergoes a volte-face. Expectations of future returns on investment and the debt obligations that they permit come to be viewed as dramatically over-optimistic. Third, 'panic' quickly follows as speculators retreat from the asset concerned and the supply of credit is withdrawn. Finally, panic leads to 'crash' as asset prices tumble sharply and debtors and their lenders are rendered insolvent. If not checked by the credit and capital provided by a 'lender of last resort', the crash may ramify throughout world credit practices and cripple future credit creation.

Market, state and civil institutions

Within modern world finance as a succession of historical structures, institutional forces stand alongside material capabilities and ideas in framing credit practices. Indeed, world credit practices have been and continue to be institutionalised within the social institutions of market, state and civil society. The relative significance of market, state and civil institutions has waxed and waned in different periods of modern world finance, with the nature of the interplay between them tending to be formalised through regulation. A focus here on the conjunctural manner in which credit practices become institutionalised and their relationships to material and ideational forces contrasts with existing research in IPE which assumes that state–market relations are the proper object of inquiry (cf. Cohen 1996;

Dombrowski 1998). Following an Historical IPE approach, it is the actual practices of world finance that are the focus of inquiry in the first instance, not their institutional manifestations or the material capital flows that they realise. 'State' and 'market' as overarching analytical categories are effectively unpacked to reveal their institutional, material and ideational bases.

Market institutions are those that are the broadly accepted institutional form for the organisation of social practices in the economic realm undertaken for profit. Throughout modern world finance and with considerable national variation (cf. Zysman 1983), credit practices have been institutionalised within various market institutional networks including commercial, merchant and investment banks. The notion of market institutional networks reflects the extent to which modern world credit practices are collectively organised in hierarchical networks of market institutions that reach throughout the relevant geographical scale of world credit practices in different periods.

The penetration of credit practices by state institutions has also followed diverse patterns across national political economies, but tends to combine 'design capacity' and 'operational capacity' (Vipond 1993: 187). The design capacity of state institutions concerns the establishment of the laws and regulations framing credit practices undertaken within financial market institutions. Once regulatory parameters have been established by the state, much of the day-to-day supervision of credit practices has traditionally been organised through a complex and nationally diverse mix of civil institutions, in particular, stock exchanges and clearing houses.[3] State institutions' operational capacity in finance is, meanwhile, concerned with the attempt to control the volume of credit creation in response to monetary and growth targets, particularly by manipulating the rate of interest on borrowed reserves in the form of fiduciary money. Operational capacity is thus closely related to the so-called 'financial revolution' of the eighteenth and nineteenth centuries in the sense that the revolution involved the first time issue of national fiduciary money in which credit also became denominated (Dickson 1967). Given that financial market institutions are first and foremost in competition for the pursuit of profits, market institutions tend to require regulation and supervision to prevent the imprudent expansion of credit. In the absence of such operational management by state institutions, the value of fiduciary money may be brought into question. Further, in the advent of panic surrounding the solvency of financial market institutions, it is also in the interest of state institutions to perform the operational role of lender of last resort by injecting liquidity. The operational capacity of state institutions has largely been the preserve of central banks, based upon their monopoly over the issuing of fiduciary money and government debt. At a world scale, credit creation and commodity transactions in different periods have tended to be largely denominated in a single national currency as 'world money' (Strange 1976; Walter 1993). The central banks with monopoly over the issue of world monies have, therefore, been key state institutions framing world credit practices. The operational capacity of key central banks has been assisted by co-operative inter-state monetary arrangements and institutions, such as those associated with the gold standard in the nineteenth and early twentieth centuries.

World financial centres

An Historical IPE advances a concern with social space as a principal category of inquiry. In terms of world finance, this leads to the recognition of the inherent spatiality of modern world credit practices. Credit practices necessarily assume and entail social space at a world-scale, with key interconnected social spaces emerging as the social loci for world credit practices. World financial centres (WFCs) are conceptualised here as the key social spaces for world credit practices. Alternative WFCs emerge in different periods and it becomes possible to distinguish WFCs from national and regional financial centres. The status of a WFC corresponds to the centralisation of world credit practices and the material, ideational and institutional forces upon which they draw.

The centralisation of capital in WFCs is partly related to the inconstant geography of capitalism. The rise of national financial centres to world status corresponds with the ascendancy of their respective national political economies in terms of capital accumulation (Kindleberger 1974/1978). Capital also becomes centralised in WFCs as a consequence of their tendency to stand as world centres for commodity exchange (Kindleberger 1983: 79–80). In addition and, in the absence of restrictions upon its movement, foreign accumulated capital becomes centralised in WFCs. This is a consequence of what Brown (1940: 154), with reference to London as the WFC of the nineteenth and early twentieth centuries, terms 'deposit-compelling power'. Foreign capital is directed to and maintained in a WFC as a result of the capacity of the credit practices centralised there to offer relatively high rates of return on investment. Meanwhile, technological innovations are centralised in WFCs, so that WFCs constitute the 'technopoles' (Petrella 1991) of world finance in two interrelated senses. Technological innovations have become centralised in WFCs to facilitate both credit practices within the space of the centre itself, and inter-linkages with the wider social space of world finance.

The centralisation in WFCs of information and market, state and civil institutions is interpreted by economists as the functional outcome of the informational efficiency gains associated with external economies of scale (Grilli 1989; Davis 1990). The centralisation of market institutional networks in particular comes to be seen as reducing the costs of access to market information. In our terms, however, as Pryke and Lee (1995: 330–1) assert, 'external economies do not just happen to exist in the air or appear automatically as geographical clustering proceeds within financial centres; they are socially generated'. Such social construction and reproduction rests on the centralisation of material and ideational forces in WFCs, and the wider production and reproduction of WFCs. In terms of shared meanings, WFCs constitute important 'epistemic communities': that is, 'occupational communities with their own specialised vocabularies, rhetorics, knowledges, practices and texts' (Thrift 1994: 349–50). WFCs are at the forefront of the formation of those shared meanings that surround the interpretation of information. It is the centrifugal spatiality of both capital and the formation of shared meanings that enables informational efficiency gains.

A conceptualisation of WFCs as key social spaces is, then, distinctive and contrasts with the understandings of financial centres usually expressed in the social sciences. Financial centres are typically defined by economists in a somewhat functional manner as 'a central location where the financial transactions of an area are co-ordinated and cleared' (Reed 1981: 1; cf. Kindleberger (1974/1978). Meanwhile, economic geographers concerned with so-called 'world cities' – 'centres of transnational corporate headquarters, of their business services, of international finance, of transnational institutions, and of telecommunications and information processing' (Knox 1995: 6) – suggest a structural–functional as opposed to social understanding of WFCs.[4] Conceptualised as social spaces, WFCs are neither reified in analysis of world finance nor configured homogeneously in a structural relationship to world finance that is the likely outcome of a functional understanding of WFCs. As Pryke and Lee (1995: 333–4) assert, financial centres 'are dynamically reproduced, not merely in a mechanical way, through their success in sustaining accumulation, but socially and culturally'. Through a conceptualisation of WFCs as social spaces, an Historical IPE demands that inquiry acknowledges the social processes which produce and reproduce specific WFCs and the relationships of these processes to the making and unravelling of world finance as a social order.

World financial orders

Following an Historical IPE, it is important that the conceptualisation of modern world finance as a succession of conjuncturally distinct sets of social practices that span irregular conjunctures is extended to the diachronic moment. Therefore, inquiry into change in modern world credit practices understands their organisation in the context of both successive hierarchical social orders ('world financial orders') and wider world orders. While grounded in an awareness of the continuities of modern world finance, comparative historical study of successive financial orders enables consideration of structural change from one order to another.

Structures of power

Each world financial order has a discernible structure of power that frames the possible organisation of world credit practices. Power in world finance has tended to be understood by IPE scholars in state-centric terms. Debates about contemporary world finance thus largely focus on the relative power of America and Japan as principal states in the contemporary era (e.g. Gilpin 1987; Strange 1990; Helleiner 1992, 2000) and the implications for state power of burgeoning financial markets (Cerny 1993a; Germain 1997; Dombrowski 1998). Helleiner's (1993b) inquiry into the nature of what he terms 'financial power' provides a clear and particularly comprehensive example of the state-centric approach. He identifies five common features of the United Provinces, Britain and the United States viewed as successive hegemonic states in world finance. Each was the leading creditor economy, 'home' to the dominant market networks, host to the dominant world financial centre, and had the key public institutions and currencies that operated as world money. Such state-centric approaches to power in world finance tend to collapse material, market and political power into state power (Ingham 1994). The significance of social power is also neglected, especially in terms of its contribution to shaping the purposes to which political power is put. The exercise of political power through states is not, therefore, the sole explanatory factor, but is a significant part of what is to be understood as part and parcel of an account of the power relations in a hierarchical world financial order.

Material power in successive world financial orders emerges from the unequal social relations surrounding capital, information and technology. Power is conferred upon those who occupy positions of ownership, control or access to these material capabilities. Given the tendency for material capabilities to be centralised in WFCs, it is no surprise that those social forces that have been materially dominant in world financial orders have also been associated with the dominant WFC. Polanyi (1944) identifies this as power of London's *haute finance* between 1815 and 1914. For Polanyi (1944: 17), *haute finance* is understood as a class and political category. At the roots of the formation of the perceived shared interests of *haute finance*, and of their position within the world financial order and wider world order of the period, was their centralisation in London. As Polanyi (1944: 11) asserts, London stood as 'the international center, *haute finance* proper'. Furthermore, the centrifugal dynamics of material power relations indicate that the rise and fall of WFCs, echoing contests between ascendant and descendant social forces, is an important dynamic in the world financial orders. As Braudel (1984: 32) highlights, the rise to prominence of one financial centre and the decline of another 'always meant a massive historical shift of forces'. A period in which one world financial order becomes decentralised and begins to unravel and another is apparently in the making can be seen as an 'interregnum' (Cox, M. *et al.* 1999: 3–4), that is, a period of considerable uncertainty marked by an uneasy balance of contending forces.

Social and political power relations also form part of the basic structure of power in a world financial order. Social power emerges from the configuration of social forces – the manner in which different social forces come together. For instance, despite the material predominance of New York's social forces in the post-1945 world financial order, the manner in which the order came to be organised did not reflect their perceived shared interests (Helleiner 1993a). Given the significance of state institutions in framing world credit practices, whoever holds political power narrowly defined, that is, 'the power to control the machinery of the state or to influence government policy' (Cox 1987: 18), is likely to be of particular importance. An understanding of the forms of state emerging from state-societal relations and the relationships between material, social and political power is essential, then, to identifying the structure of power within a world financial order.

The structure of power in a world financial order cannot be divorced from the corresponding wider world order. Aside from the dynamics of social and political power relations in the wider world order, the nature of inter-state relations is of particular significance for world financial orders. At the most extreme, periods of international war can have major implications for world financial orders. As Kindleberger (1984/1993: 7) asserts, 'Financial history cannot escape dealing with war.' In our terms, major international wars tend to contribute to broad re-articulations of power relations that resonate through a world financial order. Alternatively, periods in which there is an absence of major international conflict tend to present opportunities for inter-state co-operation in the organisation of world credit practices.

Structures of governance

An Historical IPE approach suggests that periods of relative stability emerge in social orders, marked by the broad-based acceptance of a hierarchical pattern of social forces and the associated organisation of social practices as legitimate. The informal and formal faces of a structure of governance contribute to the reproduction of relative stability through the organisational principles and authoritative technical management of social practices. For world financial orders, the significance of a structure of governance is revealed, in particular, with reference to financial crises. During periods of relative stability in a world financial order, a structure of governance is able to manage a crisis effectively so that world credit practices are not paralysed. Put another way, the 'superficial fluctuations' generated by a financial crisis do not lead to a diachronic 'structural disruption' (cf. Overbeek 1990: 19). During periods of relative instability marked by contestation between social forces over the organisation of social practices and a questioning of informal and formal authority, however, a financial crisis may contribute to further instability and ultimately to the unravelling and collapse of a world financial order.

It is posited here that a period of relative stability in a world financial order during which the prevailing power relations are broadly accepted is likely to coincide with the firm centralisation of a world financial order in a single WFC. Conversely, relative instability coincides with the decentralisation of an order and the proliferation of financial centres at its apex. Furthermore, as a somewhat fragmentary body of research suggests, it is largely as a consequence of the formal and informal authority of the social forces of the dominant WFC that a relative stability is produced and reproduced. For Polanyi (1944: 18), in the organisation of world credit practices *haute finance* held both formal authority, as exercised through the principal market institutional networks such as that of Rothschilds, and the informal authority to shape 'the universally accepted principles upon which this organization rested'. Ingham (1994) meanwhile stresses the detrimental consequences for world money and finance of the failure of New York between 1945 and 1971 to replicate the governance role played by London between 1870 and 1914. Subsequent to the publication in 1973 of his classic *The World in Depression*, Kindleberger (1974/1978; 1983) seems to have revised his initial state-centric argument that disruptions to world money and finance could be traced to the problems of the transfer of hegemony from Britain to the United States. Although based on a somewhat functional understanding of WFCs, Kindleberger (1983: 82) argues that the Great Depression of the 1920s and 1930s occurred 'in the midst of the transfer of financial leadership from London to New York'. Brown's (1940) research is, perhaps, the most suggestive. Having established that the most significant factors facilitating the smooth operation of the pre-1914 international gold standard were efficient movements of credit for adjustment, Brown argues that the very efficiency of movements of credit resulted from the firm centralisation of what he terms the 'world credit structure' in London. For Brown, the key to the disruptions to the international gold standard caused by the First World War therefore lay in the subsequent decentralisation of the world credit structure between London and an emergent New York. WFCs constitute the social loci for the reproduction of relative stability in a world financial order, the key complexes of governance where formal and informal authority comes together.

Conclusions

An Historical IPE of world finance proceeds, then, by focusing upon commercial credit, corporate credit, sovereign credit, money-market and clearance practices as the principal social practices which have constituted modern world finance since the seventeenth century. Modern world finance is conceptualised in synchronic terms as a succession of structurally distinct sets of world credit practices that have spanned irregular conjunctures. World credit practices are framed by and draw upon capital, information and technology as material resources; shared meanings as ideational forces; and market, state and civil institutional forces. In diachronic terms, world finance is understood as a succession of hierarchical social orders, that is, world financial orders. In the context of the wider world order, the structure of power in a world financial order directs the possible organisation of world credit practices. Periods of relative stability in a world financial order, characterised by the broad-based acceptance of prevailing power relations and the organisation of world credit practices in which they are manifest, are reproduced by the informal and formal faces of a structure of governance. While recognising the continuities in the *mentalité* of modern world finance, comparative Historical IPE inquiry across successive world financial orders enables consideration of significant change from one order to another.

An Historical IPE of world finance identifies the significance of WFCs in world financial orders in three senses. First, WFCs stand as the key social spaces for world credit practices. The practices that create, allocate, buy and sell credit instruments on a world-scale and the material, ideational and institutional forces which frame these practices tend to be centralised in a WFC. Second, given the centrifugal spatiality of material capabilities and the unequal power relations that emerge from ownership, control and access, the social forces that are materially predominant in the making of world financial orders tend to be associated with the predominant WFC. So the rise and fall of WFCs is closely intertwined with the making and unravelling of world financial orders and reflects contests between ascendant and descendant social forces over the organisation of world credit practices. Third, WFCs are key spaces or complexes of governance in world financial orders, the social loci for the reproduction of relative stability in an order. The informal and formal authority that comes together in a WFC is pivotal to the organisation and authoritative management of world credit practices. Relative stability in a world financial order coincides, then, with the predominance of a single WFC, while relative instability is concurrent with decentralisation between two or more financial centres at the apex of the hierarchy.

Notes

1 '[G]eographical scale is the focal setting at which spatial boundaries are defined for a specific social claim, activity or behaviour' (Agnew 1997, in Hudson 1998: 536). The spatial boundaries for world-scale credit practices will, then, be defined differently during different periods.

2 There are considerable linkages here to the work of Keynes. Keynes distinguished between two different types of economic expansion, which he termed 'virtuous' (productive expansion) and 'vicious' (speculative expansion). Vicious circles of expansion were seen as profoundly destabilising to both government policy-making and economic activity generally. For an understanding of contemporary world finance building upon this aspect of Keynes work, see Henwood (1997).

3 The categorisation of stock exchanges and clearing houses as 'civil institutions' is clearly contentious. 'Civil society' is used here in a Gramscian sense as an ideal-type analytical category that includes knowledge construction, non-state and non-market institutions, and the social forces that emerge in world order (cf. Murphy 1994). This contrasts with both the traditional equation of 'civil society' with the private realm of bourgeois interests, and the contemporary use of 'civil society' as the realm of resistance by autonomous groups that emerged first in the course of 1989 revolutions in Eastern Europe (cf. Cox 1999). Stock exchanges and clearing houses tend to be categorised as market institutions. For instance, Cutler *et al.* (1999: 10–11) class them as 'coordination services firms', that is firms that 'work closely and cooperatively with their customers' and 'promote recognised parallel practices among otherwise disconnected firms'. However, assuming that, as Cutler *et al.* and also Lütz (1997: 6–10) suggest, stock exchanges and clearing houses function primarily not as profit-making institutions but as regulatory institutions that enable the interests of a coalition of social forces, their categorisation as institutions of civil society would seem most appropriate.

4 Structural conceptualisations of space view geographical entities such as cities as having spatial effects that stem from their interrelationships with one another (Agnew 1994). Such an understanding of space is present in the world cities paradigm, where world cities become the nodal points for global control and a pre-requisite for the continuation of capital accumulation in the world-system as a result of their structural relationships to peripheral geographical areas (cf. Sassen 1991).

Part II

Modern world financial orders

3 From Amsterdam to London

The Dutch and British world financial orders

This chapter initiates our concrete historical inquiry into modern world finance. It begins with the Amsterdam-centred Dutch world financial order of the seventeenth and eighteenth centuries, and then moves to consider the London-centred British world financial order of the nineteenth and early twentieth centuries. An Historical IPE approach to world finance suggests that the Dutch financial order is the appropriate point for *longue durée* inquiry to commence. During the seventeenth century world credit practices first took on their modern form, becoming framed and legitimated by the principles of rationality and reason. The Dutch and British financial orders were, however, a complex mix of continuity and change.

In terms of the position of WFCs within world finance, the Dutch financial order was a continuation of the tendency since the fourteenth century for great mercantile cities to rise to WFC status. Amsterdam followed in the wake of Venice in the fourteenth and fifteenth centuries, and Antwerp and Genoa in the sixteenth century (Braudel 1977; Tilly 1990; Arrighi 1994). With the unravelling of the Dutch world financial order from the late eighteenth century, and the concurrent rise of London as WFC of the British financial order that became established after 1815, an important structural transformation took place in the nature of world financial orders. London stood, first and foremost, as the financial centre of the industrialising British national political economy (Kindleberger 1974/1978: 79–83; Braudel 1984: 35; Germain 1997: 45–7). With the emergence of European industrial state-society complexes during the nineteenth century, consolidated national political economies as imaginary and regulatory constructs came to form the foundations of both world financial orders and the world economy more broadly (Jacobs 1963; Radice 1984; Agnew and Corbridge 1995). As Cameron and Palan (1999: 274) summarise:

> The strongly territorial idea of the nation-state was from the outset closely bound up with the extension of regulatory control over the assets and transactions of the national population and the emergent institutions of the private and public sectors. At the same time, the state border as an economic boundary serves to separate and *create* the 'domestic' and the 'international' economies as discrete spaces.

With the consolidation of national political economies and, in particular, through the development of national currencies which formed an important element in the processes of consolidation (Giddens 1985; Gilbert and Helleiner 1999), state institutions came to assume a greater governance role in modern world finance.

Amsterdam: world financial centre

From the early seventeenth century through to the latter stages of the eighteenth century, there appears little doubt that Amsterdam stood at the pinnacle of world finance, *the* world financial centre (Barbour 1963; Braudel 1984; Kindleberger 1984/1993: 208–12; Germain 1997: 39–44).[1] Closely intertwined with Amsterdam's standing as the centre for world trade, corporate and commercial credit practices were centralised in Amsterdam. Although corporate credit practices remained relatively small-scale during this period, stocks on the Amsterdam Bourse were the first to take the form of a permanent investment as opposed to a recoverable subscription. Such modern fictitious capital supported the wide-reaching expansion of the Dutch East and West Indies companies in particular, the only two institutions in the seventeenth century that approximated to the contemporary corporation (Goldsmith 1987: 219). The creation of commercial credit took the form of the so-called 'commission' and 'acceptance trades' and involved the issue and trading of bills of exchange. The commission trade issued credit for both the purchase and sale of goods, while the acceptance trade focused on the underwriting and discounting of bills of exchange (Chapman 1984: 1–3). With the gradual decline of Amsterdam as the world's trading centre during the eighteenth century, the continued precedence of Amsterdam in commercial credit creation was closely intertwined with the expanded importance of the acceptance trade.

Accompanying the centralisation of commercial credit practices in Amsterdam, clearance and money-market practices were subject to a similar centrifugal spatiality and were institutionalised within the Amsterdam Exchange Bank and its network of private agents of collection and payment. The Bank both transferred obligations through its books, with daily transfers amounting to 10–12 million florins by 1776, and stood as a secure depository for the working balances of specie and precious metals used to make payments (Riley 1980: 28). As a secure depository, the Exchange Bank was effectively the key institution for money-market practices, attracting capital from all over Europe that sought a safe haven from social and political upheaval.

The Amsterdam capital market also stood as the 'pivot' (Braudel 1982: 395) for the provision of sovereign credit to Europe's royal and princely borrowers throughout the seventeenth century. Institutionalised through the Bourse and the networks of major market institutions such as Hope and Co., this often led to the situation whereby Amsterdam-centred credit was supporting both sides in a war (Barbour 1963: 106–11). A rapid expansion of Amsterdam-centred foreign sovereign credit creation took place during the latter half of the eighteenth century (Riley 1980: 14–16; Braudel 1984: 246–7; Arrighi 1994: 142). By the 1780s states including Britain, Sweden, Austria, Denmark, Russia, Poland, Spain, France and the United

States had become the principal debtors on the Amsterdam capital market. The escalation of wars between the European sovereigns and a significant structural shift in the nature of Amsterdam-centred practices lay at the roots of this expansion of sovereign credit creation. The horizons of Amsterdam's financiers became increasingly focused on the potential returns offered by sovereign credit creation and the acceptance trade, so that associated secondary trading practices based upon perceptions of risk and return expanded throughout Amsterdam's capital markets.

The rise of Amsterdam as a WFC was underpinned in synchronic terms by the centralisation of the material resources upon which world credit practices drew. The relative abundance of capital in Amsterdam ensured that, from the mid-seventeenth to the mid-eighteenth century at least, rates of interest on credit were lower in Amsterdam than elsewhere in Europe (Braudel 1982: 386; Goldsmith 1987: 218). The most immediate source of Amsterdam's accumulated capital was the Dutch 'agro-industrial production complex' (Wallerstein 1980: 44) that integrated primacy in high-quality textiles, shipbuilding, intensive agriculture, and fishing. Based upon Dutch colonies and naval and shipping supremacy, the centralisation of capital in Amsterdam also resulted from the city's position as mercantile entrepôt centre in the seventeenth century world economy. The Baltic, Far East and Americas trading networks intersected in Amsterdam in terms of exchange and distribution, proving mutually reinforcing (Germain 1997: 40–1). The bullion from the Americas that was used to pay for Baltic goods warehoused in Amsterdam also flowed onwards to the Far East to purchase luxury goods which were, in turn, shipped to Amsterdam. From the turn of the eighteenth century, Amsterdam's position as entrepôt centre for world trade became gradually undercut, eventually by-passed by the trading networks established by French, German and, in particular, British competitors.[2] Significantly, however, despite the gradual erosion of Amsterdam's commercial predominance, large volumes of capital remained centralised in Amsterdam (Wallerstein 1980: 57; Arrighi 1994: 138). From the 1740s in particular, Amsterdam-centred world credit practices themselves stimulated an influx of capital, as a consequence of returns on previous investments or their deposit-compelling influence on foreign mobile capital.

Information and technology centralised in Amsterdam provided further material resources upon which credit practices drew. Smith (1984) highlights that a series of more or less institutionalised world-wide networks served to establish Amsterdam as an 'information exchange' during the seventeenth century. These included the networks of private merchants, financiers and joint-stock companies, and the active commercial press that fed off these networks. Information concerning economic and political conditions throughout the world was processed both privately and publicly in Amsterdam yielding, for instance, the commodities price list of the Amsterdam Exchange.[3] Based around packet boats and stage coaches carrying regular postal correspondence between Europe's major cities (Israel 1995), established lines of communication ensured flows of information in, through and out of Amsterdam.

The making and reproduction of the Dutch financial order

Ownership and control of material resources was vital to the power relations that favoured Amsterdam's financiers. They also enjoyed social and political power that was essential to their dominant position in the making of the Dutch financial order. Amsterdam's merchants and financiers had realised a commonality of interests with the dynastic social forces of the Regent House of Orange and the anti-Rome sentiments of the Calvinists during the Dutch revolt against Spanish rule (1572–1609). Thereafter, a combination of the fragmented federal structure of the Dutch state apparatus and the importance of Amsterdam's wealth to Dutch state power ensured that Dutch mercantilism conformed to the interests of Amsterdam's social forces. Dutch mercantilism was 'the great exception among states in the era of mercantilism' (Wallerstein 1980: 58). While other European states followed protectionist–mercantilist strategies that sought to accumulate capital and generate balance of payments surpluses by importing and limiting the export of specie and precious metals, Dutch mercantilism was associated with the free flow of specie and credit to foreign borrowers. As such, Dutch mercantilism reinforced both the deposit-compelling power of Amsterdam in synchronic terms and, in diachronic terms, the capacity of Amsterdam's social forces to frame the making of the Dutch world financial order.

Considerable inter-state conflict throughout the seventeenth and eighteenth centuries did not lead to structural dislocation in the making and reproduction of the Dutch financial order. Contrary to the view of world-systems writers (Wallerstein 1980; Arrighi 1994), this was not simply the result from the hegemony of the United Provinces. The Dutch state was not hegemonic, but central in a wider world order in which inter-state relations were dominated by short-term alliances. For much of the eighteenth century up until 1770s, the United Provinces tended to ally with Britain against France, alliances built upon the accession to the British throne of William of Orange in the Glorious Revolution of 1688. Regular inter-state wars were in this sense coalition wars, with the United Provinces pivotal (Kennedy 1989: 94). As Braudel (1984: 256–60) suggests, the integral position of the United Provinces stemmed from the commercial and financial strengths of the Dutch form of state. These effectively undercut the capacity of the English and French forms of protectionist–mercantilist state to transform the Dutch financial order. Policies of disrupting Dutch commercial and financial networks tended to harm the English and French as much as they did the Dutch.

The making of the Dutch financial order was, then, framed by power relations that favoured Amsterdam's social forces and rested more broadly upon a climate of inter-state relations in which the Dutch were pivotal. Furthermore, the world financial order that emerged was characterised by relative stability, as power relations and the forms of credit practices in which they were manifest were broadly accepted as legitimate. At the core of relative stability in the Dutch financial order was the diffusion and emulation throughout the order of the shared norms and meanings that informed Amsterdam-centred credit practices as organisational principles. Considerable similarities existed between the norms and meanings surrounding credit practices in Amsterdam and those which had predominated in the major financial centres of Europe since at least the fourteenth century (Braudel 1977: 66–7). However, significant innovations were also made in Amsterdam that contributed towards the transformation of understandings of the practices of credit creation and the motivations that lay behind them. As Chancellor (2000: 9) asserts:

> Although the Dutch did not invent the institutions and practices of financial capitalism such as banking, double-entry bookkeeping, joint-stock companies, bills of exchange, and stock markets, they brought together and established them on a secure basis in a mercantile economy organised around a highly evolved profit motive.

Amsterdam-centred credit practices slowly became subject to calculations of profit and risk rooted in assumptions of rationality (de Goede 1998). Understandings of 'usury' became redefined not as the charging of interest itself, but as the charging of excessive rates (Visser and MacIntosh 1998). Financiers were no longer regarded as irrational gamblers but as men whose practices were framed by a growing science. For instance, Joseph Penso de la Vega published his *Confusion de Confusions* in Amsterdam in 1688, the first treatise on futures contracts, hedging, and options for puts and refuses (Chancellor 2000: 11–13). Assumptions of rationality provided the basis for a universalisation and intensification of world credit practices which served to set the Dutch financial order apart from pre-modern world finance (Barbour 1963: 140, 142; Braudel 1982: 390–5).

The epistemic authority of Amsterdam's social forces did not result, however, from a simple acceptance of the assumption that decisions to create credit should be based primarily upon the rational assessment of risk rather than loyalties to princes or merchants. French and British forms of mercantilism in particular mitigated the capacity of such a cosmopolitan discourse of governance to become embraced throughout the Dutch financial order in a straight-forward manner. Rather, it was the competitive emulation of the sovereign credit arrangements of their Dutch counterparts by protectionist–mercantilist state managers that lay at the cutting edge of the diffusion of modern understandings of credit practices that was essential for relative stability in the Dutch financial order. In the context of regular inter-state conflict, the protectionist–mercantilist states came to recognise that access to Amsterdam-centred sovereign credit gave the Dutch a relative competitive advantage in war making (Cox 1987: 115; Kennedy 1989: 98–111). The raising of wartime sovereign credit by protectionist–mercantilist states had traditionally been associated with a combination of emergency borrowing from a narrow pool of loyal lenders and recourse to foreign credit. Sovereign credit practices were widely regarded as hazardous and defaults were common. By contrast and buoyed by assumptions that the risks of credit creation were calculable, particularly for limited monarchies (Leyshon and Thrift 1997: 18–19), sovereign credit practices came to be regarded as a relatively safe investment in Amsterdam during the seventeenth century (Barbour 1963: 80–1). This facilitated both a widening of the pool of investors upon which Dutch sovereign credit relied, and longer-term credit planning by the state through instruments which included annuities, bonds and lottery loans (Kindleberger 1984/1993: 156). It was these alternative arrangements for sovereign credit, and the modern norms and meanings upon which they rested, that other European governments, more or less consciously and with varying success, sought to emulate alongside continued recourse to the foreign sovereign credit provided by Amsterdam's merchant bankers.

Amsterdam's market institutional networks, in particular the major merchant banks such as Hope and Co. and Clifford and Son, provided the institutional basis for the reproduction of relative stability in the Dutch financial order. The governance role of Amsterdam's market networks was rooted in their formal authority in the organisation of world credit practices. As had been the case with the networks of the Bardi and Peruzzi of fourteenth-century Florence and the networks of the *nobili vecchi* of sixteenth-century Genoa, it was broadly accepted that demands for large-scale credit could not be met without their capital, contacts and expertise. For instance, given the uncertainties and risks surrounding the direct issue of credit by sovereign borrowers, institutions such as Hope and Co. organised the technicalities of both the issue and placement of bonds directly and via the principal stock exchanges (Born 1977: 28). The interdependent intersection of market networks with the Exchange Bank and Bourse was also significant to the exercise of formal authority within Amsterdam as a complex of governance. The clearing of credit claims through the Exchange Bank acted as an unofficial form of regulation of world credit practices (Born 1977: 27). The meeting of obligations under the Bank's guidance reduced uncertainty, providing a level of security and adjustment that was rare in this period (Barbour 1963: 44–7; Riley 1980: 28–9). Such security was particularly significant in the context of the slowdown in the world economy in the seventeenth century and the associated monetary disturbances. At the same time, the capacity of the Bank to capture and hold massive volumes of specie both maintained confidence in florin-denominated credit creation and limited the basis upon which credit could be created in and through rival centres such as London and Genoa (Kindleberger 1984/1993: 52). In a not dissimilar vein, the Bourse also performed a role as a 'central regulatory mechanism' (Arrighi 1994: 140) that arose from its authority over the mobilisation of the capital necessary for long-term credit creation.

The interdependent intersection of Amsterdam's market institutions with the Exchange Bank and Bourse also lay at the heart of *ad hoc* attempts to authoritatively manipulate the organisation of world credit practices during sporadic financial crises. Market networks tended to collectively mobilise their capital resources in support of those struggling institutions whose assets inspired confidence. Further, during the 1763 crisis, the Bank took the unprecedented step of accepting gold and silver ingots in an attempt to increase the coverage of outstanding claims and, thereby, to increase confidence (Braudel 1984: 269). Crisis management was supported by the reach of the Amsterdam-centred structure of governance throughout the financial order. This led to the enlisting of the support of London-centred institutions in instances of crisis. For example, in the course of the crisis of 1763, the Bank of England and London-centred market networks granted credit to their counterparts from Amsterdam. Similarly, in January 1773 the Bank of England allowed specie to be drawn on the presentation of Dutch government stock certificates (Kindleberger 1978: 183–4). In our terms, London-centred assistance was significant as it reflected the relative stability of the Dutch financial order. Not only did London's social forces broadly accept the hierarchical Dutch financial order, but moved to support the Amsterdam-centred structure of governance that reproduced the order.

The unravelling of the Dutch financial order

The relative stability of the Dutch financial order reflected the acceptance of power relations in which Amsterdam's financiers were predominant as legitimate. Acceptance was founded upon the world-wide diffusion of the meanings surrounding credit creation from Amsterdam as the order's organisational principles. In turn, Amsterdam-centred institutions were able to perform a governance role that, by virtue of their authority in the administration and management of credit practices, entrenched and reproduced the order. Any decentralisation signalled, then, the unravelling of the order in the sense of both the disintegration of its relatively stable coalition of social forces and the erosion of the capacity of Amsterdam to stand as the key complex of governance.

The unravelling of the Dutch financial order was a slow and drawn-out set of processes. Up until the 1780s, Amsterdam's financiers continued to stand alone at the pinnacle of world finance and the intricate Amsterdam-centred edifice of governance remained intact. From the 1740s, however, a contradiction had begun to emerge that was to prove significant in the unravelling of the Dutch financial order. Given the long-term decline of Amsterdam as a commercial centre, the centralisation of capital in Amsterdam during this period came to increasingly rely upon attracting mobile capital. On the one hand, as Wallerstein (1980: 57) notes, attracting accumulated capital was a sign of the strength of Amsterdam and of the continuing material power of Amsterdam's social forces. On the other hand, however, as Braudel (1984: 246) asserts, this 'stage of financial expansion' in Amsterdam was 'a sign of autumn' in its standing as a WFC. Attracting mobile capital entailed offering the prospect of high returns through secondary trading in credit instruments, and a vicious circle of speculative expansion that was disembedded from production and trade became a structural feature of the Dutch financial order. The value of credit instruments expanded, in turn, nourishing speculative and crisis-ridden credit practices. Each crisis was followed by attempts to encourage further inflows of capital in the form of silver and gold in order to try to restore confidence (Riley 1980: 32–4; Braudel 1984: 269–72). The crises of 1763, 1772–3 and the early 1780s were the immediate manifestations of a contradiction in the material basis of Amsterdam's standing as a WFC.

The roots of the material contradiction of the Dutch financial order lay in the rise of London and the industrialising British national political economy to challenge Dutch pre-eminence. Contrary to the interpretation of world-systems scholars (Wallerstein 1980: 281), the rise of London was largely independent of the vicious circle of speculation centred in Amsterdam. Such autonomous development was closely bound to the emergence of Britain as the first national industrial political economy to dominate the world economy (Hobsbawm 1968). The Dutch financial order became increasingly decentralised between Amsterdam-centred credit creation and the largely independent London-centred financing of British trade and sovereign spending (Brewer 1989).[4] An uneasy and relatively unstable coexistence had emerged in which both Amsterdam and London stood at the pinnacle of the hierarchy of world finance. In effect, the social forces of neither Amsterdam nor London were predominant.

Changes in the wider world order accompanied the waning relative power of Amsterdam's social forces in contributing to the gradual unravelling of the Dutch financial order. Elements of the wider world order that had previously underpinned the order were no longer present. From the 1770s, the close alliance between the United Provinces and Britain that had marked inter-state relations for nearly a century unwound. This culminated in the Dutch entering the American War of Independence in 1780 on the French side. As the power of the United Provinces waned, the Dutch lost their integral position in inter-state relations. In this period of intensified mercantilist rivalry, Dutch mercantilism and the material resources of the Amsterdam capital market upon which it drew were becoming inadequate (Riley 1980: 197–8; Kindleberger 1996: 103). As a consequence, the United Provinces was no longer able to prevent inter-state wars from leading to serious dislocation in the Dutch financial order.

The combination of material and wider world order changes in the unravelling of the Dutch financial order became particularly apparent in the course of the fourth Anglo–Dutch war of 1780–3. During the war, the market institution of van Faerelinks was forced into bankruptcy after an over-extension of credit and the Amsterdam-centred structure of governance proved unable to come to its aid. The Exchange Bank collapsed as unprecedented extensions of credit in support of the Dutch East Indies Company undermined confidence in its capacity to cover outstanding deposits (Kindleberger 1984/1993: 50). Furthermore, in contrast with the previous two major crises of 1763 and 1772–3, London-centred support for crisis management failed to materialise. This was not surprising given the ongoing Anglo–Dutch war (Kindleberger 1978: 184). Indeed, in the context of the war, the collapse of the Exchange Bank was itself closely associated with the seizure of Dutch colonies and attacks on the ships of the Dutch East Indies Company by the British navy (Roberts 1995: 181). Amid relative instability in the Dutch financial order that itself arose from a combination of material and inter-state factors, then, the capacity of Amsterdam's governance institutions to reproduce the order had been finally ruptured.

The transformation that the rise of London implied for the nature of world financial orders – i.e. that national industrial political economies were to stand as the foundations for future world financial orders – was, however, far from inevitable. It was to take the defeat of French expansionism in the Napoleonic wars from 1793 to finally bring about the conditions for such a transformation. The Napoleonic wars had three principal sets of consequences that fed the concurrent processes of the unravelling of the Dutch financial order and establishment of the London-centred British financial order.

First, the successful French invasion of Amsterdam during the Napoleonic wars and the ensuing establishment of the Batavian Republic effectively dissolved the configuration of social and political power relations within the United Provinces that had benefited Amsterdam's social forces. Consequently, through a series of forced loans, levies and the regulation of foreign loans, the Amsterdam capital market came to almost exclusively service the credit needs of the Dutch state (Riley 1980: 197; Kindleberger 1984/1993: 7; Neal 1990: 225–6).

Second, the wars led to the disruption and disintegration of Amsterdam's world-wide market institutional networks. The majority of Europe's cosmopolitan financiers sought shelter in London from Napoleonic expansion (Neal 1990: 198; Kynaston 1994: 26–7; Roberts 1995: 181–2).

Third, the victory of the dynastic British state over the Napoleonic empire at last heralded a transformation in the foundations of future world financial orders. British victory rested largely upon its independence from the crumbling Dutch financial order (Kennedy 1989: 101–3). Unlike the French state's reliance upon foreign credit, the British state was able to draw upon the material resources of a consolidated and industrialising national political economy in time of war (Riley 1980: 199–200). With the emergence of dynastic, territorially bounded state-societies across Europe, national political economies came to form the foundations of both the world financial order and the world economy more broadly. British victory in the Napoleonic wars finally shattered the broad structural coherence that had marked world finance since the fourteenth century.

London: world financial centre

In the aftermath of the Napoleonic wars, London stood at the apex of the hierarchy of the world's financial centres, a position that it was to occupy throughout the 'Hundred Years Peace' of 1815 to 1914. Considerable academic debate surrounds whether London shared its position as at the apex of this hierarchy with Paris, evidenced in the main by the consistently lower levels of short-term interest rates in Paris up to 1914 (cf. Walter 1993: 89). Paris may have mounted a brief challenge to London from the 1850s through to the suspension of the convertibility of the franc in 1870 (Bagehot 1873/1991: 63; Kindleberger 1996: 136), but in the main stood alongside Berlin as a second tier of regional financial centres (Kindleberger 1984/1993: 263; Germain 1997: 55–6). Paris- and Berlin-centred credit practices serviced the commercial and industrial needs of their respective national political economies, with foreign lending directed according to their respective imperial considerations from the 1870s.

London's position as the single WFC after 1815 is revealed by its dominance of world credit practices. In contrast to the largely European reach of Amsterdam-centred credit practices during the previous centuries, London-centred credit practices were undertaken at a world-scale that to some extent embraced Africa, Asia, Oceania, Latin and North America (Held *et al.* 1999: 193–4). Commercial credit practices in support of British – and later, world – trade took the form of issuing and trading bills of exchange and commodity futures contracts, institutionalised within specialised merchant banks called acceptance houses – Barings, Brown Shipley and Co., and Wiggin Wilson and Wildes (Chapman 1984: 8–15). Of the commercial bills outstanding in London by 1913–14, two-thirds represented credit allocated for trade that did not touch British shores, even for re-export (Michie 1992: 72–3). Grounded in their role in the provision of credit for post-war reconstruction, the merchant banks of Barings, Rothschilds and JS Morgan (which became Morgan Grenfell after 1869) all emerged after the Napoleonic wars as the major institutions through which London-centred sovereign bond issues were organised (Kindleberger 1984/1993: 214–15; Kynaston 1994: 24–5). They did not relinquish their grip on foreign sovereign credit creation for much the next one hundred years. Meanwhile, particularly from the 1850s and as the demand for sovereign credit decreased during peacetime (Roberts 1995: 153–4), the very same merchant banks provided the backing for large-scale industrial ventures in conjunction with the brokers and jobbers of the London Stock Exchange. London provided huge volumes of the credit necessary for railway construction and other long-term infrastructural undertakings throughout Europe, Africa, North and Latin America. Increased demands for credit associated with more capital-intensive industrial production such as mining, iron and metal working across Europe and North America were, however, largely satisfied by domestic joint-stock and universal banks (Born 1977: 46–52). Corporate credit creation in London came in the latter stages of the hundred years' peace to focus, in the main, on the provision of credit for productive ventures that sheltered under the umbrella of British imperial expansion.

Clearance and money-market practices were also centralised in London. Clearing in the British political economy had become institutionalised in the London Clearing House and its membership of clearing banks in Lombard Street in 1773. After the Napoleonic wars, London came to stand as the 'one major clearing house of universal scope' (Anderson 1987: 33), where the world's bullion, credit, and foreign exchange markets met (Brown 1940: 142; Kindleberger 1996: 136). The world's merchants, bankers and central bankers maintained large working balances in London in order to clear their sterling-denominated claims and obligations (Brown 1940: 10–11; Germain 1997: 51). Idle working balances were also 'borrowable money' (Bagehot 1873/1991: 3) that stimulated by far the largest money-market in the world.[5] Money-market practices were able to match the supply of short-term funds searching for returns with the demand for long-term credit the world over (Brown 1940: 142; Michie 1992: 75–7), as the jobbers of the Stock Exchange in particular sought to profit from interest rate differentials.

London's rise as the key social space for world credit practices rested upon the centralisation of material resources. The relative abundance of capital in London during the nineteenth century was in part a result of its standing as the world's commercial centre. With the backing of the British navy, London's merchants had been pivotal in establishing British dominance over the Baltic, Atlantic and Far East trading networks in the course of the latter half of the eighteenth century. However, as Braudel (1984: 35) notes of the rise and fall of successive world commercial and financial centres, 'With London, we move into a completely different context; this great city had at its command the English national market'. London dominated the British national political economy and, supported by imperialism and commercial success, industrialised Britain dominated the world economy for much of the nineteenth century (Hobsbawm 1968; Kynaston 1994: 9–13). The networks of the country and joint-stock banks at home and the foreign and colonial joint-stock banks abroad channelled a vast mass of accumulated capital into London that was far in excess of that at the disposal of Amsterdam's financiers a century earlier (de Cecco 1974; Kindleberger 1984/1993: 79–81; Anderson 1987; King 1990). Somewhat paradoxically, however, the 'high period' (Germain 1997: 47) or 'golden age' (Kynaston 1995: 8) of London's standing as a WFC from around 1870 to 1914 corresponded with the relative decline of British industry in the face of German and American competition and the increased protectionism and imperial scrambles associated with the unravelling of the '*Pax Britannica*' (Imlah 1958; Hobsbawm 1968: 103–4). From the 1870s, London-centred credit creation became materially less reliant upon capital newly accumulated through British trade and industrial production. Instead, it took place largely on the back of mobile capital in general and capital accumulated through previous rounds of credit creation (Feis 1930/1964: 16–17; Brown 1940: 159; Roberts 1995: 182).[6] Echoes of Amsterdam's experience of financialisation in the latter half of the eighteenth century are clear. London displayed what Brown (1940: 154) terms 'deposit-compelling power', whereby capital was attracted to and maintained in London principally on the basis of the capacity of London-centred credit practices to offer relatively high returns. The material basis of London's high period as a WFC was not, then, simply a continued reflection of its standing as the financial centre of the British national political economy, but also closely related to its own independent development as an entrepôt WFC.[7]

Information and technology centralised in London during this period was also a key material resource for world credit practices. London rivalled Amsterdam as an information exchange by the end of the eighteenth century, and surpassed both Amsterdam and Paris by the conclusion of the Napoleonic wars (Neal 1990: 20). The information centralised in London was a consequence of the overlapping of a broad range of networks. These included the merchant networks of London's Baltic Exchange (Michie 1992: 41), the insurance networks co-ordinated through Lloyd's of London (Michie 1992: 148–54), the financial information provided by London's merchant banking networks themselves (Cassis 1994: 43), and the networks of service firms, most notably accountants, that provided information on the financial positions of joint-stock companies throughout the world (Michie 1992: 176–7). London's financial press, especially *The Economist* (1843) and the *Financial Times* (1888), supplemented these networks and reported their content throughout London. Significantly, London was also at the heart of the introduction of the telegraph and telephone from the 1850s, placing it at the centre of an internationalisation of economic and financial information during this period (Parsons 1989). The telegraph was first used by Paul Reuter in 1851 to exchange stock prices between London and Paris, while a permanent telegraph link was established between London and New York in 1866 (Michie 1992: 184–5; Kynaston 1995: 51). The first telephone exchange in Britain was introduced in London in 1879 – only three years after the telephone had first been tested (Thrift 1994: 344). The significance of these communications networks lay in their capacity to enable the more rapid transfer of information in, through and out of London and to facilitate speculative trading on price differentials between London and other financial centres.

The making and reproduction of the British financial order

The power relations that emerged from the centralisation of material capabilities in London contributed to the capacity of London's social forces to frame the making of the British financial order. London's social forces enjoyed unrivalled positions of ownership, access and control over the capital, information and technology relevant to world credit practices. Social and political power relations in British state-society took a liberal configuration that also enabled the dominant role of London's social forces in the making of the British financial order. The effective designation of 'economy' as an institutionally separate realm of self-regulating market relations both at home and abroad was crucial (cf. Polanyi 1944: 70). London's financiers and Britain's merchants and manufacturers could legitimately pursue their economic interests free from feudal or mercantilist social relations in the realm of the self-regulating market. In contrast to the political restrictions placed on credit creation by the governments of continental Europe (Feis 1930/1964: 83–186), British state officials wedded to free trade, the gold standard and fiscal rectitude sought to largely divorce the 'economy' of finance from foreign policy.

The liberal policies pursued by successive British governments that effectively bracketed economy and finance from political interference should not, however, be equated with the domination of the machinery of the British state by London's social forces in an instrumentalist sense.[8] A series of complex changes in British state-society relations from the 1820s appears to have underpinned the emergence of the liberal form of state (Hobsbawm 1968: 24; van der Pijl 1989). The intersection of various social forces in these processes suggests that the adoption of liberal policies is not reducible to the triumph of the interests of London's social forces (Ingham 1984: 101–6). For instance, while the expansion of British imperialism from the latter stages of the nineteenth century clearly benefited London, this expansion seems likely to have been driven by the general threat to British manufacturers of increased protectionism across continental Europe (Ingham 1984: 125–6). The significance of the liberal policies of the British state, then, lies not in the manipulation of the British state by London's social forces, but in the manner in which the state form was supportive of the power of London's social forces in the making of the British financial order.

Conditions in the wider world order were also conducive to London's social forces framing the possible organisation of credit practices in the British financial order. Patterns of state–societal transformation underway across western Europe and North America broadly served to legitimate the power of London's social forces. The rise of mass politics and the increased freedoms of the press and judiciary contrasted sharply with the reactionary, interventionist and militaristic nature of the Napoleonic expansion that had finally brought the Dutch financial order to its knees (Gill 1991: 280). Meanwhile, inter-state struggle and conflict did not interfere with the capacity of London's social forces to make and reproduce the British financial order. During the Hundred Years Peace of 1815–1914, an inter-state balance of power existed in Europe in which the British state was principal (Polanyi 1944; Imlah 1958; Cox 1987: 123–9). British naval superiority and diplomatic manoeuvrings through the Concert of Europe were vital to the post-1815 balance of power.

The British financial order that emerged from the first decades of the nineteenth century was characterised by relative stability, as hierarchical power relations and the organisation of world credit practices in which they were manifest were broadly accepted as legitimate. At the core of relative stability in the British financial order was the diffusion throughout the order of the shared norms and meanings that informed London-centred credit practices. The meanings and norms surrounding credit creation in London in the nineteenth century constituted organisational principles that bore close resemblance to those of the Dutch financial order. In nineteenth century London, however, Amsterdam's long-standing modern meanings and cosmopolitan values were given a firm theoretical underpinning by the classical liberalism of Adam Smith and David Ricardo and later by the neo-classicism of Stanley Jevons and Alfred Marshall. During the late eighteenth and early nineteenth centuries, the British classical economists who took up where *The Wealth of Nations* left off had, by virtue of the abnormal demands for sovereign credit emanating from successive wars, turned their attention to theorising money and credit (Deane 1978: 44). Subsequent debates about the relationship of paper money to gold and the operational capacity of the Bank of England only served to further encourage concern with issues of money and credit. Many of those economists involved, such as Jewish stockbroker Ricardo and banker and Member of Parliament Henry Thornton, were from the upper echelons of London's financial community. Economics graduates often found their way to London's financial institutions, and lectures delivered to audiences in the City often formed an important component in the working week of a British economist (Deane 1978: 72). As the marginalist revolution took hold and the emerging 'science' of economics turned to the methodology of mathematics, credit practices clearly lent themselves to the empirical testing of theories concerned, in particular, with the workings of the gold standard and the determination of prices and rates of interest.[9] The assumed allocative efficiency of the market led political restrictions on international loans to become viewed both as harmful to the prosperity and power generated by world trade, and as serving to prevent them from assisting in bringing about an equilibrium in the world's balance-of-payments.

The epistemic authority of London's social forces was not, however, a consequence of a straightforward liberal consensus in the British financial order. Contrary to *laissez-faire* organisational principles, the state-based direction of credit creation remained the norm across continental Europe and a broader shift to protectionism took hold in the world economy following Bismarck's Tariff of Rye and Iron in 1879 (Walter 1993: 90–1). Instead, relative stability based around liberal organisational principles and the governance role of London became established in the British financial order somewhat indirectly as a consequence of the adoption of the international gold standard by the governments of continental Europe (cf. Polanyi 1944: 14). Within the framework of the balance of power, Europe's governments adopted the gold standard as they sought to emulate British economic success, maintain fixed exchange rates, consolidate national monetary arrangements, compete for financial business and improve their creditworthiness (Walter 1993: 91–2, 250–1; Helleiner 1999: 140–5). The *de facto* consequences for the British financial order of the widespread adoption of the international gold standard were considerable. Albeit to a greater or lesser extent, Europe's governments chose to adhere to the discipline of the gold standard over and above domestic economic considerations (Ruggie 1982), thereby effectively accepting liberal organisational principles and the institutionalisation of the formal authority of London in the financial order's reproduction.

The international gold standard developed as part of the British financial order and wider world order and, in practice, operated as a sterling exchange standard.[10] As the complex of governance that was pivotal to the reproduction of the British financial order, then, London undertook the administration and management of both financial and monetary practices. Public and private, formal and informal authority came together to form a London-centred edifice of governance in financial and monetary affairs that Ingham (1984: 128–51) characterises as the 'City–Bank of England–Treasury nexus'. Public and private authority was interdependent with each other in the reproduction of the British financial order, underpinned by a wider world order context that was conducive to such a structure of governance. As Cox (1987: 111) contends, 'the world economy functioned through private agencies, centred mainly in the City of London, that were symbiotically related to the British state and to the Europe-centred state system'. While the British financial order saw an expanded governance role for public institutions in comparison with the Dutch financial order, this increased responsibility remained circumscribed by interdependent relationships within London as the complex of governance.

The coming together in London of public and private formal authority in an elaborate structure of governance can be seen particularly clearly with reference to the role of the Bank of England in the reproduction of the British financial order. While the crucial contribution of the Bank is widely acknowledged – the 'conductor of the international orchestra' in Keynes' famous phrase – existing accounts tend to focus rather narrowly on the position of the Bank within the workings of the gold standard. This leads to an emphasis on the operational capacity of the Bank in terms of the provision of liquidity, facilitating adjustment, guaranteeing convertibility and managing financial crises (e.g. Gilpin 1987: 123–7). However, the various facets of the Bank's operational capacity appear to have rested more broadly on its position within London as a WFC (Williams 1963: 513–14; Roberts 1995: 155–9), as the Bank's potential and actual sterling liabilities to foreigners were vastly in excess of its gold reserves (de Cecco 1974). An adequate supply of liquidity was dependent upon the provision of sterling-denominated credit, rooted in world-wide confidence in the convertibility of sterling to gold (Brown 1940; Ingham 1994). In particular, London-centred short- and long-term advances of credit and the clearance of credit and debt obligations were key to addressing adjustment (Brown 1940: 775, 777; Michie 1992: 78). The ability of the Bank to manipulate liquidity through the Bank rate rested largely on the deposit-compelling power of London's money-market practices (Walter 1993: 103–4),[11] supported by the prevalence of the sound banking practices of London's merchant banks themselves. Indeed, for Brown (1940: 778), 'the development, empirically, under the leadership of the Bank of England, of a stable and conservative type of banking management' was one of the two 'foundation stones' of the British financial order.

Furthermore, the Bank was reliant upon close co-operation with other London-centred institutions to manage the superficial fluctuations to credit practices emanating from sporadic financial crises. In short, London as a complex of governance acted as lender of last resort, not the Bank. For instance, when the solvency of Barings was threatened in 1890 following an over extension of credit to Argentina, the Governor of the Bank established an underwriting syndicate to prevent bankruptcy which included the Treasury, Rothschilds and other leading market institutions (Ingham 1984: 165–6; Cassis 1994: 6). London's deposit-compelling power lay at the roots of the capacity of the Bank to attract gold and internationally mobile capital to London without undermining the wider provision of credit to the world economy. Perhaps more significantly, as Kindleberger (1978: 183–90) highlights, commitment to the international gold standard and the European balance-of-power effectively translated into support for the authority of the Bank of England by other European central banks. Between 1824 and 1914, continental European central banks came to the assistance of the Bank of England on four principal occasions. First, in 1825 the Bank of France channelled £400,000 worth of gold sovereigns to the Bank of England via the market institutional network of Rothschilds. Second, between 1836 and 1839, the Bank of England was able to draw credit of £400,000 and £2 million from Paris and £900,000 from Hamburg in support of its own liquidity. Third, in 1890, with the collapse of Barings seemingly imminent, the Bank was able to gain assurances from the Russian government that it would not withdraw £2.4 million worth of deposits that it held with the Bank, and the Bank secured £3 million worth of loans from the Bank of France. Finally, the Bank of France assisted the Bank of England in 1907 by selling gold in the London markets. In our terms, such assistance to the Bank of England was significant as it reflected the relative stability of the British financial order. Not only was the British financial order broadly accepted as legitimate, but the structure of governance that reproduced the order enjoyed crucial support in moments of crisis.

Alongside the Bank of England, the London Stock Exchange (LSE) also formed part of the institutional edifice through which London stood as the key complex of governance in the reproduction of the British financial order. The LSE was the institution through which the capital necessary for long-term credit creation was mobilised. In particular, it was through the LSE that the vast sums of short-term capital residing in London's money-markets became organised for long-term credit creation. From the middle of the nineteenth century, the LSE emerged as the central institution in a reasonably well-integrated world securities market (Kynaston 1995: 10–11). The significance of the civil authority of the LSE lay not in the universalisation of long-term credit creating practices around the LSE as a 'model', as the norms and meanings that informed the practices of stock exchanges tended to reflect local conditions. Instead, the governance role of the LSE was rooted in its authority in long-term credit creating practices, as the practices, and to some extent capital and price movements, of other stock exchanges were defined in relation to the LSE (Michie 1992: 134). The position of the LSE in the organisation of the world's long-term credit provision itself was underpinned by the rules and norms of the LSE, especially its limited regulations, negotiable structure for commissions, and willingness to expand membership to include foreign nationals.

Within the London-centred structure of governance that reproduced the British financial order, 'The banks at the heart of the City were the cornerstone of the whole edifice' (Cassis 1994: 5). The specialised market institutional networks centralised in London formed something of a complementary intersection in the organisation of world credit practices (Cassis 1994: 5–6). The clearing banks cleared obligations, provided short-term loans and collected deposits that the discount houses accessed through money-market practices to discount bills of exchange. The acceptance of bills of exchange, along with the prudent organisation of foreign sovereign and corporate credit practices, was the preserve of the great merchant banks of Rothschilds, Barings, C.J. Hambro and Kleinworts. Securities issued through the merchant banks were, in turn, placed through the jobbers and brokers of the London Stock Exchange. Through institutional networks extending across Europe, North and South America that included between 1500 and 2000 foreign branches by 1913 (Cassis 1991: 55), London's merchant banks dominated the organisation of foreign sovereign and corporate credit during the British financial order. Between 1860 and 1904, Barings and Rothschilds alone undertook 250 sovereign and corporate issues with a value of £1.9 billion (Michie 1992: 111). In the British world financial order, then, decisions regarding the creation and allocation of credit were largely institutionalised within the market networks of London-centred banks and financial houses. The institutional edifice of London's authority guaranteed these decisions.

The governance role of London's merchant banking networks in the organisation of sovereign credit practices has tended to inform a widespread perception of their 'political identity'.[12] For instance, based on a reading of Polanyi (1944), Arrighi (1994: 167) suggests that *haute finance* as a class dominated by London's merchant bankers acted as 'the "invisible hand" of an imperial organisation', part of 'the power apparatus through which Britain ruled the world'. Born (1977: 34–5) highlights that London's merchant banking networks, largely as a consequence of their sovereign lending to Europe's governments, sought to maintain peace throughout Europe. Not dissimilarly, Polanyi (1944: 10) asserts that 'the secret of the successful maintenance of general peace lay undoubtedly in the position, organization, and techniques of international finance'. The common feature of these perceptions is an assumption that London's merchant banking networks contributed not only to the governance and reproduction of the relative stability of the British financial order, but to the balance of power within the wider world order more broadly. In our terms, not only did London's position as the key complex of governance rest upon the wider world order, but it also contributed to the maintenance of a balance of power within that order up to 1914.

Conclusions

The Dutch and British financial orders were marked by significant continuities. World credit practices took a 'modern' form in both orders, framed and legitimated by the principles of rationality and reason. Each financial order was centred in a single WFC as the key space for world credit practices and the material, ideational and institutional forces that framed them. Based upon favourable material, social and political power relations and resting upon wider world orders that enabled the power relations that emerged, the social forces of Amsterdam and London were pivotal to the making of their respective financial orders. Amsterdam and London were also the key complexes of governance in the reproduction of relative stability in the Dutch and British financial orders. Relative stability hinged upon the shared meanings and values of the dominant WFC becoming accepted as the appropriate organisational principles in each order. The epistemic authority enjoyed by the social forces of Amsterdam and London was accompanied by their more formal, institutionalised authority in the administration and management of world credit practices.

While the rise to predominance of Amsterdam and London as WFCs was underpinned by patterns of capital accumulation emanating from world trade and industrial production, both enjoyed periods of somewhat independent development as entrepôt WFCs. During their periods as entrepôt WFCs, Amsterdam and London continued to stand as key spaces of governance in their respective financial orders. A relatively narrow focus on the rise and fall of states' wealth and power is insufficient, then, to account for the organisation of world credit practices. Rather, world credit practices come to be organised across a succession of hierarchical social orders.

The period of interregnum and relative instability in world finance that coincided with the unravelling of the Dutch financial order was associated with the decentralisation of the order between Amsterdam and London. The London-centred British financial order that emerged after 1815 heralded an important structural discontinuity in world financial orders: national industrial political economies came to form the foundations of world finance and the world economy more broadly. Given the close relationship between the consolidation of national political economies and the construction of national currencies, the British financial order saw an increasing role for public institutions in the structure of world financial governance. However, the governance capacity of the Bank of England remained interdependent with London's market and civil institutions in the reproduction of relative stability. During the British financial order, then, the increased authority of state institutions did not serve to erode the significance of WFCs as complexes of governance.

Notes

1 The infamous Dutch tulip bulb mania and ensuing crash on 1637 did little to interrupt the consolidation of Amsterdam as a WFC. For the principal financiers and merchants, 'tulips remained merely an expression of wealth, not a means to an end', so they were 'largely unaffected' when the crash came (Chancellor 2000: 20).

2 Amsterdam's position as the world's mercantile entrepôt centre had been visible in the breakdown of British trade at the end of the seventeenth century, when the United Provinces were Britain's principal export market, receiving goods valued at £1,500,000 out of the total value of British exports of £3,500,000. By 1775 a major transformation had taken place as British exports and re-exports had become firmly centralised in London and Liverpool, with only £1,000,000 worth of British exports bound for the United Provinces out of a total value of £14,800,000 (Haley 1988: 160–1).

3 Capital market prices do appear to have been systematically publicly listed in London from the late seventeenth century, well in advance of a similar service in Amsterdam (Braudel 1982: 103; Neal 1990: 27–9). However, it was Amsterdam that provided much of the information which informed world credit practices relative to London's more nationally-based information networks (Meyer 1991: 101).

4 For instance, the demands of the British state for credit to finance the Napoleonic wars were met without much recourse to foreign borrowing, with only £20 million out of a total national debt of £500 million under foreign ownership in 1807–10 (Haley 1988: 168–9).

5 Bagehot (1873/1991: 2) suggests that based on those banks that published figures for deposits, London held balances to the value of £120 million, compared with £40 million for New York and £13 million for Paris.

6 The accumulation of the deposits of foreign and colonial joint-stock banks in London, totalling £1.9 billion by 1914 (almost twice the level of domestic British bank deposits), is illustrative of the general inflow of mobile capital into London. The particular significance of the centralisation of capital in London generated by previous rounds of foreign lending is visible in terms of the breakdown of British foreign earnings. By 1913, around £200 million net in interest, dividends and repayments were returning to Britain from abroad, accounting for 22 per cent of British foreign earnings in that year (figures from Michie 1992: 74, 111).

7 It was not simply that London-centred credit creation drew upon purely British capital up until the 1870s, as is illustrated by Britain's position as a marginal net-debtor state in the short term throughout much of the nineteenth century (Germain 1997: 54). See Imlah (1958: 42–81) for details of British balance-of-payments between 1816 and 1913. However, the significance of foreign capital centralised in London did clearly increase, reflected in the growing significance of the invisible earnings generated by London-centred credit creation in the British balance-of-payments (Cassis 1994: 7).

8 For such an instrumentalist view, see Arrighi (1994).

9 Liberal values did not, contrary to neo-classical economics, inform 'rational' decisions regarding everyday credit allocation. Decisions regarding creditworthiness appear likely

to have been taken on the basis of the reputation of potential debtors when assessing the risks involved in credit creation, underpinned by common class, educational and social affiliations of London's social forces (cf. Cassis 1994: 139; Pohle 1995). The prevalence of liberal principles is, then, of greater significance in diachronic terms as legitimating the organisation of credit practices and the formal exercise of authority through London's market institutions.

10 The international gold standard is usually understood as the institutional infrastructure through which the hegemonic British state actively managed the organisation of international monetary relations during this period (Kindleberger 1973; Gilpin 1987). For Kindleberger (1973), the hegemony of the British state is held as a necessary feature of monetary stability given the inherent instability of international monetary order, while for Gilpin (1987) the need for a hegemonic state to generate a stable international monetary order results from the presumed anarchy of the system of states (cf. Walter 1993). Enabled by the gold standard, the British state is viewed as providing an adequate supply of liquidity, overseeing international adjustment, playing the role of lender-of-last-resort in periods of crisis, and stimulating confidence by maintaining the convertibility of sterling to gold at a fixed rate. This conventional wisdom is itself based on a critique of the classical theory of the gold standard which, resting on Hume's identification of the specie-flow mechanism, identified the automatic adjustments of the gold standard as bringing about monetary stability. Eichengreen and Flandreau (1997: 3) provide a concise summary of the classical theory of the gold standard – 'Each country's money supply was linked to its gold reserves, and balance-of-payments adjustment was accomplished by international shipments of precious metal. Each country being subject to the same gold discipline, the system brought about a *de facto* harmonization of policies and an admirable degree of exchange rate stability'.

The view taken here is supported and informed in particular by Brown's (1940) monumental two volume study of the functioning of the gold standard as part of what he terms the 'world credit and clearing structure'. He draws a distinction between the stability of the pre-1914 gold standard that operated within a world credit structure that was firmly centralised in London, and the instability of the post-1918 gold standard which operated within a decentralised world credit structure in which neither London nor New York stood as the predominant WFC.

11 The deposit-compelling power of London meant that, particularly from the 1870s, the 'market rate' became increasingly significant, as opposed to the Bank rate, in determining foreign exchanges and therefore capital movements. As a result, the Bank was only able to make the Bank rate effective by the high price of borrowing in the market to raise the price of money or by limiting the export of gold (Cassis 1994: 81–2). The deposit-compelling power of London did not mean that increases in the rate of interest in London and the subsequent effects on international adjustment translated into deflation across the main national political economies of continental Europe. The position of Paris and Berlin as second-tier regional financial centres and their ability to attract capital from the third-tier centres of central Europe – the majority of which stood as the financial centres of national political economies which consistently ran payments surpluses up to 1914 – mitigated against the spread of deflationary pressures (Walter 1993: 102-3). Clearly, however, the deposit-compelling power of London did have detrimental consequences for those national political economies outside Europe with balance-of-payments deficits before 1914 (Eichengreen and Flandreau 1997: 10).

12 The phrase 'political identity' and its application to market institutions is taken from Sally (1994).

4 From London to New York

The British and American world financial orders

In this chapter we continue our historical inquiry into modern world finance, focusing on the demise of the British financial order and the making and reproduction of the American financial order. The Great War of 1914–18 irretrievably ruptured the London-centred British financial order. An interregnum in world finance followed that was marked by relative instability as the British financial order unravelled and finally disintegrated amid the financial crises of 1929–31. As with the Dutch financial order, the demise of the British financial order was associated with decentralisation. The rise of New York to challenge the predominance of London in the wake of the Great War ensured that the authority of London's social forces in the making and reproduction of the post-1918 British financial order was undermined.

Following the crises of 1929–31 and the apogee of the British financial order, credit creation at a world-scale collapsed. Relative stability in the American financial order only emerged after 1947 following the granting of Marshall Plan aid. Not only did it take the Great Depression of the 1930s and the Second World War, it also took perceptions of a deepening crisis of post-war west European reconstruction and the Cold War before the foundations of the American financial order became solidified. Viewed in comparative historical terms with the Dutch and British financial orders that preceded it, the American financial order heralded 'a new phase in international finance' (Nadler *et al.* 1955/1994). Three main interrelated features of this structural discontinuity are discernible.

First, bank lending and capital market practices as the previously predominant forms of world credit practices were heavily restricted. Long-term inter-governmental and corporate capital outflows from the US national political economy were a defining characteristic of the American financial order. As such, New York stood somewhat indirectly as the WFC of the order, the key space for the creation of the credit that supported American capital outflows at one remove.

Second, restrictions on world credit practices reflected the distinctive nature of the making of the American financial order. In the making of previous financial orders, the social forces of the predominant WFC had enjoyed considerable social and political power. By contrast, New York's social forces were unable to advance their interests in the making of the American financial order amid the Fordist compromise between American industry and labour and similarly unfavourable conditions in the wider world order. As a result, the making and reproduction of the American financial order became informed and legitimated not by the orthodox liberalism of New York's social forces, but by the organisational principles of 'embedded liberalism' (Ruggie 1982) that promoted free trade and monetary stability at the expense of financial flows.

Third, reflecting the epistemic authority enjoyed by proponents of embedded liberalism, the relative stability of the American financial order was largely reproduced by the formal governance supplied by US state agencies and US dominated inter-state institutions. Unlike the positions of Amsterdam and London in the previous financial orders, New York's role as a complex of governance was largely subordinated in the American financial order.

The unravelling of the British financial order

The Great War not only marked a significant rupture in the wider world order – the closing act of the Hundred Years Peace between the major states – but it had important ramifications for the British financial order. The war itself was the culmination of the gradual displacement from the 1870s of the principal role of British state in the European balance of power. The erosion of British state power in turn reflected a loss of dynamism amid intensified industrial and imperial rivalry between the major states (Cox 1987: 151–64). With the coming of the war, the British state proved no longer able to prevent inter-state contestation from impinging upon the British financial order.

The war contributed to a decentralisation of world credit practices. As the British state sought to finance its war efforts from 1914, London was temporarily closed as a WFC realising a 'vacuum in international money and capital markets' (Madden and Nadler 1935/1994: 164). It was New York that emerged as the key wartime social space for world credit practices.[1] Sovereign credit was channelled to the belligerent and neutral states of Europe by the American government, New York-centred commercial credit creation in support of foreign trade took off, and the dollar-denominated working balances of foreign financial market institutions and central banks became centralised in New York (Brown 1940: 143–5, 149, 152–3; Burk 1992: 360–1). After 1918, London did recover in large measure its position as the key space for commercial credit practices. However, for those state-societies that lay beyond the reach of the British Empire in particular, New York stood as the key social space for long-term credit creation in the British financial order after 1918. Between 1921 and 1924, the value of new issues of foreign securities in New York totalled $2,373 million, compared with $917 million in London (Germain 1997: 63). Similarly, from 1925 to 1929, foreign lending out of New York totalled $6,400 million, compared with $3,300 million from London (Kindleberger 1973: 56). The clearance of dollar- and sterling-denominated credit obligations and associated money-market practices were somewhat decentralised in the post-war years (Brown 1940: 538), although the restoration of the convertibility of sterling to gold in 1925 did lead to a partial re-centralisation of working balances in London (Kindleberger 1973: 44). From the Great War, then, a competitive duality developed between London and New York as WFCs at the apex of the British financial order.

The post-1914 decentralisation of world credit practices has tended to be noted by those who have been critical of the somewhat nostalgic assumption that restoring monetary and financial arrangements after the Great War hinged upon the reformulation of the international gold standard (Brown 1940; Kindleberger 1983; Ingham 1994).[2] While the 1925 return to the gold did appear to generate confidence in currency values, the gold exchange standard remained something of a 'façade' (Brown 1940: 389). As Brown (1940: 137–8) summarises:

> At the close of hostilities it was impossible to see the consequences of this decentralization . . . A whole new set of relations with the dollar was suddenly superimposed upon the old set of relations with sterling. The old sterling relations were based upon a long historical development and appropriate institutional techniques were established to regulate them. The new relationships with the dollar were emergency relations created by the sudden upheaval. *They were not solidified by an appropriate credit system.* [*my emphasis*]

Given that the centralisation of the British financial order in London had been pivotal to the workings of the pre-1914 gold standard, the decentralisation of the order undermined efforts to return to the redesigned gold standard. In our terms, however, the decentralisation of the British financial order also entailed a shift in the hierarchy of power relations, leading to contests over the appropriate organisation of world finance and the erosion of London's role as a complex of governance.

Changes to the structure of power in the British financial order were inextricably bound up with the shifting relative strengths of the British and American national political economies, and the extent to which those economies channelled capital to their respective financial centres. By 1913, the United States produced over a third of the world's industrial output, just under the combined total of Britain, Germany and France (Hobsbawm 1994: 97). London's high period as a WFC from around 1870 through to the outbreak of war masked the potentially destabilising consequences for the British financial order of Britain's relative industrial decline. During London's golden age, credit creation had become increasingly reliant upon the City's role as an entrepôt WFC and its deposit-compelling capacity to attract mobile capital. London's high period was associated, then, with a period of financialisation, that is, the speculative accumulation of capital through world credit practices themselves became a structural feature of the order. London-centred financialisation was closely bound up with the so-called Great Depression (1873–96) which, in the face of competitive pressures emanating from Germany and the US, struck at the established industrial heartlands of Britain and France in particular and encouraged holders of capital to turn away from productive investment (Arrighi 1994: 161–7). It took the major upheavals of the Great War to eventually expose this material contradiction in the British financial order, as New York came to undercut London's deposit-compelling capacity. Attracting and retaining mobile capital in London after the war required the Bank of England to pursue 'deposit-attracting policies' of relatively high interest rates (Brown 1940:

157). With European political economies slow to come to grips with the dislocation of wartime, such high rates of interest tended to translate into a deflationary spiral and detrimental consequences for world credit practices.

Shifts in social and political power relations in British state-society that were rooted in wartime also fed the unravelling of the order. After 1918, the exigencies of Britain's relative economic decline encouraged the Treasury to attempt to tie London-centred credit creation to the needs of the British national political economy to a greater extent (Born 1977: 231–55). For instance, between 1924 and 1928 foreign issues on the LSE accounted for only 45 per cent of total issues, compared with 82 per cent in 1913 (Michie 1992: 113). A subtle transformation had occurred in the City–Bank of England–Treasury nexus. The Bank of England came consistently to express the 'Treasury view' (Brown 1940: 160–1; Ingham 1994: 36–7), undercutting the capacity of the City to govern and reproduce the British financial order. The Bank's adoption of the Treasury view in the immediate post-war years also chimed with its fears that sterling-denominated foreign credit creation undermined efforts to return to the gold standard at the pre-1914 level (Burk 1992: 362–3; Roberts 1995: 162). By way of example, wartime demands for sovereign credit had led to an expansion in the use of treasury bills on the London money-markets at the expense of finance bills (Brown 1940: 156). Following the war, the Bank continued to restrict the use of finance bills in favour of treasury bills (Michie 1992: 79–80), thereby curbing the ability of London-centred commercial credit practices to contribute to the smooth financing of world trade.

The post-1914 changes in British state-society that eroded the power and governance role of London's social forces in British financial order were echoed throughout the wider world order. The First World War accentuated what Polanyi (1944) terms the 'counter movement' within state-societies, as those social forces that looked to state institutions to protect them from the commodifying pressures of the self-regulating market gained ground. Cox (1987) characterises this as the transition from liberal to welfare-nationalist, fascist and communist state forms. With the effective separation of economy from society and finance from foreign policy now under challenge, the consequences of these changes for the British financial order were considerable. For the majority of state-societies including Britain, the liberal organisational principles that were the basis for the London-centred stability and authoritative reproduction of the order prior to 1914 now 'stood in contradiction to the transformation in the mediating role of the state between market and society' (Ruggie 1982: 392). Shifting configurations of social forces ensured that central banks no longer necessarily supported the gold standard at the expense of domestic considerations (Ruggie 1982: 390). Support for the gold standard regardless of its domestic consequences had, prior to 1914, provided *de facto* the basis for both relative stability and the London-centred authoritative reproduction of the British financial order.

The post-1914 changes to the structure of power at home and abroad became manifest in relative instability in the British financial order. American and British state and social forces shared a commitment to rebuilding the fragmented world economy, but their contrasting positions of ascending and descending power led to considerable disagreements as to the appropriate organisation of world finance (Costigliola 1977). As Secretary of the US Treasury William Gibbs McAdoo recognised, the war offered the opportunity for New York 'to become the dominant financial power of the world' (in Burk 1992: 362), backed by unrivalled industrial strength, trade surpluses and gold reserves. Giving full vent to this predominance rested on the creation of a liberal world economy that was the mirror image of the late-nineteenth century, except that now New York would stand at its centre. By contrast:

> With faltering trade, massive unemployment, high debts and a relatively meagre gold reserve, Britain perceived its position as far more precarious. Consequently London hoped to enhance its resources and power with a system of international monetary regulation and gold conservation. By defeating this financial program, America aggravated British economic problems in the 1920s.
>
> (Costigliola 1977: 911)

Confronted by American power, London's social forces were unable to recast the British financial order to suit their changed circumstances. Given the significance of commitment to the gold standard for the relative stability and reproduction of the pre-1914 British financial order, defeat of British plans for a post-war reformulation of the standard to include currency blocs and formalised central bank co-operation proved the vital issue.

In sum, the post-1918 relative instability in the British financial order reflected changes to power relations that had accelerated during the Great War. The associated decentralisation of the order between London and New York also rendered its reproduction through the management of world credit practices increasingly problematic. This came to a head in the course of the European financial crisis of 1931 that finally marked the apogee of the British financial order. The roots of the 1931 crisis lay in the Wall Street Crash of 1929 and the Great Depression that followed feeding into the world economy. The Crash and the ensuing credit crunch accelerated falls in industrial production and commodity prices and, as the US in particular sought protection from tariffs, the deflationary spiral fed the gradual collapse of world trade (Kindleberger 1973: 108–45; Hobsbawm 1994: 91–4). In this context, the heavily indebted European political economies were clearly vulnerable to defaulting on outstanding obligations. The Austrian and German political economies were in a particularly precarious position as a result of the relatively large size of their short-term foreign credit obligations. For example, when the European crisis of 1931 broke out, 57.8 per cent of Germany's foreign debts were repayable within three months (Born 1977: 228). It was from the immediate threat of Austrian default that the crisis emanated – Credit-Anstalt, 'the greatest of Vienna's great banks' (Cottrell 1995: 96), became the first to experience problems in May 1931. Fearful foreign lenders withdrew lines of short-term credit to Austrian borrowers more broadly, such that the banking crisis fed a currency crisis. A series of loans organised by international central bank co-operation through the recently formed Bank of International Settlements (BIS) proved successful in prolonging Austria's agony.

Through June and July 1931, particularly with the waning gold reserves of the Reichsbank, the crisis spread to Germany. A rescue package similar to that provided for Austria failed to materialise to prevent a German default. The response by the German government was to introduce exchange controls and extend protectionist policies, effectively insulating the German political economy from the world economy and the world financial order (Cottrell 1995: 96–9). The post-1914 disintegration of the coalition of social forces that had previously characterised the order ensured that London's social forces were unable to enforce their will in constructing a rescue package to prevent the German default. Despite eventual French agreement to the Hoover Moratorium on German reparations, the rescue efforts floundered amid on-going sensitivity over German reconstruction and inter-governmental wrangling between the US, Britain and France over inter-allied war debts and German reparations.[3]

London's incapacity to authoritatively direct a solution to the German crisis ensured that the otherwise superficial fluctuations in world credit practices emanating from the crisis led to a major structural disruption. London financiers' assets in Austria and Germany had been frozen by the crisis and confidence in the stability of sterling evaporated (Roberts 1991: 63–4; Cottrell 1995: 100). Continental European commercial banks, who had themselves lost liquidity as a result of Austrian and German bad debts, sold sterling in an attempt to increase their gold reserves (Kindleberger 1973: 158). London itself was now the eye of the storm. Yet the decentralisation of capital in the British financial order had considerable implications for London's governance role, as it generated a 'conflict between the technical requirements of the banking process itself and the actual distribution of resources' (Brown 1940: 533). As the MacMillan Report of July 1931 made plain, the critical mass of material resources necessary for world credit practices was no longer centralised in London. As Williams (1963: 519) posits:

> In the face of external pressure, London had previously responded to demands for finance at times of general difficulty in two ways. First, by reducing its long-term foreign investment, while tending to maintain – or even increase – short-term foreign investment, and, secondly, by attempting to increase its borrowing from abroad. In the 1929–31 crisis London was successful in changing the structure of its foreign investment but failed to attract greater foreign investment in London. Only one part of the pre-1914 machinery was operative.

In our terms, London had lost the deposit-compelling power that had enabled its governance institutions to manage crises prior to 1914. In face of such structural weakness, support for the Bank of England from the Bank of France and the Federal Reserve was insufficient.

Furthermore, and reflecting the subtle changes in the nature of the City–Treasury–Bank of England nexus after 1918, the capacity of the Bank of England to increase the Bank rate in an effort to manage the crisis was also limited. Concerns with the detrimental consequences for employment in the British political economy now impinged on Bank policy (Williams 1963: 524). The Labour government was deeply divided as to the possibility of submitting to the so-called 'bankers' ramp' of cutting government expenditure in order to relieve some of the pressure on sterling. In September the link between sterling and gold was finally severed. Enacted by the newly-formed National Government in the wake of the crisis, a series of regulations and restrictions ensured that London-centred credit practices became largely confined to supporting the interests of the British national and imperial economies (Kindleberger 1984/1993: 377–8). As Roberts (1991: 65) asserts, 1931 was 'the end of an epoch' for London and its relationship to world finance.

New York: world financial centre

In the context of the Great Depression and the Second World War, world-scale credit creation lay virtually dormant throughout the 1930s and the first half of the 1940s. At the heart of the New York-centred order, credit creation was crippled by bad debts accumulated in the run up to the crises of 1929–31 and hampered by the New Deal legislation that, in the wake of the Wall Street Crash, demanded a major restructuring of American credit practices.[4] Given widespread perceptions of a direct link between the Crash and the severe depression that followed, revulsion at speculative financial excess was common and was voiced by the leading politicians of the Roosevelt administration (Buck 1992: 152; Chancellor 2000: 220–5). Based on their considerable social and political power, isolationist American farmers, organised labour and industrialists ensured that New York would not be a WFC at the heart of a reconstituted orthodox liberal world financial order during the 1930s.

The decades following the Second World War were marked by a highly significant structural change in world credit practices. Capital market and bank lending practices that had previously been the predominant forms of world credit practices played only 'a residual role' (Mendelsohn 1980: 53) in the post-war American financial order. While short-term commercial credit practices remained organised through the hierarchical institutional networks of the financial markets, long-term inter-governmental and corporate capital outflows from the US national political economy were a defining characteristic of the American financial order. As a result, New York was only of indirect importance as a key social space in the American financial order. In the main, New York-centred capital market and bank lending practices provided credit in support of American inter-governmental and corporate capital flows. Furthermore, in sharp contrast with the near global reach of London-centred credit practices during the British financial order, the world-scale of credit practices and capital flows was now subject to Cold War concerns and bounded within the western sphere of influence.

The highly distinctive organisation of world credit practices in the American financial order is revealed by reference to the provision of sovereign credit. Sovereign credit took forms that were new to peacetime, with provision primarily organised through US-influenced inter-state institutions and bilateral inter-state aid, military assistance and loan agreements in which the US state was ascendant. Between 1947 and 1954 and based upon capital contributed by the principal states, the newly created International Monetary Fund (IMF) made a total 107 loans to the value of $2 billion to provide 36 countries experiencing balance of payments problems with offsetting finance (Nadler *et al.* 1955/1994: 195–6).[5] In contrast, the World Bank, which remained reliant upon private capital markets for credit, proved an inadequate source of long-term sovereign credit (Walter 1993: 159; Frieden 1987: 63). Meanwhile, the $15 billion provided by the US Economic Co-operation Administration through the Marshall Plan defined the provision of inter-state aid by the US state. The disproportionate share of the financing of western military security accounted for by US expenditure and grants throughout the Cold War also provided, *de facto*, a source of credit for other western governments (Brett 1983: 164). Between 1951 and 1954, US grants and military supplies and services provided to other states, official purchases of foreign goods by the US military, and purchases by US military personnel stationed abroad all combined to total $19 billion (Nadler *et al.* 1955/1994: 195). In short, during the American financial order, sovereign credit provision was dominated by capital outflows from the US political economy that were organised through US state institutions and US-influenced inter-state institutions.

It was as a consequence of the mediation of sovereign credit by the US state that New York-centred sovereign credit practices were only indirectly important to the American financial order. For instance, in raising capital for the Marshall Plan in 1947, the Truman administration issued US government bills and bonds in New York which were purchased by US banks and investors. Meanwhile, the allocation of the New York-centred credit that was created for foreign sovereign borrowers remained highly circumscribed. Of the $14 billion worth of foreign issues in New York between 1946 and 1963, over half were shared between Canadian borrowers and the World Bank (Mendelsohn 1980: 209). The US state rather than Wall Street, then, held authority over the allocation of sovereign credit in the American financial order.

From the middle period of the 1950s, the long-term capital outflows from the US political economy that characterised the American financial order became predominantly private in nature. The majority of private long-term capital outflows from the US through to the early 1970s took the form of foreign direct investment (FDI) by US-owned multinational corporations (Nadler *et al.* 1955/1994: 196; Cooper 1968: 82; Germain 1997: 79). Several sets of factors combined to encourage US MNC FDI while discouraging New York-centred foreign portfolio investment or the issue of bonds and securities for foreign corporations (Cooper 1968: 84–90; Hawley 1987: 45–86). These included the inter-war experience of bond defaults; the erection of a common tariff around the European Common Market; the nature of US corporate and commercial expansion driven by Fordist mass production and mass consumption dynamics; the restoration of currency convertibility from 1958 which guaranteed the unrestricted repatriation of FDI earnings; and the unilateral imposition of capital controls in the United States from 1963.

Not dissimilar to the indirect significance of New York in terms of the provision of sovereign credit in the American financial order, an 'ambivalent relationship' (Germain 1997: 81–2) existed between New York and US MNC FDI. On the one hand, the prevalence of direct investment at the expense of large-scale foreign corporate issues, loans and portfolio investment weakened the significance of New York as a social space in the financial order. New York was 'an international capital market only at one remove' (Mendelsohn 1980: 54). The subsequent development of New York as a WFC would, therefore, be subject to competitive pressures from London and elsewhere (Germain 1997: 82–3). On the other hand, given the pivotal position of New York's financial market institutions and Stock Exchange (NYSE) in the creation of American corporate credit, the prevalence of US MNC FDI was accompanied by the development of extensive networks of New York-centred market institutions. As the scale of US MNC FDI increased and New York-centred foreign corporate credit creation continued to be discouraged, 'The multinationalization of banks followed upon the multinationalization of industry' (Born 1977: 307).[6] New York-centred market institutional networks reached throughout the space of the American financial order and predominated in the provision of corporate credit. As with the provision of sovereign aid and loans, New York's social space tended to underpin rather than directly contribute the outflows of long-term private capital from the United States.

In line with the structural transformation of long-term credit practices in the American financial order, clearing practices from the late 1940s to the late 1950s were also organised through state and inter-state institutions to a much greater extent than previously. Part and parcel of the first round of Marshall Plan aid allocated to western Europe in 1948 was the establishment of the European Payments Union (EPU) as an intra-European clearance mechanism. The EPU, organised through the BIS and the Organisation for European Economic Co-operation (OEEC), provided for multilateral clearing and, funded by the US, managed revolving credit facilities to assist deficit countries (Cooper 1968: 39–49). It was only with the adoption of full currency convertibility by the major western European states from 1958 that clearing practices came to take a similar form to that which had characterised previous world financial orders. London's position as the principal European financial centre and the continued denomination of around 40 per cent of world trade in sterling ensured that the clearance of European transactions once again became centralised in London (Nadler *et al.* 1955/1994). However, given both the continued pivotal position of the US political economy in world trade and the associated institutionalisation of the US dollar as 'world money' (Strange 1976) under the Bretton Woods fixed exchange rate arrangements, New York remained the key social space for clearing practices during the American world financial order (Germain 1997: 85). Significantly, even with the emergence from the late 1950s of Euromarket credit practices centralised in London,[7] the dollar-denomination of this credit ensured that these transactions had eventually to be cleared through New York (Bareau 1979: 57; Klopstock 1973/1994: 215).

World credit practices in New York drew in material terms on the capital, information and technology centralised in New York. US predominance in the world economy was based upon a combination of the competitive advantages accrued from labour productivity, the organisational and technological leadership associated with the techniques of Fordist mass production and the sheer size of the US political economy (Rupert 1995). The massive volumes of capital accumulated in the US political economy did become centralised in New York. However, given the sheer size of the American political economy and its greater self-sufficiency when compared, for instance, with the British political economy, the tendency for American capital to become centralised in New York as a national financial centre was to some extent undercut (Mendelsohn 1980: 205–6; Helleiner 1993b: 220; Ingham 1994: 41). This contrasts with the greater centralisation in London of capital accumulated in the British political economy under the British financial order. In response, Mendelsohn (1980: 205) suggests that the more even distribution of accumulated capital throughout the American political economy acted as a structural constraint that contributed to determining the more indirect significance of New York as the key social space in the American financial order.

It would seem tempting to account for the indirect and subordinated position of New York during the American financial order in these terms. However, material resources were centralised in New York during the American financial order in a similar way to the patterns of centralisation that had marked the Dutch and British financial orders. Financiers in New York during the American financial order enjoyed unrivalled access to large volumes of capital. New securities issues valued at between \$50 and \$100 million were routinely absorbed in New York, compared with between \$30 and \$45 million in London as New York's leading challenger at the apex of the hierarchy of WFCs (Cooper 1968: 131–2). Several sets of information networks also overlapped in New York, providing an essential material resource for world credit practices. These included New York-centred US commercial and production networks that provided a welter of information on the conditions of world trade throughout the 1950s and 1960s (Shefter 1993); the networks of New York's multinational financial market institutions that ensured the centralisation of relevant information in New York that had often been accessed from other financial centres such as London (Nadler *et al.* 1955/1994: 198–206; Reed 1981); and a wide range of financially significant institutions including the NYSE, the *Wall Street Journal* and *New York Times*, the US Federal Reserve, and the IMF and World Bank. New York's indirect significance in the American financial order was not, therefore, simply a consequence of the nature of the distribution across the US political economy of the material resources of world credit practices.

Arriving at an understanding of the indirect significance of New York in the American financial order is greatly assisted by reference to the brief period between 1958 and 1963, an interval in which New York threatened to occupy a position of more direct importance. New York-centred world credit practices began to expand considerably over this short period, as 'New York's bankers . . . had finally achieved the position of lender to the world' (Helleiner 1994: 85). In 1960, US banks had \$8 billion worth of foreign loans outstanding and loans and bond issues to the rest of the world were running at around \$1.6 billion a year. By 1963, new foreign bond issues and lending by US banks totalled over \$2 billion

(Frieden 1987: 77, 84). Net US foreign portfolio investment accelerated dramatically from $1.1 billion in 1957 to $4.1 billion by 1964 (Cooper 1968: 114). Underpinning the expansion of New York-centred credit creation was an increase in the capital centralised in New York. The centralisation of a larger volume of capital in New York was in part driven by the growth of US institutional investors throughout the 1950s (Bernstein 1992: 109–10; Buck 1992: 182). However, it was the restoration of currency convertibility and the associated removal of capital controls on current accounts by the major western European states from 1958 that led to New York's deposit-compelling power to be felt. European short-term capital in particular poured into New York in search of profitable returns (Cooper 1968: 132–4). New York's standing as the 'lender to the world' was, however, brought to an abrupt halt by the imposition of a series of US capital controls from 1963. What this suggests is that the indirect significance of New York as a key social space for much of the American financial order was largely an outcome of a structure of power that, for the most part, restricted its role. As Mendelsohn (1980: 208) notes of the period from the 1930s through to the 1970s, 'New York dominated the international capital market whenever it was allowed to and whenever there was an international capital market to be dominated.' In our terms, then, accounting for the position of New York in the American financial order requires an understanding of the making and reproduction of the order.

The making and reproduction of the American financial order

The centralisation of material capabilities in New York entailed the emergence of a structure of power in the American financial order in which New York's financiers occupied a dominant position. New York's social forces sought orthodox liberal solutions to the reconstruction of world finance which, given the strength of the US national political economy, would place New York-centred market institutional networks firmly at the heart of world-wide credit creation. The material dominance of New York's social forces was not, however, sufficient for them to play a role in the making of the American financial order that was broadly comparable to that of the social forces of Amsterdam and London in the making of the Dutch and British financial orders respectively. Unlike in previous world financial orders, New York's social forces were constrained rather than enabled by both social and political power relations and conditions in the wider world order.

The orthodox liberal vision of New York's financiers for the making of the post-war American financial order could not be reconciled with 'welfare-nationalist' (Cox 1987) social and political power relations at home or abroad. Key was the extent to which social power relations demanded a strengthening of the imaginary and regulatory edifice of the national political economy. While a broad-based consensus existed in US policy-making circles with the regard to the desirability of multilateral exchange and currency convertibility, this consensus did not extend to the organisation of world finance. The orthodox liberal views and objectives of New York's social forces and the Federal Reserve Bank of New York contrasted with the 'New Dealers' of the US State Department and Treasury (Cox 1987: 213–14; Frieden 1987: 64; Maier 1987: 136–8). Across the wider world order, a similar constellation of social and political power relations impinged on the making of the American financial order. The post-1945 wider world order itself was characterised by the bi-polarity of the Cold War, with the western sphere distinguished by the *Pax Americana*. As a consequence, US policy-makers sought to maintain an 'open', liberal world order in the western sphere where US business could dominate and prosper, while simultaneously protecting that sphere from Soviet domination. The *Pax Americana* was distinguished not just by a simple predominance of US material resources (cf. Keohane 1984: 37), but by an internationalisation of US state-society relations across the western sphere (Cox 1987: 211–68; Rupert 1995: 57). The processes of internationalisation were mediated by existing welfare-nationalist forms of state-society that had become consolidated after the Great War of 1914 (Polanyi 1944; Maier 1987). As Ruggie (1982: 388) notes:

> demands for social protection were very nearly universal, coming from all sides of the political spectrum and from all ranks of the social hierarchy (with the possible exception of orthodox financial circles) . . . the post-war international economic order would have to reflect this change in state-society relations if the calamities of the interwar period were not to recur.

Such 'demands for social protection' were to be met within separated national political economies. The maintenance of an international balance as an important priority of liberal economic orthodoxy now took second place to the creation and maintenance of high levels of domestic employment under Keynesian policies. As Helleiner (1993a: 22–3) stresses, the use of capital controls in support of the priorities of the welfare-nationalist state-society form became, for the first time, a permanent feature of peacetime with considerable consequences for world finance.

In the immediate post-war years, the disjunction between the undoubted material power of New York's social forces and the broader pattern of social and political power relations manifested itself in relative instability and considerable contestation as to the appropriate organisation of world finance. This had been starkly revealed in the course of the Bretton Woods negotiations in 1944.[8] The Bretton Woods agreements of 1944 were central to the creation of a multilateral consensus of western state and societal forces around the liberalisation of world trade and the establishment of a system of fixed exchange rates pegged to the US dollar. No such consensus marked world finance. The British delegation led by John Maynard Keynes proposed to include within the Bretton Woods agreements co-operative controls on the movement of private capital, and an inter-state framework for large-scale credit creation under the auspices of his 'Clearing Union'. New York's social forces succeeded in persuading the US negotiating team led by Harry Dexter White not to initiate unilateral capital controls, thereby precluding a co-operative capital control programme. Keynes' proposals for a Clearing Union were also rebuffed in favour of a more piecemeal approach to the provision of credit (Helleiner 1993a: 30–7). In the absence of relative stability and agreement as to the appropriate organisation of world credit practices, credit would be provided through an incremental combination of financial market institutions, bilateral loans between creditor and debtor states, and the IMF and World Bank.

This piecemeal organisation of world credit practices was found seriously wanting. The US had emerged from the Second World War as the dominant creditor economy to such an extent that the majority of capital goods necessary for western European reconstruction could only be imported from the US. After the war the western European political economies were in no position to generate large amounts of foreign exchange and, consequently, there was a massive demand for dollar-denominated credit to pay for imports from the USA.[9] The American financial order of the immediate post-war years was unable to sufficiently address this so-called 'dollar shortage' (Walter 1993: 160; Germain 1997: 70). World credit practices, restricted by the maintenance of wartime unilateral capital controls by virtually all states except the US and limited by the problems of rebuilding market institutional networks that had been shattered during the war, were unable to satisfy the demand for dollars.

Furthermore, the orthodox liberal solution to the dollar shortage promoted by New York's social forces also floundered. With the full support of New York's financial community, the Federal Reserve had put forward the Key Currency Plan as an alternative to the Bretton Woods framework. The Plan favoured the re-establishment of sterling convertibility and the associated re-emergence of London-centred credit creation to fund European reconstruction (Frieden 1987: 65). While sidelined at Bretton Woods, the Plan subsequently informed efforts to alleviate post-war British financial problems. Alongside an agreement to cancel British war debts, the British state agreed an emergency loan of $5 billion in December 1945, three-quarters of which was to be provided by the US and the remainder by Canada. The loan was designed to address the huge sterling balances held by foreign governments and colonial firms in London that had been frozen at the outset of the war (Born 1977: 299–300; Kindleberger 1984/1993: 418–21; Walter 1993: 158). In return for the loan, sterling convertibility was to be restored by July 1947. This restoration proved disastrous (Born 1977: 300–1), as efforts by the Bank of England to prop up the value of the pound in the wake of capital flight to the dollar ensured that the loan was all but frittered away. The British response was to re-impose sterling exchange controls that were to stay in place through to 1958.

It was only a significant departure by US policy-makers that finally sidelined the liberal orthodoxy of New York's social forces and also laid the foundations of relative stability in the American financial order. The granting of Marshall Plan aid to the governments of western Europe in 1947 stood in sharp contrast with the vision of the American financial order that the US state, swayed by New York's financiers, had embraced at Bretton Woods just three years previously. With the Marshall Plan, 'a new phase in international finance' (Nadler *et al.* 1955/1994) was born.[10] At the roots of this new phase was a disintegration and reintegration of social forces within US state-society that, for the first time, decisively displaced the power of New York's financiers. In the course of 1947, perceptions that a deepening crisis of western European reconstruction placed the Bretton Woods arrangements in jeopardy combined with the fear of a threat to US interests by the Soviet Union, as the contours of the Cold War began to solidify under the Truman Doctrine, to produce a shift in state-society relations (Brett 1983: 162; Frieden 1987: 67–70; Maier 1987: 139). An unlikely internationalist coalition of US social forces emerged uniting industrialists, organised labour, New Deal state managers, liberal internationalists and forces of the right concerned with the perceived Soviet threat. In the face of such a coalition, New York's social forces were unable to prevent a move away from liberal orthodoxy in US foreign economic policy.

The Marshall Plan marked, then, the beginning of the relatively stable making and reproduction of the American financial order. Relative stability was forged through the principles of what Ruggie (1982) calls 'embedded liberalism'. Embedded liberalism differed significantly from the liberal orthodoxy of New York's social forces.[11] Under embedded liberalism, capital was not accorded the same status as, and became subordinated to, movements of goods and services through the use of unilateral capital controls (Hawley 1987: 7). Embedded liberalism came to frame the organisation of world credit practices, as it was broadly accepted that US foreign economic policy should impinge on world finance. For instance, US state-directed flows of sovereign credit, whether in the form of aid or military expenditure, tended to have conditions attached that sought to reinforce the multilateral framework for trade and payments and the *Pax Americana* more broadly. By way of example, attached to Marshall Plan aid to western Europe was conditional membership of the OEEC which worked towards the liberalisation of intra-European trade (Cooper 1968: 39; Cox 1987: 214–15; Rupert 1995: 58). Furthermore, the distribution of long-term US corporate capital outflows took place beneath the umbrella of US Cold War interests. Outflows of US MNC FDI into Latin America, Africa and the former colonial areas of Asia such as South Korea and Taiwan were backed by informal guarantees of US military might and direct interventionism (Augelli and Murphy 1993; Gills 1994). The American financial order was not characterised, then, by the orthodox liberal principles that were applied to world trade. In our terms, New York's social forces did not enjoy the epistemic authority in the American financial order that had been held by the social forces of the predominant WFC in previous modern world financial orders.

The distinctive structure of power that framed the possible organisation of world credit practices in the American financial order and the forging of relative stability around the organisational principles of embedded liberalism ensured the partial displacement of the more formal authority of New York's social forces. Embedded liberalism legitimated a largely state-based structure of governance in the reproduction of the American financial order, leaving New York's market institutions to play a subordinate and yet supportive role. State-based authority in the administration and management of credit practices ensured that a key feature of the American financial order was its 'quasi-public form' (Germain 1997: 71). The Bretton Woods planners had envisaged that market-based authority would be supplemented by the IMF's governance role in managing balance of payments difficulties. However, particularly in the first decade or so after 1947, the US Treasury, State Department and Economic Co-operation Administration stood at the apex of the order, effectively managing and manipulating world credit practices (Cox 1987: 300). Welfare-nationalist state-societal forms and the strengthening of the edifice of the national political economy that they entailed, buttressed by capital controls and commitments to maintain the fixed exchange rate arrangements, underpinned this state-based structure of governance.[12] While often created through market institutions in New York, the allocation of long-term sovereign credit was subject to the authority of US state institutions. US state influence over the IMF also ensured that its formal authority extended into the provision of offsetting finance throughout the American financial order (Frieden 1987: 65). Furthermore, as the granting of a loan to the British state in the wake of the Suez fiasco of 1956 illustrated, the IMF's governance role came to involve the supervision of capital as well as current account problems (Strange 1994: 56). In contrast to the firm centralisation of authority in London under the British world financial order, then, a 'Washington–New York axis' in which the former predominated characterised the structure of governance under the American financial order.[13]

Conclusions

The unravelling of the British financial order from the Great War of 1914–18 through to 1931 was similar in several respects to the unravelling of the Dutch financial order that had taken place around 150 years previously. As with the relationship between Amsterdam and the Dutch state's relative wealth and power, the London-centred financial order outlived the relative decline of the British state by around half a century. In contrast to a narrow focus on the rise and fall of states' wealth and power, then, the utility of accounting for the organisation of modern world credit practices in terms of hierarchical social orders is once again illustrated. In addition, central to the demise of the British financial order were shifting patterns of power relations that manifested themselves in the order's decentralisation and associated changes in wider world order conditions. Just as the ascent of London was an essential aspect of the unravelling of the Dutch financial order, the rise of New York in the course of the Great War ruptured the authority of London's social forces in the making and reproduction of the post-1918 British financial order. Furthermore, with the London-centred structure of governance found wanting, the British financial order came to an end amid the European financial crisis of 1931. Echoes of the 1780s are clear, as the superficial fluctuations of the crisis could not be prevented from degenerating into a highly significant structural disruption.

The Great Depression of the 1930s and the Second World War ensured that world-scale credit creation lay virtually dormant in the first decades of the American financial order. Viewed in comparison with the Dutch and British financial orders that preceded it, the American financial order that emerged after the war was marked by three main interrelated elements of structural discontinuity. First, long-term inter-governmental and corporate capital outflows from the US national political economy rather than bank lending and capital market practices were a defining characteristic of the order. As a consequence, New York was somewhat indirectly the key social space for world credit practices. Second, the distinctive organisation of world credit practices reflected social and political power relations in both US state-society and the wider world order that constrained the role of New York's social forces in the making of the American financial order. The making and reproduction of the American financial order was informed and legitimated not by cosmopolitanism or liberalism, but by an embedded liberalism that promoted free trade and monetary stability at the expense of finance. Third and in line with the organisational principles of embedded liberalism, formal governance was supplied principally by US state institutions and US dominated inter-state institutions. New York's standing as a complex of governance in terms of the authoritative management of world credit practices and the reproduction of relative stability in the order was largely subordinated amid a state-based structure of governance.

While it is structural discontinuity that undoubtedly marks the transition from the British to the American financial order, this should not obscure an important continuity. With the rise of London and the making of the British financial order, consolidated national political economies had come to stand at the foundations of world financial orders and the world economy more broadly. An important dynamic in the restructuring of power relations that led to the unravelling of the British financial order was the transition from liberal to welfare-nationalist, fascist and communist state forms. Such transitions all implied a deepening of the consolidation of national political economies, as societies looked to their state institutions to protect them from the commodifying pressures of the self-regulating market. During the American world financial order, and particularly through the widespread use of capital controls and commitments to the fixed exchange rate arrangements, world finance became organised in such a way as to minimise the potential disruption to national economic management arising from world credit practices.

Notes

1 Prior to 1914, New York was largely a national and regional financial centre, standing as a key social space for practices which provided credit for the United States and Latin America (Kindleberger 1974/1978: 114–19). Aside from London's continued predominance, this limited role of New York in world finance was also related to the processes of the consolidation of the American national political economy. In particular, New York's standing was undercut by the absence of a central banking system and the resulting restrictions on the creation of bankers' acceptances that mitigated against its role as a space for world commercial credit and money-market practices (Madden and Nadler 1935/1994: 164; Nadler *et al.* 1955/1994: 190–1; Burk 1992: 361–2). Against this backdrop, the Federal Reserve Act of 1913 represented an important victory for New York's social forces in the consolidation of the US political economy (Henwood 1997: 93–7).

2 Restoration was complicated by the devastation of Europe's national political economies during the war and a brief post-war inflationary boom that eroded the value of the world's gold stocks (Kindleberger 1973: 32). Following the Geneva conference of 1922 it was agreed that the reconstructed gold standard would take the form of a 'gold exchange standard', in which central banks increasingly held reserves in the form of balances in foreign currencies in addition to gold.
3 The British and French governments in particular were reliant upon the payment of German reparations to assist in servicing inter-allied war debts. The distinctive feature of inter-allied war debts was that they were '"political" debts' (Born 1977: 204), in the sense that they were direct inter-state lending from government to government. The United States government was the principal lender and the only government to emerge from the war without any debt repayments. The Dawes Plan of 1924 and the Young Plan of 1929 which sought to address the issues of inter-allied war debt and German reparations had had limited success in alleviating the war debt encumbrance.
4 The Banking Act of 1933 (commonly known as the Glass–Steagall Act) divorced deposit taking by commercial banks from investment banking. The Securities Act of 1933 required that all new securities issues were registered and that basic disclosure procedures were followed to increase investor protection and transparency. The Securities and Exchange Act of 1934 tightened regulation at the Federal level by establishing a new regulatory institution – the Securities and Exchange Commission (SEC) – and empowering the Federal Reserve to regulate stock exchange profit margin rates.
5 On US influence over the IMF via the voting structure that gave the US a veto, see Frieden (1987: 65–6).
6 By 1971, the thirty largest US financial market institutions had over one hundred foreign branches in Europe alone (Born 1977: 307). Once affiliates are included, the true extent of New York-centred market institutional networks can be comprehended. For instance, between 1955 and 1965 the number of overseas offices and affiliates of the market leader Citibank tripled to 163 (Frieden 1987: 77). Further, New York-centred market institutions had undergone a period of concentration (for example, the 1955 merger between Chase National Bank and the Bank of Manhattan to create Chase Manhattan) from the immediate post-war years through to the mid-1950s which underpinned their world-wide dominance (Born 1977: 308–9).
7 The term 'Euromarket' is used here to describe a specific period in the development of offshore finance, that is, credit creating practices which take place beyond the reach of the regulations which apply in the 'home' national political economy of the currency in which the credit created is denominated. Within the Euromarkets, distinctions are made between 'Eurocurrency markets' (offshore money-markets), 'Eurobonds' (offshore bond issues and trading) and 'Eurocredits' (offshore bank lending) (Mendelsohn 1980). What distinguished the Euromarkets was that while banks had accepted deposits in non-local currencies for centuries, credit denominated in non-local currencies (especially US dollars) was created for the first time instead of returning deposits to their respective money-markets. The 'Euro' prefix reflected the centralisation of these offshore dollar-denominated practices in Europe's financial centres, especially London (Strange 1976: 180).
8 This view contrasts with those who cast the American world financial order as part of the liberal international economic order or 'Bretton Woods system' established at the Bretton Woods Conference of 1944 (Krasner 1976). It is supported by writers such as Helleiner (1993a, 1994) who, concerned primarily with the organisation of world credit practices during the post-war world order, highlight the unilateral use of capital controls as one of the defining features of that order. In this sense, then, to cast the American world financial order as part and parcel of a liberal world order established under the auspices of the 'Bretton Woods system' is misleading.
9 Between 1946 and 1949, foreign countries purchased $72 billion worth of US goods and services (not including military goods shipped under aid programmes), while the

value of US imports of foreign goods and services over the same period was less than half this amount (Nadler *et al.* 1955/1994: 194).

10 Such a view of the political significance of the Marshall Plan is not undermined by the debates surrounding the contribution of the Plan to western European economic reconstruction. In challenging the orthodox view that stresses the fundamental contribution of Marshall Plan aid to western European economic reconstruction (cf. Kindleberger 1987), Milward (1984) has highlighted that recovery was already underway. This was based upon high rates of domestic capital formation and the booming West German political economy providing both markets for European exports and relieving European dependence upon imports of US capital goods. In this context, the effect of the Marshall Plan was to provide 'offsetting finance' which resolved balance of payments problems generated by a thirst for US imports. Helleiner (1994: 58–62) builds on Milward's (1984) revisionism by highlighting the large volumes of western European capital flight to the US which coexisted alongside Marshall Plan aid. Hence, for Helleiner (1994: 58–9), 'the economic significance of Marshall Plan aid was, in effect, simply to compensate for the US failure to institute controls on inflows of hot money from western Europe'.

11 What Ruggie (1982: 393) describes as the 'essence' of 'embedded liberalism' was that 'unlike the economic nationalism of the thirties, it would be multilateral in character; unlike the liberalism of the gold standard and free trade, its multilateralism would be predicated upon domestic interventionism'.

12 Even after the fixed exchange rate monetary system became operative following the restoration of currency convertibility by western governments from 1958, unilateral controls tended to remain in place on capital accounts. These prevented the purchase of foreign securities and the making of foreign loans. The only exception was West Germany that restored convertibility on both current and capital account. Having restored currency convertibility in 1964, Japan retained even more restrictive controls as all current and capital account transactions were carried out through state institutions or authorised foreign exchange banks (Helleiner 1994: 71–5).

13 The notion of a 'Washington–New York axis' is an attempt to capture the interdependent nature of state, civil and market authority under the American world financial order while recognising that US state authority centralised in Washington predominated. The roots of the notion are in a reversal of what Shefter (1993: 11) terms a post-war 'New York–Washington Axis', as 'New York and Washington were complementary, not competing, centers of power during the New Deal and the post-war decades' (Shefter 1993: 15).

Part III

The contemporary world financial order

5 From New York to 'global finance'

In this chapter we begin our inquiry into contemporary world finance. Following an account of the unravelling of the New York-centred American financial order, the contemporary restructuring of world credit practices that tends to be explained as the emergence of 'global finance' is addressed. As in the preceding chapters, comparative historical reflection across modern world finance is the key to our understanding of contemporary world finance.

The roots of the unravelling of the American financial order lay in two key interrelated contradictions. First, as Robert Triffin (1960) famously identified in what became known as the 'Triffin dilemma', the organisation of credit practices stood in tension with the Bretton Woods fixed-exchange rate arrangements. Long-term US capital outflows that manifested themselves in continual balance of payments deficits could not be indefinitely maintained alongside continued confidence in the value of the dollar in which they were denominated.[1] Second, New York's social forces were only supportive of the embedded liberal organisational principles and state-based reproduction of the American financial order while their dominant position in credit creation was guaranteed. New York's social forces' shared interests were threatened once the US state responded to the Triffin dilemma by imposing unilateral capital controls from 1963, thereby limiting New York centred credit practices. As with previous world financial orders, the ensuing disintegration of the relatively stable coalition of social forces in the American financial order was associated with decentralisation. London re-emerged as a WFC to challenge New York at the apex of the world finance as the American order gradually crumbled during the 1960s.

The decentralisation that characterised the unravelling of the American financial order was highly distinctive by comparison with previous orders. The rise of London to challenge Amsterdam during the latter stages of the eighteenth century and the rise of New York to challenge London in the decades that followed the Great War of 1914–18 were both underpinned by notable geographical shifts in power relations that favoured the social forces of the ascendant WFC. By contrast, London's re-emergence as a WFC was not grounded primarily in the growing material power of London's social forces. The adoption of capital controls by the US state and their detrimental impact on the interests of New York's social forces – alongside the continued promotion of London as a WFC by the British state – presented

London with a structural opportunity. American financiers were the key players in London-centred credit practices that were, significantly, organised in the offshore regulatory space of the Euromarkets. The decentralised American financial order finally collapsed in 1973–4 amid the disintegration of the fixed exchange rate system and the incapacity of the state-based structure of governance to manage demands for credit arising from the oil crisis.

In the wake of the unravelling of the American financial order, world credit practices have undergone significant restructuring. The contemporary prevalence of world-scale bank loans and capital and equity market practices contrasts sharply with the idiosyncratic, largely state-managed credit practices of the American financial order. At the same time, there are considerable similarities between the contemporary organisation of world credit practices and that of the Dutch and British financial orders. However, restructuring has not prompted 'back to the future' processes of change. Rather, the contemporary organisation of credit practices is conjuncturally distinct. Orthodox neo-liberal explanations of contemporary world credit practices tend to emphasise 'global finance', that is, the unprecedented emergence of a genuinely integrated 24-hour global marketplace for credit. The marketisation of contemporary finance underlined by the notion of global finance is indeed apparent. Yet the orthodoxy serves to obscure important developments in world credit practices, particularly qualitative changes to their scale, form, institutionalisation and spatiality, and, therefore, must be challenged as an inadequate representation of contemporary world finance.

The unravelling of the American financial order

Long-term inter-governmental and corporate capital outflows from the US economy were a defining feature of the American financial order. Such US capital outflows manifested themselves in continual long-term balance of payments deficits that were effectively financed by both the willingness of foreign central banks to hold dollars as reserves, and of individuals and firms to transact their business in dollars. As Hawley (1987: 8) notes, 'These *de facto* loans by foreign governments, individuals, and firms transformed the United States into a *de facto* central bank able to create global liquidity, promote trade expansion, and simultaneously run a long-term payments deficit.' As the effective demand for dollar-denominated credit increased in a world economy experiencing unprecedented levels of growth and, as Charles de Gaulle highlighted at the time, the US state exploited its position of seigniorage by printing dollars, so too did the US deficit increase. While confidence in the convertibility of the dollar into gold under the Bretton Woods arrangement remained, the willingness of foreigners to hold dollar-denominated assets continued. However, from the early 1960s confidence in the value of the dollar began to slowly evaporate, reflected in a series of speculative attacks, and with it the willingness of foreigners to hold dollars declined.

The emergence of this unsustainable 'dollar overhang' became widely recognised in the early 1960s, particularly as a consequence of Robert Triffin's reports to the US Congress. Rebuilding confidence in the US dollar and ultimately in the system of fixed exchange rates required a reduction in the US deficit. In addition to growing capital outflows, the US deficit was stoked by a gradual increase in purchases of imports from Germany and Japan in particular. Policies aimed at increasing the industrial competitiveness of the US political economy and thereby encouraging exports and dampening imports would have entailed large wage cuts. Such restructuring would have constituted a direct challenge to the welfare-nationalist form of state and 'the politics of productivity' (Maier 1987) which characterised US Fordist state-society relations. Cutbacks in military expenditure against the backdrop of US Cold War aspirations were equally unattractive (Calleo 1982), and a devaluation of the dollar was likely to trigger the devaluation of the other major currencies. In short, policies to address the US deficit were constrained by the US state-societal form and its insertion into the structures of the wider world order. This served to condense the dollar overhang problem into a straight-forward contradiction between the value of the dollar against gold on the one hand, and the supply of liquidity in the American financial order on the other.

In line with the organisational principles of embedded liberalism, US state managers chose from 1963 to attempt to solidify the Bretton Woods monetary arrangements through a programme of unilateral controls on capital account that reduced US outflows.[2] The imposition of capital controls reflected the predominance of the US Treasury in the making of foreign economic policy (Mendelsohn 1980: 35), which, in turn, rested on US state-society relations that tended to cut against the interests of New York's social forces (Hawley 1987: 21, 64–5; Helleiner 1994: 86–7). For a decade and a half following the Marshall Plan, New York's social forces had been willing to accept their subordinated position and not question the authority of US state policy makers in the American financial order. However, the capital controls programme impinged directly on New York's shared material interests such that the relative stability of the American financial order was effectively sacrificed in favour of the multilateral framework for trade and payments. The 'basic dislocation of state and market' (Ingham 1994: 45) that had been papered over during the period of relative stability in the American financial order had been exposed.

While market authority within the Washington–New York axis remained centralised in New York, it remained subordinated to, and broadly supportive of, the largely state-based structure of governance that reproduced the American financial order. Yet with the capital controls programme, 'American international banking was pushed out of Wall Street by a US government afraid of its domestic consequences' (Frieden 1987: 82). Restrictions on US capital outflows generated a demand for alternative sources of dollar-denominated credit that were not met through state-managed credit creation. Hampered from conducting New York-centred credit creation, American bankers' credit practices came to focus on the London-centred offshore Euromarkets that circumvented both US and British capital controls. The outflows of US long-term capital that characterised the American financial order became increasingly supplemented by dollar-denominated short- and medium-term credit based upon short-term holdings of dollars already residing offshore in the Eurocurrency markets.[3] The gradual break up of the Washington–New York axis throughout the 1960s, then, saw the emergence of an alternative offshore space of credit creation and foreign exchange practices centred in London that organised credit practices through largely market forms of authority.[4] The American financial order unravelled and became increasingly decentralised between New York and London.

The decentralisation that characterised the unravelling of the American financial order from the late 1950s and particularly after 1963 was highly distinctive by comparison with previous financial orders. London's re-emergence as a WFC was not grounded primarily in the growing material power of London's social forces. The capital centralised in London that framed credit practices was largely foreign and short-term in nature, restricting the volume of long-term credit creation in the Euromarkets (Strange 1976: 176–9; Born 1977: 306; Frieden 1987: 79; 93–4; Germain 1997: 89–90). London's social forces' relative lack of material power ensured that, rather than constituting a nascent uni-centric world financial order in the making, the London-centred Euromarkets remained subsumed within the unravelling of the American financial order.

The significance of offshore Euromarket credit practices lay primarily, then, in the manner in which they circumvented the state-based structure of governance that administered and managed the reproduction of the American financial order. In this sense it is tempting to cast the emergence of the Euromarkets and their contribution to the unravelling of the American financial order as a supranational or 'stateless' development (cf. Wachtel 1990). The Euromarkets, however, were not a stateless occurrence. Governments often searching for an alternative source of sovereign credit to finance imbalances did little to control, and much to encourage, the formation of these markets. In particular, US policy makers did little to restrict and actually gave their blessing to Euromarket practices (Strange 1986: 47–50; Helleiner 1994: 84–91). Given the contribution of the Euromarkets to the unravelling of the American financial order, US state support for their development would seem somewhat paradoxical. Yet, US support reflected the very contradictions of the American financial order discussed above. First, the attractive rates of interest available in the Eurocurrency markets encouraged foreigners to hold US dollars. This, in turn, allowed US policy makers to maintain greater monetary autonomy and to further postpone addressing the issues of US industrial competitiveness that fed the deficit and threatened the dollar's position in the monetary order. Second, following the imposition of capital controls from 1963, US policy makers recognised that the Euromarkets were necessary to finance the continued overseas expansion of US MNCs.[5] The Euromarket practices of New York's financial market institutions also ensured that they retained their dominant position in world finance (Frieden 1987: 85).[6] In a similar manner to the adoption of capital controls, then, US support for the Euromarket exacerbated the contradictions that lay at the roots of the unravelling of the American financial order.

In addition to the support of the US state, the London-centred Euromarkets also rested, of course, on the support of the British state officials within the

City–Bank–Treasury nexus. Harold Wilson as President of the Board of Trade had allowed the post-war re-opening of London's commodity markets for international trading in 1951, effectively re-opening London as a financial centre for sterling-denominated commercial credit creation and foreign exchange dealing (Strange 1986: 37–8). However, a series of sterling currency crises ensured that conventional sterling-denominated credit creation was problematic. In contrast to the rise of London as a WFC in the late eighteenth and early nineteenth centuries, it was the nature of the response to this problematic that facilitated the standing of London as the centre of the Euromarkets. As Moran (1991: 85) states:

> When London re-emerged in the 1950s as a great world centre it did so in a very different way. London's new prominence rested neither on the strength of the British economy, nor on the competitive capacities of British firms. It was, instead, largely a regulatory creation: the informal and consensual style practised by the Bank of England made London attractive to the emerging 'Euromarkets', especially to the American institutions trying to escape a complex home regulatory system.

In particular, the Eurocurrency markets in London rested upon the decision in 1957 by the Bank of England to permit market institutions to organise clearance and commercial credit practices in US dollars. This followed the suspension of both the clearance of sterling transactions and the creation of sterling-denominated commercial credit for third party trade amid the Suez crisis, as the Bank of England prepared for currency convertibility in a situation of depleted reserves (Cooper 1968: 117–18; Strange 1976: 180, 1986: 36–7; Mendelsohn 1980: 19–20). Similarly, the decision by the Bank of England in 1962 to permit foreign market institutions to organise the issue of foreign securities denominated in foreign currencies stimulated the growth of London-centred Eurobond practices (Burn 1997). As Helleiner (1994: 84) summarises, by shifting their business to a dollar basis, the London operators found a way to preserve their international business without being encumbered by British capital controls. London's social forces and British state officials ensured that the structural opportunity offered to them by the contradictions of the American financial order was seized, producing and reproducing London as an entrepôt offshore financial centre.

Despite the wavering commitment of US and British state officials to the American financial order, embedded liberal organisational principles continued to inform policy makers in the major states. The order retained its broad structural contours throughout the 1960s, a decade of continuity as well as change. Even with the imposition of capital controls from 1963, the US political economy remained a net provider of long-term capital. In spite of the London-centred Euromarkets, New York maintained its position throughout the 1960s as the key social space for the recycling of capital (Germain 1997: 88–9). New York remained the key social space for clearing practices (Frieden 1987: 102–3), and the relatively high rates of interest in the Euromarkets compared with rates for new long-term bond issues in New York also reinforced New York's position (Cooper 1968: 132). It was only in the course of 1968 that new issues of Eurobonds marginally exceeded new foreign issues in New York (Mendelsohn 1980: 211). Meanwhile, the state-based structure of governance in the American financial order remained largely intact. States tended to hold unilateral controls on capital accounts in place in an attempt to preserve policy-making autonomy and fixed exchange rates in the face of the increased volatility carried through the institutional channels of the Euromarkets (Helleiner 1994: 91–5). This was accompanied by increased recourse to sovereign credit for offsetting finance, provided through the expanded role of the IMF and BIS, that served to circumvent the need to impose exchange controls to maintain macroeconomic policy-making autonomy in the face of disequilibrating short-term capital flows (Helleiner 1994: 96–9). The decentralisation of the American financial order between New York and London did not realise an abrupt collapse.

The gradual unravelling of the American world financial order culminated in 1973–4 amid the disintegration of the Bretton Woods monetary arrangements and the oil crisis. As Strange (1986: 5–6) notes, 1973 was a benchmark year that 'seemed to mark a sort of change of gear'. The escalation of the Vietnam War in the late 1960s had increased pressure on US balance of payments. In August 1971 President Nixon suspended the convertibility of the dollar into gold, the relationship that lay at the heart of the Bretton Woods arrangements. While the dollar had been subject to speculative attacks in the Euromarkets, this so-called 'Nixon shock' was underpinned by the assumption that a relatively over-valued dollar was contributing towards weakening US industrial competitiveness, increasing unemployment and balance of payments problems (Brett 1983: 164; Maier 1987: 151). Attempts to maintain the fixed exchange rate system through the Smithsonian agreement, which negotiated the realignment of the US dollar to the Japanese yen and German deutschmark and managed rates through central bank co-operation, finally collapsed in 1973 with the adoption of floating exchange rates. Taken together, the Nixon shock, the failure of the US state to fully support the Smithsonian agreement, and US preference for floating exchange rates constituted monetary policy 'non-decisions' that effectively served to increase market authority over the organisation of credit practices (Strange 1986: 38–40; Walter 1993: 209–10; Germain 1997: 98–9).[7] In short, the collapse of the Bretton Woods monetary order precipitated by US policy makers was a necessary precondition for the final collapse of the American financial order.

The end of the fixed exchange rate arrangements ensured that the risks of fluctuating exchange rates would now be addressed by large-scale foreign exchange market practices. In the face of the oil crisis, the paralysis of the state-based structure of governance that had previously managed credit practices ensured that market-based authority in the organisation of world credit practices was extended further. The four-fold increase in the price of oil from late 1973 generated both a demand for credit to maintain consumption among oil importers, and a supply of capital accumulated by oil exporters. It was left to the market institutions of the London-centred Euromarkets to undertake so-called 'petrodollar recycling'. Much of the capital accumulated by oil exporters became deposited in the Euromarkets and formed the material basis for sovereign and corporate credit creation in the wake of the crisis. In terms of sovereign credit practices, the Euromarkets displaced the authority of the IMF in financing balance of payments deficits after 1974 (Germain 1997: 92–3). Eurocredits were dramatically expanded to sovereign borrowers in underdeveloped state-societies in particular, a set of practices that was to culminate in the so-called 'debt crisis' of the early 1980s. The London-centred Euromarkets also provided much of the credit for MNC restructuring in the wake of the crisis, with the value of new issues of Eurobonds increasing from $2.1 billion in 1974 to $17.6 billion by 1977 (Mendelsohn 1980: 211).

Market authority, largely subordinated in the hey-day of the embedded liberal American financial order, had been reasserted in the organisation of world credit practices. US state officials effectively vetoed several sets of proposals made by their west European and Japanese counterparts in the early 1970s that would have strengthened the state-based structure of governance. This included US opposition to more co-operative forms of capital controls (Helleiner 1994: 102–111), reigning in the Euromarkets (Helleiner 1994: 104–6), and proposals which would have placed the IMF at the heart of a 'quasi-public' recycling of petrodollars (Strange 1986: 43–5; Helleiner 1994: 111–2). In comparison with previous orders, the unravelling of the American financial order was, then, highly distinctive. Like the Dutch and British financial orders, the unravelling of the American order was associated with decentralisation. But changes in the policies of the US state, rather than the rise of the competing state and societal forces of an ascending WFC, were pivotal in the unravelling of the order.

Underlying the shift away from embedded liberalism in US policy was a reconfiguration of US state-society relations. The integrated coalition of US societal forces that had found its expression in the embedded liberal compromise and the politics of productivity since the 1930s began to disintegrate from the mid-1960s. US industry was experiencing competitive pressures from German and Japanese consumer goods producers (Block 1977: 144–9), placing considerable strains on the tripartite internationalist coalition of industrialists, organised labour and welfare-nationalist state managers. As world economic downturn became crisis in the early 1970s, 'Economic stagnation brought out underlying conflicts of interest' (Cox 1987: 225). Confronted by a situation in which industrial capacity was surplus to demand, US industry sought to raise productivity and lower costs. Alongside further multinationalisation, key to the restructuring of US corporations was increased recourse to credit, especially that provided through the Euromarkets (Cox 1987: 245–6, 249–50). At the same time, US Treasury officials were convinced that a liberalisation of financial and monetary arrangements would preserve US macroeconomic policy-making autonomy in the face of growing trade and budget deficits (Parboni 1981: 90; Strange 1986: 7; Helleiner 1994: 112–15). US corporate-industrial and state interests, along with the social forces of New York, came to coalesce around support for the Euromarkets and the expanded role of market institutions in the organisation of world credit practices. The embedded liberal experiment in world finance had finally crumbled.

Contemporary world credit practices

The decades since the end of the American financial order have been characterised by a highly significant structural transformation in world credit practices. Capital market and bank lending practices that were heavily circumscribed under the American financial order have once again come to prevail. Considered over the *longue durée*, considerable parallels can be drawn with the Dutch and British financial orders in terms of the preponderance of market institutional networks in the organisation of credit practices. This should not, however, obscure the conjunctural distinctiveness of contemporary world credit practices. The relative importance of commercial credit as against corporate credit practices has reversed, with the latter of much greater weight in contemporary times. Furthermore, the transformation of contemporary world credit practices is widely represented as 'global finance', that is, the unprecedented emergence of a genuinely integrated, 24-hour global marketplace for finance characterised by near-perfect capital mobility. Such an image of contemporary credit practices is furthered in the statements of the IMF, BIS and other international organisations, the policy pronouncements of the leading states, and the vast popular literature that seeks to promote successful business and individual financing in a perceived global era. While seeking here to challenge the orthodox representation of contemporary world credit practices as global finance, emphasis is placed on discontinuity and the historically unparalleled features of current practices.

Key to the global finance orthodoxy is the claim that contemporary world credit practices have become marketised at a genuinely global scale. Increased marketisation can indeed be seen quantitatively in the changing private and public shares of net long-term capital movements. Under the American world financial order, the ratio of private to public was approximately 1:1. During the period 1972–6 this was transformed to roughly 2:1, and by 1992–3 stood at 83 per cent private and 17 per cent public (Germain 1997: 119). While the marketisation stressed by the orthodoxy is apparent, the notion of 'global finance' also serves to obscure important developments that, for an Historical IPE approach that focuses in the first instance upon world credit practices, are vital to an understanding of contemporary world finance. In particular and following from our inquiry into previous world financial orders, understanding contemporary credit practices requires that attention is drawn to qualitative changes in their scale, form, institutionalisation and spatiality.

The scale, form and institutionalisation of practices

The structural transformation of contemporary world credit practices is far more uneven than the global finance orthodoxy tends to suppose. The prevalence of the global finance assumption has fuelled a research programme that through empirical investigation seeks to 'test' the claim that a shift from an international to a genuinely integrated global market for finance has taken place (e.g. Allen 1994; Epstein 1996; Hirst and Thompson 1996; Perraton *et al.*1997: 265–71). Such empirical testing by quantitative measurement has, not surprisingly, only realised an inconclusive set of results. This has led some IPE scholars to move towards a more nuanced position that stresses increased but uneven market integration and capital flows (Underhill 1997d; Dombrowski 1998). Furthermore, contemporary uneveness concerns not only the partial market integration of sets of credit practices, but also the supposed global scale of credit practices. As in previous world financial orders, the world-scale of credit practices is framed by the wide-reaching physical presence of those hierarchical networks that institutionalise them and is enabled by contemporary innovations in information and telecommunications technologies that undermine geographical barriers.[8] The emergent and uneven 'global' space of credit practices is characterised not by a single universal global market, but by multiple and distinct hierarchical institutional networks for different sets of credit practices (O'Brien 1992; Picciotto and Haines 1999). In our terms, then, to cast the world-scale of contemporary world credit practices as 'global' obscures the extent to which large sections of state-societies remain marginalised from the allocation of credit. For many underdeveloped state-societies in particular, access to sovereign credit is often denied and commercial and corporate credit tends to be allocated to highly selected borrowers on a volatile short-term basis through inter-bank lending and portfolio investment practices (Hoogvelt 2001: 80–9). The use of global finance as an all-encompassing notion clearly obscures a more complex situation in which a single, integrated and universal global market has not been realised.

The notion of global finance also serves to shroud specific conjunctural forms taken by contemporary credit practices in terms of the credit instruments employed. The form of credit practices since the mid-1970s has been far from static. Prior to the debt crisis of the early 1980s that proved to be the 'watershed' (Plender 1987: 43) for contemporary bank lending, sovereign credit practices tended to take the form of syndicated loans that sought to share the risks of lending between consortia of banks operating principally in the Euromarkets (Mendelsohn 1980: 65–6). Euromarket practices were also the main source of short-term offsetting finance for alleviating balance-of-payments problems during this period (Helleiner 1994: 114). Unlike sovereign credit practices, corporate credit practices in support of the multinational strategies of the principal corporations took the predominant form of issues of Eurobonds and short-term capital instruments as opposed to syndicated loans. While the provision of corporate credit continues to display important national variations (Doremus *et al.* 1998: 22–58), the 'disintermediation' implied by corporate credit practices during the 1970s has become far more widespread since the early 1980s, engulfing sovereign and corporate credit provision both onshore and offshore (IMF 1998a: Annex V; Strange 1998b).[9] The disintermediated provision of credit through capital and equity instruments concentrated on the developed political economies of North America and western Europe throughout the 1980s, expanding to include a select group of underdeveloped political economies as so-called 'emerging markets' from the early 1990s (Krugman 1995; IMF 1997).

The uneven expansion of contemporary world credit practices has not only occurred in terms of geographical scale, but also in terms of a rapid increase in the volume of credit created. The sheer volume of disintermediated credit available dwarfs the capacity of bank loans to provide a competitive alternative. For instance, based on OECD figures, Lewis (1999: 102) calculates that the value of total bond and note issues grew from $45 billion to $1,168.7 billion between 1981 and 1996. As several commentators have shown (Allen 1994; Shutt 1998; Watson 1999), ever more amounts of accumulated capital have been absorbed by world credit practices as the material basis for this expansion. Palan (1993) terms the increase in the value of credit instruments the 'debt for growth syndrome', as corporations and states have increasingly relied upon credit rather than existing revenues to fund investment against a background of slow economic growth since the early 1970s. While partly resulting from contemporary state and corporate financing requirements, the increased volume of credit created through world credit practices and associated capital movements also arises from financialisation. As with the periods from the 1740s to the 1790s and the 1870s to 1914, a structural feature of contemporary world finance is the expansion in the value of credit created due to the speculative accumulation of capital through world credit practices themselves.

The perception that contemporary world finance is marked by financialisation is fairly common. For instance, Drucker (1986: 781–8) posits that 'the changed world economy' has been marked by the emergence of what he terms the 'symbolic economy' of massive volumes of capital and credit flows alongside the flows of goods and services in the 'real economy'. Gordon (1988: 55) traces the roots of contemporary financialisation to the early 1970s and the combination of falling levels of corporate manufacturing profitability (cf. Brenner 2001), increased interest rate and exchange rate instability, and the re-cycling through the Euromarkets of the large volumes of petrodollars generated by the first oil crisis. Meanwhile, for Strange (1986), the de-coupling of the symbolic and real economies is such that the contemporary world economy comes to be described as 'casino capitalism'. Even the IMF have noted 'a pyramiding of financial transactions on a relatively small base of real transactions' (IMF 1990, in Roberts, 1994: 96).

Our historical inquiry suggests that the contemporary bout of financialisation is conjuncturally distinct. During previous instances of financialisation, important sets of credit practices remained at a certain remove from financialisation. For instance, during the Dutch financial order, the creation of British sovereign and corporate credit was, in the main, isolated from Amsterdam-centred financialisation. Similarly, during the British financial order, German and US corporate credit was by-and-large detached from London-centred speculation. What marks contemporary financialisation is the extent to which, to varying degrees but to almost universal extent, world credit practices are subject or respond to speculative motivations. This was most starkly revealed by the Asian financial crisis of 1997–8 as, contrary to the expectations of world-systems scholars in particular (e.g. Arrighi 1994: 337; Amin 1996: 242), eastern Asian corporate credit was shown not to be shielded from the impulses of financialisation. Contemporary world credit practices are characterised, then, by what might be termed 'generalised financialisation'.

Current financialisation is evidenced by the sheer extent of secondary trading practices. In 1975, the value of cross-border transactions in bonds and equities expressed as a percentage of GDP in the US, Japan, Germany, France, Italy and Canada amounted to 5 per cent or less for each economy, growing to between 100 per cent and 700 per cent for each by 1997 (IMF 1998a: 186–7). While partly associated with the creation of fresh credit, the value of these transactions is primarily the result of the speculative arrangement and re-arrangement of ownership claims. The most widely recognised indicator of contemporary speculation is the degree to which increases in foreign exchange trading have outpaced the growth of world trade. According to BIS (1999a) figures, the daily turnover realised by foreign exchange trading practices in 1998 averaged $1.5 trillion, around seventy times that necessitated by world trade. Back in 1973, daily turnover varied between $10 and $20 billion, around twice that necessitated by world trade. The collective and hierarchical organisation of these practices is considerable, with over half of all transactions undertaken by the top ten dealers in London and New York (BIS 1999a: 19).

Closely intertwined with disintermediation and financialisation is 'securitisation', that is, the unbundling, repackaging, pricing, and secondary trading of the claims and obligations arising from the creation of credit. The focus for securitisation has been the displacement of the risks arising from outstanding claims and obligations including exchange rate, interest rate and credit risks. Contemporary world finance has witnessed a rapid increase in practices that seek the displacement of such risks by hedging price fluctuations, utilising an ever-widening range of derivatives instruments that include financial futures, options and swaps (Strange 1998a: 22–42).[10] Enabled by innovations in information technologies, such practices have been informed by the development of complex mathematical risk management models. While these practices have been a feature of modern world finance since the seventeenth century, what is striking is the extent to which they have increased with securitisation. BIS (1996) figures show a phenomenal growth in derivatives practices from the 1980s such that, by the end of 1995, financial institutions participating in the survey were involved in $64 trillion worth of outstanding derivatives contracts. To put this in perspective, the aggregate market value of all bonds, equity, and bank assets in Japan, North America and the fifteen European Union state-societies totalled $68.4 trillion at the end of 1995 (IMF 1998a: 192). Given that they are often purchased on the margin, derivatives instruments facilitate high-risk and potentially high-yield speculation (Shutt 1998: 121; Strange 1998a: 94–5). The spectacular growth in the use of derivatives instruments has, then, been closely bound up with the disintermediated and financialised form of contemporary world credit practices.

Today's world credit practices rest upon and bring together a wide range of market institutions that, taken together, constitute an unprecedented pattern of institutionalisation. Three interrelated principal developments have characterised change. First, so-called 'non-bank' financial market institutions, particularly institutional investors such as pension funds, insurance companies and mutual funds, have come to play an important role in world credit practices (OECD 1994; IMF 1995; Minns 1996a; Clark 1999). Either directly or through fund management institutions, institutional investors are key in the collective allocation of capital and secondary trading in support of disintermediated practices (Harmes 1998). The rise of institutional investors has been grounded primarily in changes to saving patterns since the 1950s, whereby the traditional dominant position of commercial banks has been undermined. While the 'Anglo-American' (i.e. US, UK, Canada, Australia) political economies have been at the forefront of change, reflected in the high profile of their institutional investors in world capital and equity market practices, such developments are discernible to differing degrees throughout the developed political economies.

Second, the institutionalisation of sets of credit practices in specific institutions, for example, the making of bank loans on the basis of deposits in commercial banks, has become increasingly eroded. In particular, the distinction between commercial and investment banks maintained in Anglo-American and 'Roman Law' (e.g. France, Japan, Italy) political economies, principally through strict legal and regulatory codes that compartmentalised credit practices according to institution-type, has been largely dissolved (Cerny 1993b: 56–62). Contemporary major banks have increasingly come to approximate to those institutions traditionally associated with the 'universal banking' political economies of Germany and the Netherlands, undertaking all manner of credit practices. Such 'decompartmentalisation' has been essential in enabling commercial banks, as the principal intermediary institutions, from playing a role in the organisation of disintermediated practices (*Economist* 1994). Commercial banks are now less likely to rely on loan practices, with profits accruing to a greater extent from the fees earned from so-called 'off-balance sheet' practices – investments, mergers and acquisitions, transfers and trading – undertaken on behalf of customers (IMF 1997: Annex III).

Third, the changing institutionalisation of credit practices has been enabled by a wave of alliances, mergers and acquisitions that has led to the formation of massive universal financial market conglomerates, or what the IMF (1998a: 180) terms 'global banks' such as Citigroup, ING Group, Credit Suisse, Deutsche Bank, and J.P. Morgan Chase and Co. Reference to developments across European political economies is illustrative of the range of motivations framing alliances, mergers and acquisitions. Cross-border alliances, mergers and acquisitions have tended to be characterised by Europe's commercial and universal banks developing links with, or purchasing, smaller institutions. The principal motivation has been to augment profits through specialisation (Vipond 1993: 202). Although some of Europe's largest universal banks such as Deutsche Bank may approximate to the model pan-European universal bank, forging institutional relationships with or the purchase of London-centred investment banks in particular has enabled greater involvement in disintermediated world credit practices. High profile alliances, mergers and acquisitions have brought together, for example, Deutsche Bank and Morgan Grenfell (1989), Dresdner Bank and Kleinwort Benson (1995) (with both subsequently swallowed up by the German insurance group Allianz), and Swiss Bank Corporation and S.G. Warburg (1996). Ultimately, such institutional reorganisation has led to consolidation and an intensification of the collective and hierarchical tendencies of financial markets (Smith 1992).

Spatiality

With the exception of interregna periods in modern world finance associated with the simultaneous fall from prominence of one WFC and the rise of another, the spatiality of world credit practices has been characterised by centralisation in Amsterdam, London and New York as a succession of single WFCs. The orthodox representation of contemporary credit practices as 'global finance' implies an unprecedented transformation of this spatiality. Powered by information and telecommunications technologies, the inference is that the 24-hour global marketplace for finance is 'spaceless' as it follows the sun from East to West. In the words of a British Telecom television advertisement from the mid-1990s, 'geography is history'. A range of research from across the social sciences (Sassen 1991; Pryke and Lee 1995; Germain 1997; Leyshon and Thrift 1997) and also commentaries in the popular media (*Economist* 1998) have effectively challenged the 'end of geography' argument. In our terms, the integral relationship between modern credit practices and financial centres as key social spaces continues in the contemporary era. At the same time, however, this should not obscure an important transformation in the spatiality of contemporary credit practices that combines two related dynamics. The asymmetrical decentralisation of credit practices across a multi-centred financial order appears, for the first time, as more than a transient development associated with interregna periods of the decline of one WFC and the rise of another. Closely associated with decentralisation is the advent of offshore as a qualitatively new social space of world credit practices.

The vast majority of world credit practices are now undertaken offshore. Based on BIS figures, Lewis (1999) calculates that, at June 1997, 88 per cent of world-scale bank lending practices and 85 per cent of bond issues take place offshore. As with the London-centred Euromarkets that lay at the roots of offshore, the social space of offshore is not given its character by a new set of world credit practices. Equally, while some offshore credit practices may become associated with visible territories – so-called offshore financial centres (OFCs) and tax havens such as London, Hong Kong, Singapore, the Cayman Islands, Jersey, Guernsey, Panama and the Bahamas – OFCs are not the defining feature of offshore. Rather, the boundaries between onshore and offshore are distinguished by 'a position of differentiation within the regulatory realm of the state', the former as 'fully regulated and taxed' and the latter 'where some regulations and taxation are withheld' (cf. Roberts, S. M. 1994; Palan 1999: 21; Picciotto 1999). Offshore, then, is a space of world credit practices denominated in non-local currencies that lies beyond the jurisdictional regulatory parameters of the local state, but remains within legal frameworks.

The advent of offshore as a new 'regulatory landscape' (Hudson 1998) has been highly significant to the other key transformation in the spatiality of contemporary world credit practices, that is, asymmetrical decentralisation. The contemporary financial order has been marked by the coexistence of New York, London and Tokyo as a 'triad' at the apex of hierarchy of WFCs – or what Hamilton (1986) has termed 'the three-legged stool'. Prior to the current era, the changing spatiality of world credit practices had followed a centralisation–decentralisation–(re)centralisation dynamic. By contrast, no single WFC appears likely to emerge as dominant at present (Drennan 1996; Sassen 1999). Pivotal to the rise of financial centres to world status during modern world finance has been the relative ascendancy of their respective national economies in terms of capital accumulation and the use of their currencies as world money. Offshore, as 'the bifurcating of sovereign space into relative realms distinguished by degrees of regulations' (Palan 1998: 626), has the effect of fracturing and reconstituting the national economy as a territorially-defined regulatory construct (Cameron and Palan 1999). Since the early nineteenth century, national economies had formed the foundations of the British and American financial orders and the world economy more broadly. With the Euromarkets, the space of national economic units defined through state territoriality began to be overlain and permeated by offshore regulatory space. As a consequence, the rise and fall of WFCs becomes partially de-coupled from the relative ascent and decent of their respective national economies, and 'the necessary nexus' (Lewis 1999: 83) between the key social space of world credit practices and the currency in which those practices are denominated is severed. In short, the emergence of offshore and OFCs contributes to a conjunctural distortion of the centralisation–decentralisation–(re)centralisation dynamic of modern world finance.

Alongside the advent of offshore, developments in the contemporary world economy have also contributed to the conjunctural distortion of the tendency for modern world credit practices to display a uni-polar spatiality. From the 1960s, the relative competitiveness of South East Asia in particular and also Germany reshaped the parameters of the post-1945 world economy in which the US had been ascendant. The result is that the contemporary world economy is more multipolar in nature, characterised in particular by MNC production networks and flows of trade that have generated distinct patterns of economic regionalisation in North America, Europe, and Asia (Ruigrok and van Tulder 1995; Hirst and Thompson 1996; Zysman 1996). In both North America and Europe, regionalisation has been facilitated respectively by the regionalism of the North American Free Trade Agreement (NAFTA) and the European Union's Single Market Programme. Given the continuing close relationships between commercial banks and their medium-sized corporate customers (Pauly and Reich 1997), regional arcs of production and trade have tended to be mirrored by a regionalisation of banking practices (Germain 1996b, 1996c). Such a regional orientation of commercial credit practices in particular is encouraging the consolidation of regional financial centres across North America, Europe and Asia.[11]

The relationships between offshore and regionalisation on the one hand and the asymmetrical decentralisation of world credit practices on the other are revealed by close examination of London, New York and Tokyo as WFCs. Each WFC stands as a key social space for different world credit practices.

London

Based upon its re-emergence at the heart of the Euromarkets during the unravelling of the American financial order, London is the exemplar entrepôt OFC. As such, London has been the key social space for disintermediated offshore credit practices. In 1998, 32 per cent of foreign exchange trading practices were London-centred, far outstripping New York as the next largest centre with 18 per cent (BIS 1999a: 15). London accounted for 60 per cent of primary bond syndication and 75 per cent of secondary bond trading at the end of 1994.[12] In 1997, approximately 60–5 per cent of world turnover in foreign equities trading took place in London, compared to 30–4 per cent in New York.[13] This is a consequence of both the comparatively world-scale orientation of listings on the LSE and the centralisation in London of the over-the-counter trading practices of the principal investment banks, institutional investors and fund managers.[14] Around two-thirds of London's equity trading practices are in European equities, adding a regional dimension to London's standing (Honeygold 1989: 59–61; Coakley 1992: 65; Stafford 1992: 48).[15] London-centred European equities trading has been facilitated by mergers, acquisitions and alliances between major continental European universal banks and London's investment banks. Furthermore, the recent advent of the European single currency (euro) appears not to have undermined London's standing as the centre for European capital and equity market practices (Corporation of London 2000: ch. 5). This would seem largely as a consequence of the British government's decision to retain sterling at present, and therefore the offshore status of London in terms of credit creation denominated in euros (Talani 2000).

Three broad phases can be distinguished in London's contemporary standing as a key space for banking practices. First, from 1974 through to the early- to mid-1980s, London dominated banking by virtue of its position as the key OFC for syndicated lending, accounting for 27 per cent of the total volume of cross-border bank lending among BIS reporting countries in 1980 (Davis and Latter 1989: 518). Second, from the early- to mid- 1980s through to the end of the decade, the value of outstanding cross-border bank lending out of London almost doubled while London's share of the total volume of cross-border bank lending among BIS reporting countries fell to 20.5 per cent by 1989 (Davis and Latter 1989: 518). London's relative decline as a key space for banking practices during this period appears to have been related to disintermediation and regionalisation. The disintermediation of London- and New York-centred practices after the debt crisis was not paralleled by developments in Tokyo. On the contrary, Tokyo experienced an increase in banking practices that provided the credit for the expanding regional arc of production and trade in Asia and saw its share cross-border bank lending increase from 5 per cent (1982) of the total volume among BIS reporting countries to equal that of London by 1989 (Davis and Latter 1989: 518). At the same time, Japanese banks became important market institutions in London-centred banking practices, providing short-term inter-bank funds for longer-term regional 're-lending' (Nakao 1995) by their Tokyo-centred counterparts.

The period from the beginning of the 1990s has marked a third, current phase of London's standing as a key social space for banking practices. BIS statistics show that in the course of the 1990s London has once again regained its position as the key social space for banking practices, accounting for 18 per cent of cross-border lending in 1997, compared with 14 per cent for Japan and 9 per cent for the USA.[16] London continues to stand as an off-shore entrepôt WFC for banking practices broadly, providing non-capital market corporate credit and commercial credit for the world's major MNCs. What characterises this current phase particularly, however, is that London's standing has been partially eroded by second-tier continental European financial centres. As such, while London has regained its comparative position as the principal WFC for banking practices among the triad, its overall share of the total continues to decline. Paris and Frankfurt especially have increased in significance as social spaces for regionally-orientated banking practices as European production and trade networks have become consolidated (CRP 1995: section 10).[17] Europe's medium-sized companies have intensified their trade and investment links with neighbouring European economies, encouraging their 'home' banks to expand their pan-European institutional networks and re-organise practices by replacing nationally-based institutional divisions with various functional market divisions (Canals 1993: 162; Germain 1996c: 368). A presence across Europe's financial centres is necessary to service the commercial and corporate credit needs of Europe's companies (Bröker 1993). The relative importance of France and Germany within European production and trade translates into the significance of Paris and Frankfurt respectively as spaces for banking practices in Europe.

New York

Despite its displacement from the apex of the hierarchy of WFCs as part and parcel of the unravelling of the American financial order, New York continues to be a key social space for credit practices in the contemporary financial order. While the largest share of world credit practices are London-centred, the lasting primacy of the US dollar as world money ensures that clearing practices are New York-centred.[18] As Nakao (1995: 79–80) asserts:

> No matter how much the Euromarket expands, all transactions denominated in dollars can only be completed through transfers of funds in and out of US-based dollar accounts: no matter how multipolar international finance may become, New York remains the hub as long as dollar-denominated transactions predominate.

Outstanding dollar-denominated obligations are settled by automated electronic transfers organised through the Clearing House Interbank Payments System (CHIPS) of the New York Clearing House Association, in conjunction with the Federal Reserve Bank of New York. In 1999, CHIPS cleared 95 per cent of all dollar-denominated world credit practices (Corporation of London 2000: ch. 5). The centralisation of clearing practices in New York feeds the significance of New York as a key social space for money-market practices. Financial market institutions, corporations and central banks all hold working balances in New York to facilitate clearance that also find their way into the money-markets (Vogel 1993:

58). Consequently, the significance of New York as a space for money-market practices has increased alongside the vast expansion in the volume of dollar-denominated credit in the contemporary financial order.

New York has been at the forefront of the contemporary disintermediation of world credit practices. In terms of sovereign credit practices and given the US state's insatiable appetite for credit during the current era, the US Treasury bond (T-bond) market is the largest single bond market world-wide and the benchmark against which other investment opportunities are judged (Taggart Murphy 1996: 111). New York's deep and highly liquid capital markets have more broadly been a fulcrum for both the placement of foreign government and corporate bonds issued elsewhere, and the portfolio investment practices of foreign fund managers and institutional investors (Corporation of London 2000: ch. 5). Further, New York has been very much at the cutting edge in the development of the securitised credit instruments, including innovations such as certificates of deposit (CDs), mortgage-backed securities, and bonds with warrants attached. In terms of equity market practices, the disclosure rules governing new listings on the NYSE set by the Securities and Exchange Commission (SEC) have served to limit, at least to some extent, foreign issues and secondary trading in New York in the contemporary financial order (Lütz 1997). Much of the considerable secondary trading that takes place does so through the over-the-counter electronic platform provided by the National Association of Securities Dealers' Automated Quotation system (NASDAQ) established in 1971 (Smith, R.C. 1989: 7–29). By 1996, 416 foreign corporations had listings on NASDAQ, second only to the LSE with 533.[19] NASDAQ has, however, not simply contributed to the significance of New York as a social space for equity trading practices. The electronic link-up between London and NASDAQ via London's SEAQ International system, in place since 1985, has also been important in facilitating the centralisation of over-the-counter foreign equity trading practices in London.

In terms of banking practices which provide commercial and non-capital market corporate credit, New York appears to occupy a relatively insignificant position when compared to London and Tokyo. In 1997, New York accounted for only 9 per cent of banking practices by lending volume, compared with 18 per cent for London and 14 per cent for Japan.[20] Attempts during the 1980s to promote New York as a space for banking practices, particularly through the creation of offshore International Banking Facilities (IBFs), seem to have been relatively unsuccessful (McGahey *et al.* 1990: 136–7). However, a simple comparison between the WFCs of the triad obscures the extent to which New York has stood throughout the contemporary period as North America's banking centre (Germain 1996b). New York has been the key space for the regional expansion of banking practices, institutionalised particularly within the networks of American, Canadian and Mexican commercial banks. Commercial credit practices that service the credit needs of a regional arc of production and trade have, in particular, been centralised in New York. This has facilitated the capacity of Canadian and Mexican banks to cater for the credit needs of their domestic customers who themselves have become increasingly drawn into producing for the US market.

Tokyo

At the outset of the contemporary period, Tokyo was of marginal significance as a space for world credit practices. From the early- to mid-1970s, Tokyo-centred practices did become of considerable importance both as a source of Japanese sovereign and corporate credit and for the north-eastern Asia region more broadly (Reed 1980; Kalder 1997). The gravity of Tokyo as Asia's principal regional financial centre subsequently expanded to South East Asia throughout the 1980s, as Tokyo-centred commercial and corporate banking practices accompanied the regionalisation of Japanese production networks (cf. Bernard and Ravenhill 1995). The profile of credit practices undertaken in the other principal financial centres of the region came to reflect this domination, as Japanese banks and corporations emerged as the principal borrowers in Hong Kong and Singapore (Suzuki 1992: 102; Nakao 1995: 134–5). Such was the extent of the rise of Tokyo in eastern Asia that it came to stand alongside London at the apex of world bank lending by volume at the end of the 1980s.

While Tokyo-centred banking practices in support of Japanese regional production networks continued throughout the 1990s, an important shift also occurred. Lending to foreign corporations, financial market institutions and states increased considerably. For instance, outstanding Japanese loans to South Korea, Taiwan, Thailand, Indonesia, Malaysia and the Philippines grew by 76 per cent between the end of 1993 and the end of 1996 (Bevacqua 1998: 415). Tokyo-centred banking practices were, then, firmly embroiled in the early 1990s 'credit boom' (Goldstein 1998) throughout Asia, especially South East Asia, that sowed the seeds of Asian financial crisis which took hold from July 1997.

Alongside its position as the key space for regional banking practices, the development of Tokyo as the third leg of the triad of WFCs during the 1980s also resulted from Tokyo-centred capital allocation that supported the securities issues and trading practices of Japanese banks in New York and London. Japanese net long-term capital outflows increased dramatically during the early- to mid-1980s, as Japan became the principal creditor economy in the world economy. Indeed, for the period between 1986 and 1988, Japanese net long-term capital outflows that were predominantly portfolio investment were between three and four times greater than those of the next largest creditor economy (Helleiner 1993b: 209; Nakao 1995: 29; Germain 1997: 113). Such capital supported the high profile buying and placement of US T-bonds by Japanese investment banks operating in New York (Emmott 1993: 144–51). Furthermore, as Nakao (1995: 37–42) highlights, the majority of the capital channelled by Japanese market institutions from Tokyo to New York went via their offshore networks centred in London. London stood more broadly as 'the second financial capital of Japan' (Warner 1991: 196), with between 40 per cent and 60 per cent of the overseas assets of Japanese banks created in London during the 1980s (Nakao 1995: 110). Issues of Eurobonds by Japanese investment banks and corporations in London underpinned Japanese expansionary direct investments world-wide.

The relative incapacity of Tokyo to offer a space for the disintermediated practices of issuing and trading securities at a world scale has reflected comparative weaknesses in terms of restrictive regulations, money-market practices and the on-going indebtedness of Japanese financial market institutions. By comparison with London and New York and despite the 'big bang' in Tokyo which began on 1 April 1998, the regulations framing Tokyo's capital and equity market structures remain relatively restrictive.[21] While the main legislative planks of the big bang are now in place, implementation remains partial and incomplete as a consequence of embedded sectoral coalitions of interests that link politicians, bureaucrats and financiers (Cerny 2000). Given the significance of money-market practices in building the critical mass of liquid capital in a WFC, the relatively slow development of money-market practices has also limited Tokyo's standing as a space for disintermediated world credit practices (Honeygold 1989: 107–15). The relative weakness of Tokyo's money-markets is, in turn, rooted in the denomination of Japanese trade and payments with the US and Europe in currencies other than yen (Eken 1984/1994: 327; Warner 1991: 187–8).

Finally, the capacity of Tokyo to stand as a key space for disintermediated credit practices was hampered in the 1990s by the continuing malaise of Japanese financial market institutions. The huge volumes of bad debts bequeathed upon Japanese financial market institutions by the collapse of 'bubble economy' in 1989 have been compounded by losses incurred as a result of the Asian crisis of 1997–8. The collective bad debts of Japanese financial market institutions are estimated to stand at around $1 trillion.[22] The state-led restructuring of Japanese financial institutions in the wake of the Asian crisis has involved temporary nationalisation of several banks, mergers between and the foreign acquisition of major institutions, the creation of a new Financial Services Agency to oversee reform, and spending around 70 trillion yen of public money (equivalent to 14 per cent GDP) to re-capitalise ailing institutions (IMF 2000: Annex 1). Given the on-going practice by Japanese financial market institutions of holding huge stock portfolios in the belief that gains will offset bad debts, the fall, at the time of writing, of the Nikkei 225 index to a sixteen-year low in March 2001 would seem to spell particular danger. The consequence is that Japanese involvement in world credit practices is significantly curtailed and the attraction of Tokyo to foreign financial market institutions and mobile capital is undermined.

Conclusions

In contrast with the Dutch and British financial orders, the American financial order was marked by an idiosyncratic organisation of world credit practices in which New York-centred bank lending and capital market practices were heavily circumscribed; a distinctive structure of power in which, despite their material predominance, New York's social forces were constrained in their capacity to frame the making of the order; and a unique structure of governance characterised by the organisational principles of embedded liberalism and state-based formal governance that subordinated the authority of New York. It was perhaps not surprising, then, that the unravelling of the American financial order was also highly distinctive. As in previous world financial orders, the contradictions and unravelling of the American order manifested themselves in decentralisation. The decentralisation of the American financial order was, however, unlike that which had coincided with the unravelling of the Dutch and British financial orders. The demise and associated decentralisation of the American order were not driven principally by the rise of competing social forces associated with an ascendant WFC. The London-centred Euromarkets were not a nascent uni-centric world financial order in the making. Rather, US and world economic problems in the late 1960s and early 1970s revealed the strains and stresses present in the embedded liberal compromise between US state and societal forces. The restructuring of US state-societal relations in favour of New York's social forces, not the rise of London's social forces to challenge the predominance of New York, underpinned the unravelling of the American financial order. As such and once again, the utility of focusing on hierarchical social orders as opposed to the rise and fall of states' wealth and power in accounting for the changing organisation of world finance is illustrated.

Contemporary world credit practices have undergone significant restructuring since the collapse of the American financial order in 1973–4. The final years of the American financial order were characterised by the incapacity of the state-based structure of governance to manage demands for credit, particularly those arising from the oil crisis. The organisation of credit practices was ceded to market institutional networks, particularly those that operated offshore in the London-centred Euromarkets. As the orthodox representation of contemporary world credit practices as 'global finance' suggests, the subsequent restructuring of practices since the early 1970s has furthered this marketisation. The current prevalence of world-scale bank loans and especially capital and equity market practices both contrast sharply with the largely state-managed credit practices of the American financial order and is reminiscent of the Dutch and British financial orders. 'Global finance' remains, however, an inadequate representation of contemporary credit practices.

From the perspective of an Historical IPE approach that focuses upon world credit practices as opposed to capital flows, the notion of global finance obscures conjuncturally distinct qualitative features of credit practices that are vital to an understanding of contemporary world finance. The marketisation of world credit practices incorporates credit instruments and patterns of institutionalisation associated with disintermediation. The world-scale of contemporary credit practices is far more uneven than the universal reach suggested by the global finance orthodoxy. The volume of credit created has increased considerably, particularly as a consequence of generalised financialisation, that is, a structural expansion in the value of credit created due to world credit practices becoming subject or responding to speculative motivations. Furthermore, contemporary world credit practices entail a distinctive spatiality. Contemporary practices are decentralised, with the 'triad' of London, New York and Tokyo standing as WFCs. Prior to the current era, the spatiality of world credit practices had followed a centralisation–decentralisation–(re)centralisation dynamic. The prospect of another process of (re)centralisation appears remote at present. As the asymmetrical differentiation of each WFC as a key space for different sets of practices serves to illustrate, decentralisation is closely bound up with the other transformation in the spatiality of contemporary world finance, that is, the consolidation of offshore.

Notes

1 Germain (1997: 7) provides a concise overview of Triffin's position – 'He argued that continued US balance of payments deficits would create a dollar overhang that must inevitably outgrow US gold stocks and prompt a crisis in the fixed value of dollar related to gold. The solution to this problem became known as the "Triffin Dilemma", on the basis that any attempt to narrow or eradicate the US balance of payments deficit would necessarily compromise the provision of credit to the international economy.'

2 The major legislative planks of the controls programme were the Interest Equalisation Tax (IET), Voluntary Credit Restraint Program (VCRP) and Mandatory Control Program (MCP) (cf. Hawley 1987).

3 While partly a consequence of foreign dollar holdings such as those of the Soviet Union and communist China (Frieden 1987: 81), the build up of offshore short-term dollar deposits was also a consequence of the profit-making aspirations of US bankers. This led to the identification of the returns available by circumventing the Federal Reserve's Regulation Q that dated from the 1930s. Regulation Q imposed interest rate ceilings on short-term deposits of less than 90 days, whereas dollar deposits in foreign banks were not subject to the same ceilings. While Regulation Q stimulated the growth of the Eurocurrency markets, US capital controls built on this and stimulated the issuing of Eurobonds and Eurocredits (Cooper 1968: 118–9; Strange 1976: 180; Mendelsohn 1980: 23–5).

4 London's position as the key social space for Euromarket credit practices is reflected in the domination of Euromarket transactions. Born's (1977: 307) claim that 75–80 per cent of all Euromarket transactions were conducted in London in the 1960s does, however, seem overstated. While Eurodeutschmark transactions were centralised in Luxembourg and Eurosterling in Paris, London predominated as the key space for Eurodollar transactions. London's domination of the Euromarket, then, reflected the prevalence of Eurodollar business within the Euromarkets. For instance, between 1963 and 1977, 60 per cent of Eurobond issues were denominated in dollars (Mendelsohn 1980: 137). Therefore, Germain's (1997: 89) suggestion that by 1971 40 per cent of all Euromarket transactions regardless of their currency of denomination took place in London is probably an accurate representation of London's dominance. Following from London's dominant standing as the key space for Euromarket practices was its ascendancy as a space for foreign exchange trading practices. This was a consequence of the nature of Euromarket practices – i.e. borrowing on the Euromarkets for the purpose of re-lending to 'onshore' banks and businesses required the 'swapping' of dollar-denominated Eurocredits and Eurobonds for domestic currencies. By the late 1960s, around one-third of all world-wide foreign exchange trading took place in London (Cooper 1968: 125–6; Coakley 1992: 62).

5 The reliance of US MNCs on Euromarket credit practices more broadly is evidenced by their domination of Eurobond issues. Between 1965 and 1974, US MNCs accounted for one-third of all Eurobond issues valued at $9 billion out of a total of $27 billion (Mendelsohn 1980: 136).

6 Hudson (1998: 543–4) highlights that the same US regulatory restrictions (Regulation Q, Tax Equalisation Act) that encouraged the rebirth of London also offered a structural opportunity to the Bahamas, Cayman Islands and other offshore financial centres. This opportunity was grasped by these micro-states as smaller US banks in particular, confronted by the high cost of London offices, were attracted to the Caribbean.

7 For Strange (1986), 'non-decisions' are those made by states that increase non-state and, in particular, market forms of authority. For Strange (1986: 7), the immediate motivation for these non-decisions represented a belief 'that the markets could be used as allies, helping the United States to engineer a devaluation of the dollar which other countries could neither resist nor match'. Under floating exchange rates, the burden of international adjustment was effectively turned on its head, with countries in current and capital account surplus with the US now expected to face adjustment pressures rather than the deficit prone US political economy.

8 On the spatial implications of contemporary innovations in information and telecommunications technologies, see especially Giddens (1990) and Castells (1996).

9 Credit practices become 'disintermediated' when 'flows of funds between borrowers and lenders avoid direct use of financial intermediaries, for instance, in cases in which companies withdraw their funds from banks and lend them directly to each other, or when corporations issue commercial paper that may be merely underwritten by a bank or investment bank' (Sinclair 1994a: 136).

10 Derivatives are 'contracts specifying rights and obligations which are based upon, and thus derive their value from, the performance of some underlying instrument, investment, currency, commodity or service index, right or rate' (Cornford 1995, in Strange 1998a: 30). Strange (1998a: 30) suggests that around 98 per cent of derivatives practices are related to attempts to either avoid risks arising from, or to profit from, fluctuations in interest rates and exchange rates. Also, see Bank of International Settlements (1996, 1999a).

11 On this last point, I am indebted to an interview with representatives of the research and strategy departments of a major German universal bank, Frankfurt, 1 September 1997.

12 Figures provided by the Bank of England, private correspondence, 12 June 1998.

13 Figures provided by the Bank of England, private correspondence, 12 June 1998.

14 On the latter point I am indebted to the insights of a London-based representative of an American owned investment bank, confidential interview, 2 June 1998. See also Corporation of London (2000: ch.5).

15 According to the Bank of England, some 90 per cent of foreign equity turnover within Europe involved LSE member firms in 1996, private correspondence, 12 June 1998.

16 Figures provided by the Bank of England, private correspondence, 12 June 1998.

17 This view is also supported by a range of confidential interviews conducted with representatives of major German universal banks, Frankfurt, September 1997.

18 While the predominant position of the dollar is clear from the share of dollar-denominated official central bank reserves and world trade (Frankel 1995), the dollar-denomination of credit practices has declined somewhat. In particular, the share of dollar-denominated capital market practices has been eroded, largely as a consequence of the growing volume of new bond issues denominated in the Japanese yen during the latter half of the 1980s and European currencies during the 1990s (IMF 2000: 15). However, the apparent decline of the share of bond issues denominated in dollars obscures the practice of quickly 'swapping' bonds issued in other currencies into dollars (Walter 1993: 199–200). A 'swap' is 'a financial transaction in which two parties agree to exchange a predetermined series of payments over time . . . which serves to circumvent market imperfections and inefficiencies' (Leyshon and Thrift 1997: 125). In this instance, 'imperfections and inefficiencies' stem from the perceived exchange rate risk of holding bonds denominated in currencies other than the dollar. For example, 80 per cent of the 3.5 trillion yen worth of Euroyen bond issues in 1989 were accompanied by swaps into dollar-denominated bonds (Nakao 1995: 84). The combination of the dollar standing on one side of 83 per cent of foreign exchange transactions and over half of foreign exchange turnover being accounted for by 'forward' business, which is principally swaps related, is also illustrative of these practices more broadly (Bank of International Settlements 1996: 7).

19 Figures provided by the Bank of England, private correspondence, 12 June 1998.
20 Figures provided by the Bank of England, private correspondence, 12 June 1998.
21 For details of the Japanese 'big bang', see *Financial Times*, Survey, 'Japan's Financial Revolution', 26 March 1998.
22 *Guardian*, 'Big Bang Stock Takes a Tumble in Edgy Tokyo', 10 June 1998, p. 21.

6 The making of the contemporary world financial order

Contemporary world credit practices have undergone a significant structural transformation. Alongside new disintermediated forms of credit instruments and patterns of institutionalisation, contemporary practices are subject to financialisation and marked by a distinctive spatiality that combines the asymmetrical decentralisation of practices between the principal WFCs with the emergence of offshore space. As with our inquiry into previous world financial orders, an Historical IPE approach leads us to account for contemporary credit practices by shifting our inquiry to the diachronic moment. The purpose of this chapter is, then, to consider the structure of power that has and continues to frame the possible organisation of practices.

According to the neo-liberal orthodoxy of 'global finance', the restructuring of contemporary world credit practices has been driven by the expansionary tendencies of markets and enabled by innovations in information and communications technologies (Wriston 1988; McKenzie and Lee 1991; Ghosh and Ortiz 1997). In contrast to these somewhat naturalised and 'technicist' explanations, IPE scholars have done much to restore questions of power and politics to our understanding of change. The making of the contemporary world financial order tends to be interpreted as shaped by the rise and fall of hegemonic states. US academics in particular have argued that key to the making of the contemporary world financial order lies in the decline of the US and the rise of Japan. Such a view is common to orthodox IPE (Vogel 1986; Gilpin 1987) and world-systems scholars (Arrighi 1994) alike. For instance, based on Japan's position as the world's largest creditor economy and the relative size of Japanese financial markets and market institutional networks during the late 1980s, Gilpin (1987: 340) boldly asserts that 'Now it is Japan's turn at financial leadership'. Meanwhile, Arrighi (1994: 335) identifies 'the Japanese capitalist class . . . as new leaders of systemic processes of capital accumulation'. While subsequent developments in world finance and the world economy more broadly have exposed claims of pre-eminent Japanese power as overblown (Helleiner 2000: 232–4), the opposing view has been advanced throughout by new IPE scholars including, in particular, Susan Strange (1982, 1986, 1990). For Strange, the roots of change lay not so much in American decline, but rather the unwillingness of US to act as a responsible and benevolent leader.

Despite the state-centric nature of much of this existing work when compared to our focus on hierarchical social orders of which states-societies are part, it does serve to raise some important questions. How are we to account for the marketisation of contemporary world credit practices when hegemonic stability theory (HST) predicts that a decline of US hegemony will coincide with the increased protectionist impulses of resurgent economic nationalism (cf. Gilpin 1987: 88)? Should we speak of a 'contemporary' era in world finance that is distinguishable from the American financial order, or can the contemporary restructuring of credit practices be interpreted as reflecting the continued unravelling of the American financial order? Following Arrighi (1994), the current financialisation and decentralisation of world credit practices could appear as comparable to that which has coincided with previous interregna in world finance. Alternatively, drawing on the work of Strange (1986, 1990), should we view the contemporary period as the remaking or renovation of the American financial order?

Drawing on our historical knowledge of the previous 300 years or so of modern world finance, the current transformation of world credit practices is understood here as framed by an emergent and conjuncturally distinct structure of power. At the roots of the unique pattern of power relations in the contemporary financial order is the highly distinctive unravelling of the American financial order. As Chapter 5 has already made clear, the unravelling of the American order was exceptional. Decentralisation and demise were not driven principally by the rise of competing social forces associated with an ascendant WFC leading to contests over the appropriate organisation of world finance. Rather, US state and societal forces were pivotal to the unravelling of the American order and, as a consequence, have indeed been crucial in the making of the contemporary financial order (Strange 1990; Helleiner 1992; Walter 1993: 240–4; Germain 1997: 164–8). Yet to cast the contemporary financial order simply as the remaking of the American order would obscure significant changes in the very nature of financial power and conditions in the wider world order that, together, are at the heart of the making of the current organisation of credit practices.

The structure of power

Material power

Against the backdrop of conditions in the wider world order, a structure of power in world finance has framed the possible organisation of credit practices across modern world financial orders. In previous financial orders, the centralisation of capital, information and technology in the dominant WFC has been essential to the centralisation of world credit practices and significant in conferring material power upon the social forces associated with that centre. The centralisation of capital in WFCs has been due to a combination of factors: the rise of national financial centres to world status, linked to the ascendancy of their respective national political economies; the tendency for WFCs to be major centres for commercial trade; and the diversion of foreign mobile capital to WFCs in search of relatively high rates of return. The centralisation of information and technology in the dominant WFCs has, meanwhile, reflected the spatiality of a range of more or less institutionalised networks and the social relations of technology. As in previous financial orders, material power relations have been of considerable importance in framing the manner in which contemporary credit practices have come to be organised. Significantly, however, the very nature of material power has changed in contemporary world finance leading to a less hierarchical structure of power than in previous financial orders.

Change in the nature of material power in contemporary world finance combines two principal aspects. First, the consolidation of offshore as a regulatory space following its emergence during the unravelling of the American financial order has had important ramifications for contemporary material power relations. In previous financial orders, mobile capital tended to become centralised in WFCs that, largely as a consequence of the relative growth trajectories and strength of their respective national economies and currencies, already enjoyed a wealth of capital. The deposit-compelling power of a WFC effectively served to reinforce and further consolidate the material power of the social forces associated with it, tending to perpetuate their power at a time when the relative strength of their national economy had begun to wane. In contrast, in the contemporary financial order, OFCs that provide spaces for practices undertaken in non-local currencies can have deposit-compelling power regardless of their national economic weight. The centralisation–decentralisation–(re)centralisation dynamic of modern world finance is ruptured by offshore. While the rise to world status and the fall of national financial centres and their attendant implications for material power relations continues in the contemporary financial order, the distribution of capital and the material power relations that emerge are partially re-articulated by the advent of offshore.

Second, although unequal relations of ownership, control and access to information and technology have been important to material power throughout successive world financial orders, these have become of greater consequence in the contemporary order. In general terms, capital accumulation in the world economy has become more information-intensive (Castells 1989; Carnoy *et al.* 1993; Daniels 1993). As Cox (1987: 244) notes:

> Knowledge, in the form of technology and market information, is the principal resource in the world economy, especially knowledge in its dynamic form as the capacity to generate new technologies and to market new products.

Ownership, access or control of cutting edge information and technology is of expanded importance in establishing the parameters for economic competition. The greater consequence of information and technology in contemporary world finance both reflects this broad development and is amplified specifically by the long-standing significance of such material resources to world credit practices. In particular, information and technology facilitate new innovations in capital market instruments, the proliferation of all kinds of short-term trading practices that are often speculative in nature, and the assessment of the increasingly complex risks arising from the creation of credit. It is largely as a result of the expanded importance of information and technology and their continued centrifugal spatiality that geographers such as Thrift (1994) assert that WFCs have retained their standing as the key spaces for credit practices. The power relations that emerge from the contemporary centralisation of information and technology in WFCs become of greater consequence in contributing to the capacity of WFCs to stand as 'command posts' (Leyshon and Thrift 1997: 201) in framing the organisation of credit practices.

The changing nature of material power in the contemporary financial order has, particularly against the backdrop of a regionalising and more multi-polar world economy, been at the heart of the decentralisation of credit practices and the emergence of a structure of power that is less hierarchical than in previous orders. The social forces associated with each WFC of the triad all enjoy material power that has been consequential to the making of the contemporary order. Such power has not contributed primarily to determining the making of the order in a relational sense – that is, the social forces of the triad have not forced other state and societal forces to act according to former's perceived self interests, but has served to constrain the possible organisation of world credit practices. Furthermore, consideration of the position of the social forces of each WFC of the triad in terms of material power relations suggests that, relative to their counterparts in Tokyo, the social forces of New York and London are preponderant. While the contemporary structure of power has become decentralised and less hierarchical, asymmetries of power continue.

Among the WFCs of the triad, New York has stood as the 'capital of capital' (Hamilton 1986: 113) throughout the contemporary financial order. This is usually expressed by reference to the depth and liquidity of its capital, equity and money-markets (e.g. Corporation of London 2000: ch. 5). Capital is centralised in New York as a result primarily of the continued weight of the US economy and position of the US dollar as world money, both in the world economy broadly and the North American region in particular. The disintermediated nature of American retail finance helps to ensure that pools of accumulated capital within the wealthiest economy in the world are centralised in New York, channelled through the networks of institutional investors (Henwood 1997). New York also enjoys considerable deposit-compelling power, evidenced by the increase in foreign claims on US borrowers throughout the contemporary era (IMF 2000: 10).

New York's position as the capital of capital is accompanied by the centralisation of several more or less institutionalised information and technological networks. New York heads London and Tokyo in the implementation of fibre-optic networks and advanced digital communication systems (McGahey *et al.* 1990: 171–3). On its inception in 1971, NASDAQ became the first electronic stock exchange and has subsequently remained the market leader, linking over-the-counter traders from around the world (Warf 1995). Taken together, the centralisation of several networks including those of US MNCs, the quality press (Parsons 1989), 'producer services' industries including accountants, legal services and management consultants (Sassen 1991), and financial wire services such as *Reuters*, *Dow Jones* and

Bloomberg combine to ensure that New York is home to key information industries. More specifically and closely bound up with the disintermediation of current credit practices, the intersection of more specialised networks has conferred considerable material power upon New York's social forces. The major US investment banks are widely regarded as pivotal to New York's strong competitive position as a space for information-intensive disintermediated credit practices (Hamilton 1986; Noyelle 1989b). These have been supplemented by the expertise of the NYSE, Moodys and Standard & Poors as the principal credit rating agencies (Sinclair 1994a, 1994b), and the Securities and Exchange Commission (SEC) that, according to Moran (1991: 34), is 'the single most important repository of information about the securities industry'. The centralisation of capital, information and technology confers material power on New York's social forces that has and continues to provide the basis for their integral influence on the making of the contemporary financial order.

In contrast with New York, the centralisation of capital in London is primarily reliant upon London's deposit-compelling power, itself rooted in its standing as the exemplar OFC. During the 1980s, Japanese and continental European market institutional networks tended to funnel huge amounts of capital into London largely in support of their own credit practices (Nakao 1995: 37–42; Leyshon and Thrift 1997: 109). These massive inflows of mobile capital have been boosted since the early 1990s by those carried by institutional investors, collectively providing the deep and liquid resources for London's standing as the principal centre for securities issuing and trading practices.[1] The foreign mobile capital centralised in London has been supplemented by that of the British economy that, disproportionate to its relative size, contributes consistently and considerably to long-term international capital movements (Germain 1997: 113). The centralisation in London of information and especially telematics technology has also been of importance in facilitating capital and equity market practices.[2] The development of the SEAQ international trading system by the LSE, based on and linked with NASDAQ, has been particularly significant in enabling these practices.[3] The privatisation and deregulation of telecommunications from the early 1980s has ensured the centralisation of new innovations in London more broadly, replacing previous commitments to universal provision throughout Britain (Graham 1992). In terms of information networks and not dissimilarly to New York, London is a key space for the market networks of producer services firms (Sassen 1991). London's long history as a WFC has enabled the development of specialised services such as insurance and accountancy which assist world credit practices (Michie 1992: 176–7). London has increasingly become a key space for the world's financial press, with *Euromoney*, *The Banker*, *The Economist*, and *Financial Times* all headquartered in London (Thrift 1994: 350). In addition, the research departments of continental European market institutions have come to be centralised in London, both accessing and contributing to London's information base.[4] As with New York, then, the centralisation of capital, information and technology in London provides the foundation for the important influence of London's social forces on the making of the contemporary financial order.

The capital centralised in Tokyo in the course of the contemporary financial order, meanwhile, has had three major sources. First, in direct contrast to both New York and London, large volumes of capital are centralised in Tokyo for investment as the flip-side of the massive current account surpluses of the Japanese economy (Vogel 1993: 61; Germain 1997: 118).[5] The second major source of the capital centralised in Tokyo arises from the Japanese population's unrivalled propensity for saving. Japanese personal savings of 1,200,000 billion yen are the equivalent of one-third of the world's total.[6] The third source of the capital centralised in Tokyo is dollar-denominated borrowing by Japanese financial market networks. The overseas branches of Japanese market networks in London, New York, Hong Kong and Singapore have, largely through short-term inter-bank borrowing, channelled capital back to their home market. Such practices were particularly prevalent during the period of the 'bubble' of booming stock prices on the Tokyo Stock Exchange (TSE) from the middle to the end of the 1980s, and again from the early 1990s through to the Asian financial crisis of 1997–8 (Nakao 1995; Bevacqua 1998). In our terms, what these practices suggest is the extent to which, unlike New York and London, Tokyo lacks considerable deposit-compelling power. As Eric Helleiner also notes through a more state-centric comparison of the contemporary standing of Japan with that of the United Provinces, Britain, and America in previous financial orders:

> Because of Japan's emergence as an international financial intermediary in the 1980s – importing short-term capital and re-lending long-term capital – many have concluded that Japanese markets have been increasingly developing this kind of 'pulling power'. This interpretation is, however, inaccurate. Japan's short-term capital inflows came, *not* from foreigners looking to Japanese financial markets as an attractive and safe place to hold money, as was true in the Dutch, British and American cases. Rather they represented Japanese bank borrowing in London and New York markets where short-term financial instruments were cheaper and more attractive than those in the overregulated Japanese financial system.
>
> (Helleiner 1993b: 213)

Tokyo's relative lack of deposit-compelling power ensures that the material power enjoyed by Tokyo's social forces is limited and somewhat parochial in comparison with that of the social forces of New York and London.

The relatively weak position of Tokyo's social forces is compounded by the comparatively poor standing of the city as a centre for accessible information and technological networks. McGahey *et al.* (1990: 161) identify a general absence of information networks informing Tokyo-centred money-market and sovereign credit practices. Closer linkages between credit practices and western-style information networks are broadly discouraged by the tendency for decisions regarding creditworthiness to be less transparent than in the other WFCs of the triad. This is a consequence of several factors: the greater gravity of banking practices as opposed to capital and equity market practices in Tokyo; the particular importance of familial and non-contractual relationships to credit allocation decisions in Asia (Crawford 2001); and the traditional role of the Ministry of Finance as a central information exchange that provides so-called 'administrative guidance' to market institutions on credit creation and allocation (Brown 1999). The lack of transparency may well have been a source of strategic effectiveness for Japanese finance during the 1980s (Cerny 2000), but has hampered the standing of Tokyo as a WFC throughout the contemporary financial order. While it does appear that a marginal increase in transparency has occurred as a consequence of the post-Asian crisis restructuring of Japanese finance, Taggart Murphy's (1996: 49) assertion that 'external oversight by accountants, investment analysts, financial journalists, or stock market participants is largely ceremonial' continues to hold. Furthermore, technological networks facilitating the greater integration of Tokyo with the social space of the world financial order also appear to have been slow to develop. For instance, Tokyo was relatively slow when compared to Hong Kong and Singapore to develop fibre-optic cable linkages to the US (Moss 1987: 83–4). In sum, while the structure of material power in the contemporary financial order is less hierarchical than in previous orders, unequal power relations that favour New York and London have and continue to mitigate against the capacity of Tokyo's recently ascending social forces to occupy a predominant position in framing the organisation of credit practices.

Social and political power

The contemporary material preponderance of the social forces of New York and London has not itself been sufficient to ensure their influence on the making of the contemporary financial order. In previous financial orders, the capacity of social forces associated with the dominant WFC to frame the making of the orders was dependent upon favourable patterns of social and political power relations. Such a situation was absent in the American financial order, as the configuration of social and political power placed New York's social forces in a subordinate position. The significance of social and political power relations for framing the possible organisation of credit practices continues to be apparent in the contemporary financial order.

The contemporary American and British forms of state have been characterised in ideal-typical terms by Cox (1991/1996: 199–201) as displaying 'hyperliberal' tendencies.[7] Such tendencies are rooted in a change in the pattern of social power that has realised the ascendancy of the perceived interests of the social forces of capital, particularly those groups, including financiers, seeking to expand their involvement in the world economy. The development of the hyperliberal form of state entails considerable restructuring of welfare-nationalist state-societal relations that become reflected in the institutions of the state. Gill (1991, 1995) terms this process 'new constitutionalism'. New constitutionalism is the discourse which seeks to sustain the institutionalisation of neo-liberal political economy, casting market efficiency and discipline as binding constraints on the conduct of fiscal, monetary, trade and investment policies (Gill 1995: 412). In contrast with the hyperliberal tendencies of the American and British states, the contemporary

Japanese form of state seems far less certain (Cox 1989/1996: 265–6; Bello 1998; Bevacqua 1998). This has considerable consequences for the social and political power of Tokyo's social forces. Japanese finance occupied a 'repressed' (Lapavitsas 1997) position within the post-war Japanese 'capitalist developmental state' (Johnson 1982). While this has changed somewhat with the deregulation of Japanese finance, the erosion of the existing state form's coherence as Japanese production networks expanded throughout South East Asia, and the fall out from the Asian financial crisis, the social and political structures of the Japanese state have not come to take a hyperliberal form (Bello 1998).

The divergent American and British forms of state on the one hand and the Japanese form of state on the other are not significant in terms of illustrating the contrasting social and political power of the social forces of the triad in an instrumentalist sense. Rather, what is significant is the manner in which a hyperliberal form of state broadly buttresses the material power of the social forces of New York and London. As Martin (1994: 271) asserts, American and British hyperliberalism represents 'a reassertion by the state of *an underlying disposition towards financial interests* after several decades of welfare and national industrial-economic concerns' [my emphasis]. Such an underlying disposition combines commitments to market making liberalisation and deregulation on the one hand with market conforming 'embedded financial orthodoxy' (Cerny 1993c, 1994b) in state policy and the privileging of so-called 'shareholder value' in corporate production (Aglietta 2000; Boyer 2000). Embedded financial orthodoxy itself combines commitments to fiscal austerity, a balanced budget and the anti-inflationary manipulation of interest rates to manage so-called 'sound money'. The form of the American and British states, then, at once reflects and underpins the relatively greater power of the social forces of New York and London than that enjoyed by their counterparts in Tokyo in the making of the contemporary financial order.

Liberalisation and deregulation

The contemporary financial order is characterised in the first instance by the marketisation and disintermediation of credit practices. The melding of material, social and political power that has framed the emergence of marketised and disintermediated world credit practices has, given the design capacity of state institutions in world finance, been crucially carried forward by policies of liberalisation and deregulation. As IPE scholars in particular have been at pains to stress, the same state institutions that were vital to restricting the role of financial market networks during the American financial order have also enabled the role of market networks in the contemporary age (Strange 1986; Underhill 1991; Helleiner 1994). This is not to deny the importance of market institutions taking advantage of regulatory loopholes or the significance of innovations in information and telecommunications, but to stress that, at base, states make markets. In this sense, as Cerny (1993b) highlights, 'deregulation' is, in effect, 're-regulation' as states make new rules framing practices undertaken in market institutions while continuing to guarantee property rights, contracts and currencies.

The liberalisation of capital controls by their respective states has been a 'pre-condition for the dominant position of New York, London, and Tokyo in the open global financial system of the 1980s' (Helleiner 1994: 147). Yet in-depth analyses of policies of financial liberalisation and deregulation across the major states reveal that such policies have often cut against the grain of the perceived self-interests of the social forces of finance in the short-term (Moran 1991; Vogel 1996). State managers have often been the instigators for policy change, responding in large part to international competitive pressures. As Helleiner recognises, such pressures stem from the unique nature of inter-state competition in world finance:

> the dynamics of state-to-state interaction in the financial sector are the opposite of those in trade. Whereas collective action – in the form of collective adherence to liberal rules – is said to be necessary to maintain an *open* order in trade, it is the move towards *closure* which requires co-operation in the financial sector.
>
> (Helleiner 1992: 35)

Against this backdrop, the US government's decisions to unilaterally liberalise capital controls in 1974 and deregulate the NYSE in May 1975 set in motion a competitive 'deregulatory dynamic' (Helleiner 1994: 18) in the contemporary financial order.[8] Against the backdrop of widespread capital controls and wide-reaching regulation that had developed across the welfare-nationalist state-societies of the American financial order, the deregulation dynamic was especially virulent. Alongside the removal of capital controls, the dynamic has come to embrace the abolition of fixed brokerage commissions and interest rate restrictions on credit practices; the demolition of barriers that previously compartmentalised practices according to institution; the legal formalisation of the regulatory roles of civil institutions; and the granting of freedoms for the creation of new distintermediated and securitised forms of credit instruments.

Liberalisation and deregulation have been by no means uniform in pace or extent and have not brought about the convergence of national financial arrangements (Moran 1991; Taggart Murphy 1996; Vogel 1996; Coleman 1997; Loriaux *et al.* 1997; Story 1997). For instance, it was only in 1999 that the Glass–Steagall Act that had compartmentalised US investment and commercial banking practices since 1933 was finally repealed. The relatively slow pace of American reform contrasts sharply with the rapid changes associated with London's 'big bang' of 1986 and also the so-called 'little big bang' in Paris (Cerny 1989).[9] Meanwhile, fixed brokerage commissions were only abolished in Japan in 1999, nearly a quarter of a century after similar deregulation in New York's 'May Day' restructuring. Such on-going differences have, however, done little to restrict the marketisation and disintermediation of the contemporary world financial order.

Several factors have shaped the manner in which the US-initiated deregulatory dynamic has worked itself through the contemporary financial order. The zeal with which the British state has sought to follow the American lead in liberalisation and deregulation, largely in the wake of the election of the Conservative government of Margaret Thatcher in 1979, has had considerable ramifications for the making of the contemporary financial order. Particularly as a consequence of its standing as the principal OFC but also with the big bang, London has accentuated the competitive deregulatory pressures emanating from the US. Given the capacity of foreign financial market institutions to avoid regulatory restrictions at 'home' and undertake credit practices in London and other OFCs, London has been 'the most important arena through which the American financial services revolution has been exported' (Moran 1991: 121).

> national authorities were forced to scrap long-established interest rate ceilings, lending limits, portfolio restrictions, reserve and liquidity requirements, and other regulatory paraphernalia. These instruments acted on the supply side of financial markets by limiting the ability of private sector players to seek capital gains, hedge risk, or undertake arbitrage. They could all be circumvented by the new freedom to pursue offshore transactions. All had to be abandoned.
>
> (Eatwell and Taylor 2000: 37–8)

While London has, in effect, acted as a kaleidoscope for deregulatory competitive pressures, the result has not been a simple 'race to the bottom' in terms of minimising financial regulations. Deregulatory pressures have been cross-cut by similar competitive demands for new market-orientated regulations to mirror US arrangements, largely as a consequences of asymmetries in information and technological networks that favour New York. A 'diffusion' (Moran 1991: 121) of US regulatory practices, particularly in terms of the legal standing of supervisory institutions based upon the SEC as a model for change in capital and equity market practices, has also marked regulatory policy initiatives.

National liberalisation and deregulation policies have been further shaped by a range of collective initiatives, such that the competitive deregulatory dynamic has been negotiated internationally. It is in this sense that Moran (1991: 133) talks of 'coalitions' that are 'cross-national in character' as driving liberalisation and deregulation, 'uniting fragments of the state, fragments of particular industries and even fragments of particular firms in a world-wide network'. Similarly, Underhill (1997a: 3–4) characterises change as driven by a 'financial policy community' that includes a range of particularistic interests that seek, through more or less institutionalised negotiations, to either further or limit change. From their position of material strength and buttressed by favourable social and political power relations, the social forces of New York and London have been the vanguard of change. The General Agreement on Trade in Services (GATS) has ensured that financial regulation has and continues to feature in the considerations of the World Trade Organisation (WTO) (Underhill 1993; Key 1999). Signatories to GATS are committed to negotiating future rounds of deregulation, while the WTO's strong dispute settlement mechanism ensures that a withdrawal from previous commitments cannot be made without encountering compensation claims. Meanwhile, NAFTA contains certain chapters that serve to extend pre-existing bilateral agreements on financial regulation and capital movements between the US and Canada to Mexico (Maxfield 1997a: 116–18; Porter 1997). The 2001 Summit of the Americas holds out the prospect of similar arrangements being extended across Latin America more broadly in the future.

Furthermore, since the late 1980s financial liberalisation and deregulatory issues have been negotiated in great depth and detail under the auspices of the EU Single Market Programme (Story and Walter 1997; Tsoukalis 1997: 92–102; Underhill 1997c). This has led to a range of binding agreements including: the Capital Movements Directive that outlaws capital controls; the Second Banking Directive that enshrines the universal banking model; the Investment Services Directive that guarantees the cross-border operations of investment banks; and the Capital Adequacy Directive that establishes a formula to calculate capital adequacy requirements for securities practices. While all negotiations have not yielded agreements in line with the expressed preferences of British state officials and London's social forces, the effect of London as a contiguous kaleidoscope for deregulatory competitive pressures has ensured that

> the EU markets will be quite unlike the traditional restricted financial markets of the European continent in the postwar period. The focus and spiritual home of the emerging EU market is London. The central position of the City markets and the progress of EU legislation combined with domestic reform programmes in the key countries of France and Germany have yielded a highly 'marketised' (if as yet uneven) financial order in Europe.
>
> (Underhill 1997c: 102)[10]

In short, the making of the European financial area has and continues to be consistent with the making of the contemporary world financial order.

While underdeveloped state-societies have been subject broadly to the competitive deregulatory dynamic and the lure of gaining access to the credit allocated through world credit practices (Krugman 1995), liberalisation and deregulation have also been associated with the so-called 'structural adjustment' programmes and conditional lending of the IMF and World Bank. In these instances, the disciplinary effect of the competitive deregulatory dynamic is not negotiated but becomes largely a formal obligation. Capital controls and restrictive financial regulations had been central to underdeveloped state-societies that during the immediate post-war decades practised policies of economic nationalism, state socialism and self-reliance. In the contemporary financial order, World Bank lending conditions and development advice have included financial liberalisation and deregulation alongside the stabilisation of exchange rates, fiscal austerity, privatisation, and trade liberalisation (Biersteker 1992: 108–10). Meanwhile, the remit of the IMF has gradually broadened and deepened from its previous responsibilities during the era of Bretton Woods (Pauly 1997). As the IMF emerged from the sovereign debt crisis of the early 1980s as the principal institutional forum for crisis management and was subsequently given the role of overseeing the restructuring of the former Soviet bloc, its policy prescriptions have come to include financial liberalisation and deregulation. This has been starkly illustrated in the wake of the Asian financial crisis of 1997–8, as so-called 'financial sector reform' under the guidance of the IMF has gripped the effected state-societies.

Wider world order

The wider world order either reinforced or constrained the pivotal position of the social forces of the dominant WFC in the making of the Dutch, British, and American financial orders. While changes in the nature and distribution of financial power in the current era have been significant, then, they have not displaced the potential of the wider world order to shape the making of the contemporary financial order. Several features of the wider world order have effectively served to magnify the power of the social forces of New York and, to a lesser extent, London in the making of the contemporary financial order. Taken together, the neo-liberal politics of economic slowdown, intensified inter-state rivalry for market shares in the world economy, and continued US predominance in terms of both security and economic consumption, have all contributed directly and indirectly to the pivotal position of New York and London and, therefore, to framing the distinct organisation of contemporary credit practices.

The neo-liberal politics of slowdown

The disruptions to the world economy that followed the oil crisis of 1973 manifested themselves in what Vogel (1996: 39–41) terms 'the politics of economic slowdown'. The governments of the major states were confronted by the end of the so-called 'long boom' of the 1950s and 1960s and a 'fiscal crisis' (O'Connor 1973) of the state that resulted from a combination of economic 'stagflation' (i.e. concurrent stagnation and inflation) and growing demand for public expenditure. These developments struck at the heart of the politics of productivity and the configuration of social and political power relations that constituted the welfare-nationalist form of state-society (Cox 1987: 270–9; Maier 1987: 187–224). Under the influence of the monetarist doctrine of Milton Friedman and to a greater or lesser extent in different state-societies, stagflation and fiscal crisis became manifested in a turn away from Keynesian macroeconomic policy-making and a questioning of state intervention in the economy (Clarke 1987; van der Pijl 1989).

The monetarist experiment of the late 1970s and early 1980s proved to be the first movement of a newly predominant neo-liberal political economy. Neo-liberalism blamed organised labour and governments for the cycle of excessive wage demands and spending that 'crowded out' private investment. Both the labour market and government were, it was argued, in need of the commodifying discipline provided by the market mechanism. Such ideas that find popular expression in the mantras of competition, efficiency and flexibility and rely, at base, on a belief that marketised social relations are a natural product of people's inherent economic rationality, continue to frame the economic strategies of the major state governments today. As a broad political and ideological strategy, the turn to neo-liberalism in the major states has, of course, rested on 'a succession of negotiated settlements . . . concessions to the rigidities and dynamics of structures, as well as the political possibilities of the moment' (Drainville 1994: 116). The neo-liberal politics of slowdown thus has a different face in each state-society, shaped by different national political and social relations (Overbeek and van der Pijl 1993). In some instances neo-liberalism has amounted to the dominant policy discourse, while in others, most notably Britain and the US following the victories of the social forces associated with Margaret Thatcher and Ronald Reagan, it has been associated with a transformation of the state-societal form. Here the politics of slowdown was forged around a coalition of forces that drew on both neo-liberal political economy and the moral traditionalism, xenophobia and family values of neo-conservatism.

The broadly neo-liberal course taken by the politics of economic slowdown has had several important ramifications for the making of the contemporary financial order. First and most obviously, neo-liberal political economy has been at the heart of the emergence of the US and British hyperliberal state-societal forms that, as already noted, have done much to underpin the position of the social forces of New York and London in the making of the contemporary order.

Second and more generally, neo-liberal policies designed to enable capital to confront the economic slowdown have also been significant in enabling the generalised financialisation of world credit practices. The world economic slowdown was such that by the close of the 1970s world manufacturing had reached a 'profound impasse' (Brenner 2001: 23). With the profits available in the 'real economy' increasingly undercut by intensified competition and surplus capacity across the major corporations of a more multi-polar world economy, a huge shift into financial activity ensued (Gordon 1988; Boyer 2000; Brenner 2001: 24–5; cf. Cutler and Waine 2001: 100–1).[11] Under neo-liberal politics and made possible by policies of liberalisation and deregulation that strengthened the economic significance of financiers in general and the social forces of the principal WFCs in particular, money, like labour and land, is subjected to the pressures of commodification (cf. Polanyi 1944). Such commodification enables the speculative accumulation of capital through world credit practices that lies at the heart of financialisation.

Third, world credit practices have occupied a close strategic relationship to contemporary state restructuring. Confronted by fiscal crisis and rejecting increases in taxation to fund expenditure, governments initially became far more reliant than during the American financial order upon recourse to sovereign credit practices to meet budget deficits. As a consequence, OECD sovereign borrowing alone has increased nearly seven-fold since the early 1970s, reaching a peak in 1995 (Shutt 1998: 112; Granville 1999: 716–17). States in their various forms became 'a supplicant in the financial markets' (Picciotto and Haines 1999: 356). Neo-liberal arguments in favour of financial liberalisation and deregulation were effectively supplemented by political expediency and gained credence throughout the governments of the western world. For the Japanese state in particular, demand for sovereign credit actually set in motion the deregulation of national financial arrangements (Eken 1984/1994: 304–8; Kalder 1997).

Privatisation programmes and policy initiatives to stimulate private pension provision have subsequently ensured a close relationship between deregulated disintermediated financial market practices and efforts to re-articulate the socio-economic role of the state (Minns 1996a; Martin 1999b). The alignment of disintermediated world credit practices, efforts to shift the burden of pension provision away from the state, and the neo-liberal politics of slowdown more broadly is especially clear. It is not simply that public 'pay as you go' pension provision is discouraged while occupational pensions are encouraged, but that the neo-liberal variant as practised in the Anglo-Saxon political economies is tending to be promoted as 'best practice'.[12] For instance, the European Commission's Internal Market Directorate recently made the following revealing statement:

> By operating freely in capital markets, pension funds can optimise their investment policy and help accelerate EU capital market integration. Increases in pension fund investment returns will benefit employers (decrease in pension contributions) or employees (increase in pension benefits). This can be achieved without compromising pension security. In the context of the ageing population, this can help Member States preserve the long-term financial stability of existing pension systems and provide risk capital to promote jobs and growth.[13]

With the cumulative investment assets of pension funds estimated to be in the region of $12,000 billion at the turn of the millennium (OECD 1994), families and individuals from the upper echelons of Anglo-American societies today effectively own a large share of the instruments created by world capital and equity practices (Minns 1996b).

Fourth and related, neo-liberal policies that have responded to the economic slowdown by broadly providing greater freedom for capital have fed the further development of the offshore space of contemporary world credit practices. Offshore space at once frees MNCs and the major banks to restructure along the lines suggested by neo-liberalism while at the same time meaning that onshore socio-economic practices can continue to be taxed. The latter is essential in enabling state institutions in the major state-societies to continue to undertake social expenditures. As Palan (1999: 19–20) summarises:

> 'Offshore' can be thought of . . . as an ingenious device, reconciling two incompatible trends. Instead of confronting the state directly, the more mobile economic sectors are provided with a separate regulatory space where the flow of economic activities can develop more or less without government interference. And since the more mobile elements are increasingly bracketed out of the state, the state can carry on discharging its traditional roles as if nothing had happened.

Furthermore, during the early 1970s in particular, offshore sovereign credit practices also acted as a 'good servant' (Strange 1976: 176) in providing much of the credit that facilitated state restructuring. In sum, the neo-liberal politics of economic slowdown constitute conditions in the wider world order that have and continue to encourage the liberalisation and deregulation of world credit practices and, *de facto*, the pivotal position of the state and societal forces of New York and London in the making of the contemporary financial order.

Inter-state rivalry for market shares

The contemporary emergence of a more multi-polar, information-intensive world economy marked by slower growth relative to the long boom has contributed to a shift in the nature of inter-state rivalry in the wider world order (Cox 1987: 304). Inter-state rivalry that previously focused on the expansion of territory or gaining access to raw materials has been largely displaced by 'the imperative necessity of acquiring a more or less secure share in one or another sector of the world market' (Strange 1990: 266). This 'de-territorialisation' of inter-state rivalry has been closely associated with the set of tendencies that Cox (1987: 253–65; cf. Panitch 1994) terms the 'internationalisation of the state', that is, the adjustment of state policies and institutions to the perceived competitive imperatives of the changed world economy. Similarly, Cerny (1990) identifies a shift from welfare to 'competition state' preferences in government policies. The simple correlation that tends to be maintained by orthodox IPE scholars (e.g. Gilpin 1987: 88) for all but hegemonic states between economic nationalism and preferences for protectionist-mercantilism has begun to unravel. Policies of economic nationalism are shifting as 'competitive advantage' (Porter 1990) comes to embrace not only the promotion of 'national' businesses as under strategic trade theory, but also the marketing of the national economy as a space from which to conduct world economic practices.

The shifting nature of inter-state rivalry has had particular implications for the making of the contemporary financial order. Given the inherent mobility and fungibility of accumulated capital, the expanded importance of finance under information-intensive production, and the potential balance-of-payments problems generated by capital flight, inter-state rivalry for market shares is especially acute in world finance. International competitive pressures for the liberalisation and deregulation of finance are intensified. Inter-state financial rivalry increasingly hinges not only on raising the market shares enjoyed by 'home' market networks, but on the promotion of national financial centres as spaces to undertake world credit practices. Important here is the extent to which local information networks can be said to be necessary for world credit practices (Thrift 1994; Crawford 2001), and the creation of an enticing regulatory environment (Martin 1994). The relatively recent re-articulation of German financial policy in order to elevate the standing of Frankfurt as a European financial centre provides a remarkably revealing instance of this change (cf. Story 1997). World credit practices that support German borrowers or invest capital in the German economy are likely to be constrained by the availability of information, information that is often only present in Frankfurt-centred networks. This underlying attraction of Frankfurt as a space for credit practices has tended to be undercut by a regulatory environment that has been regarded by both German and foreign financiers as burdensome. As a result, the various policy initiatives of 'Finanzplatz Deutschland' have, in large part, turned on the careful and partial deregulation of German financial arrangements, promoting Frankfurt as a financial centre while at the same time protecting the tradition of close relationships between German banks and industry. Elsewhere, the deregulatory thrust has been pursued to its zenith, as offshore space has been fostered and opened up by 'competition in regulatory laxity' (Palan 1999: 32). For instance, in the face of competition from London and other regional OFCs, efforts to promote New York and Tokyo as spaces for banking practices in the early- to mid-1980s were dependent on the creation of IBFs and the Tokyo Offshore Market (TOM) respectively. In short, inter-state rivalry for market shares in the wider world order compounds and reinforces the US-initiated competitive deregulatory dynamic at work in the contemporary financial order.

Inter-state rivalry for market shares has not only or simply been played out through unilateral policy change, but has also been a significant factor in shaping regionalist initiatives. In a similar vein to the contemporary demise of protectionist-mercantilism at the national scale, the regionalism undertaken through the EU, NAFTA and broadly comparable forums in Asia has not created protected economic blocs but has remained 'open' to the wider world economy (Payne and Gamble 1996). The creation of intra-regional regulatory spaces for economic practices has tended to be seen, particularly by proponents of the European Union's Single Market Programme, as leading to increased economies of scale and thereby enhancing the competitiveness of Europe's corporations. Given that access to relatively cheap and reliable credit is an important determinant in the creation of corporate competitiveness, finance has occupied a key strategic position within the Single Market legislation (Tsoukalis 1997: 93). In our terms, inter-state competition for market shares underlines the regional negotiation of the competitive deregulatory dynamic in world finance.

Furthermore, the creation of a single currency also became increasingly linked with the competitiveness of Europe during the 1990s, offering up the prospect (according to neo-liberal political economy) of ending exchange rate risks, reducing transaction costs and increasing price transparency in intra-European trade and investment (Healey 2000: 89–93; cf. McNamara 1998). Cast in these terms and as taking effect through the creation of the European single currency in 1999, inter-state rivalry for market shares does not only impact on the making of the contemporary financial order in terms of reinforcing the competitive deregulatory dynamic. Rather, regional rivalry in the monetary sphere may potentially impact on the pattern of material power relations over the medium- to long-term. For instance, the advent of the euro and the European Central Bank (ECB) based in Frankfurt have already served to strengthen the competitive position of Frankfurt *vis-à-vis* London as a centre for regionally orientated banking practices.

Security and consumption

Dutch and British relative economic decline during their respective financial orders led to their displacement from previously pivotal positions in inter-state relations. Such displacement was an important dynamic in the unravelling of the Dutch and British orders and a prerequisite for ascending state and societal forces to contest the organisation of world finance. By contrast and in spite of relative economic decline, the continued predominance of the United States in the security and economic structures of the wider world order has tended to act as a buttress to the position of the social forces of New York and London in the making of the contemporary financial order. In particular and unlike the manner in which the other identified features of the wider world order have directly reinforced the making of the contemporary financial order, US influence in world security and economic matters has constrained the capacity of other state and societal forces to make an alternative financial order.

Throughout the Cold War context of the 1970s and 1980s, the dependence of western Europe and Japan on US military protection worked against the making of an alternative to the contemporary marketised financial order. Collective, state-based alternatives were forestalled (Walter 1993: 237–40). In particular, attempts by various French governments to take the lead on such collective initiatives were undercut by an inability to persuade German and other western European governments that there was a viable security substitute to the US-led NATO alliance. Similarly, reliance on the US security umbrella largely ruled out Japanese efforts to bring the growing power and preferences of Tokyo to bear in the making of the financial order. Indeed, as Cold War tensions intensified, the massive investment of Japanese capital in US T-bonds from the early- to mid-1980s reflected, albeit somewhat indirectly, this dependence.

In the wake of the end of the Cold War, the continued weight of the US economy in the world economy, especially in terms of consumption, has continued to constrain the making of the contemporary financial order. Today's world economy is in many respects far less US-centric than during the 1940s, 1950s and 1960s, marked instead by multi-polarity and the regionalised transnationalisation of production networks across North America, Europe and Asia. However, the US economy remains disproportionately important as a destination for the world's exports. Arguably, since the latter half of the 1990s, the significance of US consumption to the world economy has increased further, as a US consumer boom fuelled by rising household borrowing and runaway share prices has coincided with slow or negative growth in Europe and Asia. US consumption tends to mitigate against the temptation to move towards the political creation of European and Asian regional economic blocs that, presumably, could enable alternatives to the neo-liberal politics of slowdown (Hettne 1997). Regionalist initiatives in Europe and Asia in terms of world finance have, then, tended to remain largely consistent with the making of the contemporary financial order.

This was starkly illustrated during the Asian financial crisis of 1997–8. The Japanese government's preferred response to the crisis was regionalist in nature, seeking to take the lead in the establishment of an Asian Monetary Fund (AMF) to organise the bail out of heavily indebted market institutions. An AMF would have performed a similar crisis-management role to that eventually taken up by the IMF but, importantly, an AMF would have weakened the influence of US state and societal forces over the making of world finance in the region. The crisis was a critical juncture in this respect, as the planned AMF seemed far less likely to impose IMF-style conditions of liberalisation and deregulation that are essential for the marketisation and disintermediation of world credit practices. It was not unexpected that the US Clinton administration sought to kill off the plan (Higgott 1998; Gill 1999; Helleiner 2000: 234–6). 'The defeat of the Asian Monetary Fund proposal showed once again the enormous subordination of Japan to U.S. power' (Gill 1999: 7). In our terms, it should be no surprise that subsequent economic recovery in the region has in large part been reliant upon the US Federal Reserve Board's management of interest rates, buoying US consumer demand and its thirst for imports. In a similar manner to the centrality of the US to western security relations during the Cold War, then, the current US position as what might be termed 'spender of last resort' in the world economy constrains the capacity of other state and societal forces to make alternatives to the contemporary financial order.

Conclusions

As with our inquiry into previous world financial orders, we have sought to account for the structural transformation of contemporary world credit practices by developing an understanding of the power relations that have and continue to frame their possible organisation. Our point of departure was the existing work by IPE scholars that, in contrast with the de-politicised explanation of change offered by the neo-liberal orthodoxy, serves to restore questions of power. At the same time and by virtue of a conceptualisation of world finance as a succession of hierarchical social orders, we sought to move beyond the focus on the rise and fall of state power that tends to predominate in IPE scholarship. The result has been to highlight several important aspects of structural discontinuity that characterise the making of the contemporary financial order.

The making of the contemporary financial order has diverged from previous orders in the sense that it has been driven, in the first instance, by formerly predominant state and societal forces rather than by those associated with a newly emergent WFC. For many new IPE scholars in particular, this discontinuity has been interpreted as reflecting the continuation of US structural power. Under such a reading, the contemporary financial order would become the remaking of the American financial order. This view would, however, neglect to recognise the important, conjuncturally distinct change in the structure of power in world finance. The advent of offshore serves to both fragment the national economy as a regulatory construct and alter the nature of deposit-compelling power, with the effect that the centralisation–decentralisation–(re)centralisation dynamic that has characterised modern world finance becomes partially distorted. Alongside the multi-polarity and erosion of the foundational position of national economies in today's world economy, offshore capital is the key to the uneven decentralisation of contemporary credit practices.

Furthermore, given that deposit-compelling power has been important in conferring material power on the social forces associated with WFCs in previous orders, the advent of offshore has also ensured that power relations in world finance, while still characterised by stark asymmetries, are now less hierarchical and also do not simply follow a pattern of centralisation–decentralisation–(re)centralisation. As the continued importance of New York and the ascent of Tokyo serve to illustrate, the rise of national financial centres to world status and the implications that this has for material power relations remains important. Yet, as the continued standing of London also shows, the social forces of a WFC that is largely reliant on its position as an offshore space also have and continue to have a notable influence on the making of the contemporary financial order. Rather than a straightforward continuation of US power, then, the material power relations that have framed the making of the contemporary financial order favour the social forces of New York and London. In this sense, the contemporary order is more an 'emerging Anglo-American financial order' (Crawford 2001: 47) than the remaking of a continuing American financial order.

As with previous world financial orders, social and political power relations have also been an important factor in the structure of power that has framed the possible organisation of world credit practices. Despite their growing material power, the potential capacity of Tokyo's social forces to influence the making of the contemporary financial order has been undermined by the persistence of a Japanese state-societal form that continues to repress their perceived interests. Meanwhile, the hyperliberal tendencies of American and British state-societies have and continue to further the perceived interests of New York and London respectively. Given the manner in which the marketisation and disintermediation of world credit practices has been crucially carried forward by policies of liberalisation and deregulation, social and political power relations have been of particular importance to the making of the contemporary financial order. US policies of liberalisation and deregulation set in train a competitive dynamic, while the enthusiasm with which British governments have followed the American lead has positioned London as a kaleidoscope for competitive pressures. The state and social forces of New York and London have been to the fore in the transnational coalitions that have both negotiated the competitive deregulation dynamic across a range of international and regional forums, and sought to impose the dynamic on underdeveloped state-societies under the auspices of IMF conditionality and World Bank structural adjustment.

A conceptualisation of contemporary world finance as a social order has also led to an understanding of the framing of the organisation of credit practices that is firmly grounded in an analysis of the way that conditions in the wider world order impinge on the making of the financial order. Three features of the wider world order have been especially significant, all contributing directly and indirectly to the pivotal position of New York and London and, therefore, to framing the distinct organisation of contemporary credit practices. The neo-liberal politics of slow-down have served to firmly intertwine strategies for economic restructuring and the re-articulation of the economic role of the state with furthering the interests of Anglo-American world finance. Meanwhile, the changing nature of inter-state economic competition has intensified pressures for financial liberalisation and deregulation as they have been felt both nationally and collectively at a regional scale. Taken together, neo-liberal politics and the de-territorialisation of inter-state rivalry have reinforced and magnified the capacity of the social forces of New York and London to frame the contemporary organisation of credit practices. At the same time, continued US predominance in security and consumption has constrained the capacity of other state and societal forces to make alternatives to the contemporary financial order.

In short, the key to understanding the making of the contemporary financial order does not lie in a simple focus on the relative decline or otherwise of the US state, but rather on changes in the very nature of financial power and developments in the wider world order.

Notes

1 I am indebted to a London-based representative of an American-owned investment bank for highlighting the somewhat circularly reinforcing nature of the relationship between London's deposit-compelling power and its standing as a key social space for capital and equity market trading practices, confidential interview, London, 2 June 1998.

2 This view is reinforced by a range of surveys that, alongside the significance of London's relatively benign regulatory environment, identified communications linkages as most important in framing the decision to locate world credit practices in London (HMSO 1991; CRP 1995).

3 Confidential interview with a London-based representative of an American-owned investment bank, London, 2 June 1998.

4 On this point I am indebted to the insights provided by representatives of the research department of a major German universal bank, confidential interviews, Frankfurt, 1 September 1997.

5 Japanese current account surpluses which grew dramatically in the latter half of the 1980s are themselves largely the outcome of merchandise trade surpluses. While generated in part by Japanese competitiveness in the production of steel, automobiles and other consumer goods and the rise of the Asian region in a more multi-polar world economy (Kindleberger 1996: 195–200), pivotal to the realisation of Japanese merchandise trade surpluses on such a huge scale has and continues to be the stagnation of merchandise imports (Nakao 1995: 9–28). This explains how the Japanese economy has been able to generate such comparatively huge current account surpluses while accounting for a smaller share of world exports than the other major national economies.

6 Figures from *Financial Times*, Survey, 'Japan's Financial Revolution', 26 March 1998.

7 'The hyperliberal tendency actively facilitates a restructuring, not only of the labor force, but also of the social relations of production. It renounces tripartite corporatism. It also weakens bipartism by its attack on unions in the state sector and its support and encouragement to employers to resist union demands in the oligopolistic sector. Indirectly, the state encourages the consolidation of enterprise corporatist relations for the scientific-technical-managerial workers in the oligopolistic sector, a practice for which the state itself provides a model in its treatment of its own permanent cadres.

Finally, state policies are geared to an expansion of employment in short-term, low-skill, high-turnover jobs that contribute to further labor-market segmentation' (Cox 1991/1996: 199–200).

8 Others have asserted the presence of this dynamic in world finance. See, for example Hawley (1987: 142–3) and Strange (1988: 108). According to Strange (1998a: 169), it was originally recognised in the 1840s by the German political economist Friedrich List.

9 The 'big bang' eliminated fixed commissions on equity market practices, opened the LSE to foreign membership, and introduced the computerised SEAQ trading system (Vogel 1996: 100–8).

10 For highlighting this point, I am also grateful to a representative of the Bundesbank, confidential interview, Frankfurt, 3 September 1997.

11 For instance, recent estimates suggest that there is a 30 per cent over-capacity in the world's car production facilities alone (*The Economist*, 'Bavarians at the Gates', 13 February 1999, p. 22).

12 The extent to which so-called 'pensions reform' has come to be a common policy objective of governments across the developed world states is illustrated by their efforts to learn from each other's implementation experiences. For instance, the OECD recently formed its 'Working Party on Private Pensions', and on 11 October 2000 the European Commission made a proposal for a Directive on occupational pensions to form part and parcel of the future development of the internal European market (COM 1999 134).

13 <http://europa.eu.int/comm/internalmarket/en/finances/pensions/index.htm> October 2000.

7 Stability, crises and governance in the contemporary world financial order

By contrast with prior world financial orders, the making of the contemporary order has and continues to be highly distinctive. Rather than the ascendant social forces associated with a newly emergent WFC framing change, a reconfiguration of those state and societal forces that had been pivotal in the previous American order has been at the heart of the making of the contemporary order. Grounded in asymmetrical patterns of material, social and political power relations and enabled by conditions in the wider world order, the social forces of New York and London, and not those of recently emergent Tokyo, have been at the forefront in framing the possible organisation of contemporary world credit practices. Power relations are, however, less hierarchical than in previous financial orders, with change in the very nature of material power relations contributing to the asymmetrical decentralisation of credit practices across the triad of WFCs. Crucial to carrying forward the marketisation, disintermediation and changing institutionalisation of credit practices has been a US-initiated competitive liberalisation and deregulation policy dynamic, reinforced by the neo-liberal politics of slowdown and the de-territorialisation of inter-state rivalry in the wider world order. As with our inquiry into previous world financial orders, an Historical IPE approach encourages us to ask whether this current financial order is characterised by relative stability and, if so, to identify those organisational principles and formal governance institutions that serve to reproduce the order.

Our conceptualisation of world finance as a succession of hierarchical social orders has realised some significant insights into stability and governance across modern world finance. Relative stability and the reproduction of financial orders is not simply a matter of inertia. Rather, consideration needs to be given to structures of financial governance as the ideas and institutions that forge periods of relative stability and enable the legitimate and authoritative management of credit practices, thereby contributing to the reproduction of financial orders. It has been shown that periods in previous world financial orders characterised by relative stability, that is, by broad-based acceptance of power relations and the organisation of credit practices as legitimate, have coincided with the centralisation of the order in a single WFC. In the somewhat exceptional New York-centred American order, relative stability hinged upon the principles of embedded liberalism that subordinated finance to money and trade and ensured a secondary position for New

York in the largely state-based structure of governance. Meanwhile, relative stability was forged around the cosmopolitan and liberal shared meanings framing credit practices in Amsterdam and London during the Dutch and British orders respectively, while the state, market and civil institutions centralised in these WFCs served to govern their respective orders. The institutionalised administration and management of credit practices was especially important in preventing fluctuations in practices generated by financial crises from leading to the structural disruption of each order.

Given the decentralisation of the contemporary financial order between the triad of New York, London and Tokyo and the resulting absence of a single complex of governance, comparative historical inquiry raises several questions with regard to the current era. First, if the contemporary decentralised order is characterised by relative stability, how has stability been forged and upon what organisational principles is it based? Second, how are we to account for the high incidence of financial crises endemic to the contemporary financial order? Third, in what ways has the decentralised order been marked by change in the formal institutions of governance and to what extent has this change been adequate for the reproduction of the current order? We address each question in turn.

Relative stability and neo-liberal principles of governance

The contemporary world financial order is characterised by emerging relative stability. Acceptance of the current organisation of credit practices as legitimate has been gradually forged around neo-liberal organisational principles of governance.[1] Neo-liberal political economy offers a set of organisational principles or discourse of governance that is contested throughout the wider world order in the current era (Murphy 1994; Langley 2001). Such organisational principles are significant in carrying forward the restructuring that has marked the neo-liberal politics of slowdown. Neo-liberal organisational principles of governance are rooted in foundational beliefs in the role of the market mechanism and market mode of behaviour as the fair and rational arbiter in society. Particularly as a consequence of the claims to universalism made by neo-liberalism, market institutions are deemed 'apolitical' and become 'naturally' the most appropriate institutional loci for governance. Institutionalised practices take on a legitimate form once they are framed by market signals and subject to market-reinforcing self-regulation. Within state institutions, practices become organised less according to bureaucratic professionalism and more according to a new public managerialism such that social and political issues become technical and procedural matters, that is, matters to be managed. Furthermore and by virtue of the empiricist and positivist bases of neo-liberal political economy, neo-liberal organisational principles of governance also legitimate the governance role of particular experts that are seen as holding, producing and verifying relevant forms of knowledge. When combined with the predilection for self-regulation, certain experts, most notably auditors and accountants (cf. Power 1997), are deemed to be the most appropriate supervisory institutions.

Research in IPE serves to reveal various and wide-ranging ways in which neo-liberal principles have come to permeate contemporary world financial governance. First, neo-liberal principles of financial governance sit at the heart of the so-called 'Washington consensus' that since the 1980s has prevailed as the explanation of economic development (cf. Krugman 1995; Wade and Veneroso 1998; Williams 1999). The 'Washington consensus' refers

> not only to the American government, but to all those institutions and networks of opinion leaders centred in the world's de facto capital – the International Monetary Fund, World Bank, think tanks, politically sophisticated investment bankers, and worldly finance ministers, all of those who meet each other in Washington and collectively define the conventional wisdom of the moment.
>
> (Krugman 1995: 28–9)

Carried forward in particular through the World Bank's structural adjustment programmes and IMF conditionality, the Washington consensus has combined financial liberalisation and deregulation that enables governance by the market mechanism with a range of other market-reinforcing principles. These include fiscal discipline, tax reform, competitive exchange rates, trade liberalisation, privatisation and, not least, private property rights.[2] Second and on a similar note, Helleiner (1994: 19) highlights the monthly meetings of central bankers at the BIS as forming an 'epistemic community'. Membership of this community leads to a convergence of normative frameworks around neo-liberalism, such that central bankers have come to share 'a similar knowledge base, common causal and principled beliefs' (Helleiner 1994: 19). Kapstein (1994) and Pauly (1994b) also draw attention more broadly to the cognitive and normative contribution of international organisations in shaping the governance of the contemporary financial order.

Third and in a different vein, for Sinclair (1994a, 1994b) the influence of neo-liberalism is clear in the authoritative assessments of risk, 'based on their possession of specialized forms of knowledge from which they derive control' (Sinclair 1994b: 447), undertaken by Standard & Poors and Moodys as the principal credit rating agencies. Not dissimilarly, Picciotto and Haines (1999: 360–1) stress the extent to which neo-liberal organisational principles have been carried forward in world finance through 'the professional practices of various kinds of specialists: economists, accountants, scientists and lawyers'. To this list of professionals we could add the business advice dispensed by the major consultancy firms such as Andersen and McKinsey (cf. van der Pijl 1998: 160–2). Meanwhile, Harmes (1998) draws attention to the role of the collective investment decisions of Anglo-American institutional investors in encouraging the acceptance of neo-liberal social relations of production. While reasoned and rational financial criteria have always been important in modern world finance, in the current (neo-liberal) era other forms of evaluation become de-legitimated to an unprecedented extent. The effect is that the governance of finance becomes a technical and specialist mathematical exercise, largely divorced from public debate (cf. de Goede 2001).

This existing IPE research serves to challenge the de-politicised and naturalised representation of a convergence in world financial governance that is promoted by the neo-liberal discourse. It also serves to remind us that a structure of governance does not develop in a functional manner, but remains contested and constructed by the principal state and societal forces. Not surprisingly given the asymmetrical pattern of power relations in the contemporary financial order and conditions in the wider world order, the social forces of New York and London have been at the forefront in forging acceptance of the organisation of credit practices as legitimate. Directly and indirectly underpinning the various and wide-ranging mechanisms highlighted by existing research in IPE, neo-liberal organisational principles have come to permeate the contemporary financial order as a consequence of the diffusion of the shared meanings informing New York-centred and, to a lesser extent, London-centred credit practices. While the shared norms and meanings surrounding contemporary credit practices in New York and London draw on long-standing modern assumptions of rationality and reason, they are characterised by the 'market fundamentalism' (Soros 1998) of neo-liberalism.[3] In broad terms, the epistemic authority of New York is clearly felt in its contiguous influence as part of the Washington consensus (Wade and Veneroso 1998). Further, the US Federal Reserve and Bank of England have been at the heart of neo-liberal cooperation in central banking networks (Baker 1999). Meanwhile, the epistemic authority of New York and London is carried through the world-wide reach of the networks of investment banks, credit rating agencies and institutional investors centred in these WFCs. For instance, for Moodys and Standard & Poors, 'New York remains the analytical core, where rating expertise is defined and reinforced' (Sinclair 1994b: 453). The epistemic authority of New York has also echoed across the deregulation of contemporary credit practices, a key component of the institutionalisation of neo-liberal organisational principles of governance. As Moran (1991: 121) asserts:

> The resemblance to American practices emphasises a notable feature of recent regulatory change. It is tempting to represent what has been happening as a world-wide convergence. The image of convergence suggests, however, that all the financial centres in question are moving, at a significant pace, to a common point. This is not so. 'Diffusion' rather than 'convergence' best catches the nature of regulatory change: there is occurring an export of regulatory innovation from the United States to other countries.

As with the British and Dutch financial orders, then, the epistemic authority of the social forces of the WFCs of the day is crucial to the emerging relative stability. The decentralisation of the contemporary order has not proved necessarily to be a structural impediment to the establishment of relative stability. The spatiality of credit practices and the structure of power in the contemporary financial order may be decentralised and multi-polar, but the discourse that legitimates power relations and the organisation of world credit practices in which power is manifest is largely and increasingly univocal.

In a similar manner to the Dutch and British financial orders, the key to the diffusion of neo-liberal principles from New York and London throughout the contemporary order would seem to be competitive emulation. Given the perceived competitive success of New York-centred and London-centred market institutions, neo-liberal organisational principles have gradually come to be recognised throughout the contemporary financial order as 'best practice' in an ideal-typical sense. This was not clear for much of the 1980s, as the dramatic growth in the market share of Japanese market institutions fuelled the view that they constituted a 'hegemonic threat' (Nakao 1995: 103–23) to Anglo-American market networks. Such views were buttressed by debates in the wider world order that suggested the possible superiority of the Japanese 'model' of developmental state-capitalism (cf. Thurow 1992; Albert 1993). However, the collapse of the Japanese bubble economy in 1989, the subsequent malaise of Japanese finance and questioning of the Japanese model have served to gradually extinguish debate in world financial circles. This mood swing reached its zenith in the course of the Asian financial crisis, as any lingering doubts as to the apparent competitive superiority of Anglo-American credit practices were largely washed away.[4] The seeming long-standing weaknesses of Japanese and Asian credit practices were exposed by the crisis, particularly the predilection for expanding corporate credit creation without concurrent increases in industrial productivity taking place (Krugman 1994). Simultaneously and as US triumphalist commentaries of the time were keen to point out (e.g. Zuckerman 1998), New York-centred credit practices and the American economy were enjoying the bull market boom of the so-called 'new economy'.[5] Gradually throughout the financial order and increasingly since the mid-1990s, the perceived competitive success of Anglo-American finance has lain at the roots of the neo-liberal legitimation of the contemporary organisation of credit practices.

Acceptance of contemporary power relations and the organisation of credit practices as legitimate remains, however, narrow in several respects. In terms of the coalition of social forces involved, the neo-liberal consensus is far less inclusive than that which underpinned and coalesced around the embedded liberal principles of the American financial order. Acceptance of the organisation of credit practices extends to members of the transnational financial community in which the social forces of New York and London predominate, and excludes organised labour in particular and the state and societal forces of the majority of underdeveloped state-societies more broadly. While the growth of occupational pensions and mutual funds in Anglo-Saxon political economies serves to link the material interests of privileged workers with the performance of institutional investors, the extent to which this also contributes to the legitimation of the organisation of world credit practices is limited. As the debate in the UK during the 1990s over endowment mortgages illustrates, linking everyday saving to world credit practices hinges on the performance of the latter rather than a broad-based acceptance of their legitimacy. Once it became clear that calculations made concerning the capacity of the performance of securities investments to meet mortgage repayments were overly optimistic, the link between everyday saving and world credit practices was seriously questioned.[6]

The principal transnational state and social forces of world finance are bound together by a 'bottom line' perceived shared interest in perpetuating the contemporary financial order and an awareness, fuelled by the experience of the Great Depression of the 1930s, of the potentially radical social and political consequences of collapse. Agreement as to the appropriate organisation of credit practices remains fragile and not based on organisational principles that are simply immutable. Relative stability forged around neo-liberal organisational principles has been subject to instances of destabilisation and reaffirmation. For example, in the wake of the Asian crisis of 1997–8, a group led by high profile economists including Jagdish Bhagwati and Paul Krugman and, most notably, by the (then) World Bank chief economist Joseph Stiglitz strongly questioned the neo-liberal preference for the universal removal of exchange and capital controls. Their objections received partial support from the financial ministries of Japan and, to a lesser extent, some continental European state-societies. By virtue of their 'state-capitalist' (Cox 1991/1996: 201–4) form and associated Roman Law national financial structures, these governments were normatively predisposed to give credence to at least limited versions of capital controls (cf. Pauly 1994a).[7] However, debates over capital controls among the narrow transnational community did not lead to a serious questioning of neo-liberal organisational principles and contestation as to the appropriate organisation of world credit practices in any fundamental sense. Instead, agreement was fashioned around the assumption that capital controls should be neither retained or put in place, but that so-called emerging markets should ensure the soundness of their national financial governance arrangements before dismantling capital controls (BIS 1999b; Eichengreen 1999). Key here was the juxtaposition of the 'bad' Malaysian response to the crisis of limiting currency convertibility and putting in place capital controls with the 'better' example of Chile (Germain 2000). Based on the Chilean experience in particular, a potentially heated debate was effectively reduced to the technical question of the correct 'sequencing' of financial restructuring. Acceptance of the organisation of credit practices remained among the transnational coalition of forces as neo-liberal organisational principles evolved to largely absorb the capital controls question.

Acceptance of the organisation of credit practices as legitimate is also narrow in terms of the extent to which neo-liberal organisational principles are institutionalised across market networks. This is especially the case as divergent norms and shared meanings informing credit practices persist across the triad, with Tokyo standing as the exemplar of 'a distinct regional financial culture' that 'challenges many neo-liberal economic principles' (Crawford 2001: 46, 48). For instance, Taggart Murphy's (1996: 43–59) investigation into 'the credit decision' reveals differing understandings of the assessment of risk between New York and Tokyo. Assessments of risk that in New York hinge upon market fundamentalist expectations of future profitability contrast with those in Tokyo which, in the first instance, focus upon collateral. New York-centred and Tokyo-centred financial market institutional networks also differ in terms of the understandings that frame their competitive strategies. New York-centred market networks tend to focus on their capacity to generate value-added services for their corporate customers and upon trading, deal-making and the creation of new financial instruments. In contrast, the competitive strategies of Tokyo-centred market institutional networks tend to focus upon increasing market share and reducing the cost of capital to their customers (McGahey *et al.* 1990: 142–3). At the root of the distinct understandings of risk and competitiveness in Tokyo is Japan's 'banking-industrial complex' (Carnoy *et al.* 1993: 82), built upon the persistence of cross-shareholding *keiretsu* relationships between financial market institutions and corporations (Taggart Murphy 1996: 28–42). The different understanding of credit practices in Tokyo was highlighted once again in the aftermath of the Asian financial crisis (Bello 1998: 434). Technical assistance provided by the IMF has subsequently been in large part an attempt to transform the shared meanings that frame credit practices in Japan by calling for greater transparency and disclosure by market institutions.

According to the neo-liberal discourse, credit practices must embody the rationality of the market mode of behaviour in order to enable the governance role of the market mechanism. On the one hand, then, the considerable extent to which Tokyo-centred practices diverge from New York and London's neo-liberal norms would seem to represent not narrowness of agreement over the legitimate organisation of practices, but disagreement. On the other hand, however, as with the Dutch and British financial orders, alternative shared meanings informing credit practices are able to co-exist within a situation of relative stability as long as this does not manifest itself in elemental contestation over the appropriate organisation of practices. Put another way, acceptance of the organisation of credit practices as legitimate in the diachronic moment does not necessarily translate into a convergence in day-to-day credit practices. As Perraton *et al.* (1997: 270–1) stress, the significance of neo-liberalism in the contemporary financial order does not lie in its capacity to inform rational and objective credit practices. Instead, it provides a governance discourse to legitimate inherently subjective credit practices organised through hierarchical market institutional networks by reifying the façade of the market mechanism.

Crises and contradictions

Throughout modern world finance, financial crises have tended to stand as important moments in the reproduction or unravelling of successive financial orders. The resolution of financial crises through structures of governance has been integral to the reproduction of financial orders, preventing the superficial fluctuations to credit practices that arise in a crisis from escalating into structural disruption and the unravelling of an order. As the financial crises of the late eighteenth century and 1929–31 illustrate, crises that occur during periods of relative instability – that is, when considerable contestation surrounds the appropriate organisation of credit practices – may expose weaknesses in the ability of formal institutions of governance to manage credit practices and thereby contribute to the unravelling of a financial order.

The contemporary financial order is crisis-ridden. Prior to the Asian crisis, a study by IMF economists (Lindgren *et al.* 1996) found that of the Fund's 181 member states, 133 had experienced disruptions to banking practices between 1980 and early 1996. Overall, the findings classified 108 instances of disruption as 'significant', and 41 instances in 36 states as 'crisis'. In many instances of 'crisis', disruptions generated a sizeable reduction in GDP. Both the high frequency of crises and the extent of their detrimental consequences for economic growth were found to be worse than for any similar period since the Great Depression of the 1930s. More significant in our terms, the contemporary financial order itself has lurched from one major crisis to another. Such major crises are widely interpreted as each holding a so-called 'systemic threat', that is, whereby disruptions to credit practices could be sufficient to lead to world structural disruption. To date these crises have included the debt crisis of the early 1980s, the stock market crash of 1987, the European Exchange Rate Mechanism debacle of 1992–3, the Mexican crisis of 1994–5, the Asian crisis of 1997–8 and the subsequent Russian and Brazilian crises of late 1998 and early 1999. Alongside these major crises have been high-profile instances of the failure of market institutions operating at a world-scale including the Franklin National Bank, the Banco D'Ambrosiano, the Bank of Credit and Commerce International (BCCI), Barings Bank, Yamaichi, and Long Term Capital Management (LTCM).

A common sense explanation of the major crises of contemporary world finance has emerged, at once reflecting and contributing to the forging of relative stability around neo-liberal organisational principles of governance. Grounded in empiricism and positivism, the neo-liberal orthodoxy has sought to explain crises in terms of causal connections between externally observable phenomena in the national political economies concerned. In the first instance the causal factors in all crises are, in effect, domestic and non-market. Certain domestic policy decisions and/or institutional arrangements are deemed to be inappropriate as they are cast as perverting or forestalling the market mode of behaviour and the capacity of the market mechanism to rationally determine exchange rates and the availability or otherwise of credit. World credit practices would, from this reading, ensure the efficient recycling of capital from areas of surplus to areas of demand in the absence of political impediments to the market mechanism. Not surprisingly, 'one size fits all' prescriptions for crisis resolution follow, exemplified in IMF conditionality. An extract from a speech made to the NYSE on 21 September 1998 by British Prime Minister Tony Blair represents a concise summary of the orthodoxy. As crisis spread from Asia, engulfed Russia and threatened to spread further to Latin America, Blair asserted:

> The lesson from the current crisis is not that market disciplines have failed, but that in a global economy, with huge capital flows, the absence of such disciplines can have devastating effect. Countries must put in place the right policy framework – monetary policy targeted at low inflation, sound and sustainable fiscal policies and structural reforms to improve the supply side performance of the economy. Tax systems that work. Strong, properly regulated and fully transparent banking and financial systems.[8]

The explanation of crises as the outcome of domestic institutional inefficiencies and policy mistakes contributes to the legitimation and acceptance of the organisation of world credit practices.

The neo-liberal orthodox explanation of contemporary world financial crises first found its expression in the course of the debt crisis of the early 1980s. Blame for the debt crisis was placed firmly at the door of the underdeveloped sovereign borrowers themselves, rather than with the commercial banks that organised syndicated petro-dollar recycling. Latin American states were, in particular, accused of economic mismanagement that rendered the repayment of loans impossible (IMF 1986). Mismanagement was held to combine misguided policies of Import Substitution Industrialisation (ISI) that protected domestic industries, thereby reducing their competitiveness and capacity to generate the foreign exchange necessary for loan repayment; expansionary monetary policies that increased inflation, reduced domestic saving rates, and ultimately encouraged foreign borrowing to purchase imports; and poorly judged investment decisions, such as Brazil's nuclear energy programme, that did little to stimulate development and instead lined the pockets of a corrupt élite. Similarly, the 1994–5 Mexican peso crisis is interpreted by the orthodoxy as rooted in another combination of inadequate macroeconomic policies (especially with regard to the informal fixing of peso–dollar exchange rates at unrealistic levels and irresponsible current account deficits) and funding consumption through unsustainable foreign sovereign borrowing (Granville 1999; White 2000).

Meanwhile, the common sense explanation of the Asian crisis of 1997–8 places less causal emphasis on macroeconomic policies. The dangers inherent in the policy throughout the region of pegging exchange rates to the US dollar, leading to massive unhedged world-scale private borrowing denominated in foreign currencies (typically the US dollar or Japanese yen), are highlighted by the orthodoxy. However, the focal point for neo-liberal explanations has been 'internal financial sector weaknesses' (Goldstein 1998: 7–14; cf. IMF 1998a), and in particular so-called 'crony capitalist' patterns of lending that promoted irrational and poorly regulated credit creation and investment based on social and political relationships rather than rational risk analysis. The causes of the most recent crises in Russia and Brazil have, once again, been interpreted as residing in domestic policy and institutional configurations. Russia's profligate fiscal policies are held to have been unsustainable and to have led inevitably to the devaluation of the rouble in August 1998 (cf. Granville 1999: 724). Meanwhile, the dominant explanation of the Brazilian crisis 'calls attention to the distortions of macroeconomic fundamentals and government failures to put in place the "right" policy conditions which would enable a national economy to participate effectively in the globalized international economy' (Higgott and Phillips 2000: 363).

By proportioning blame on domestic policies and institutions that are perceived either not to reflect or to act as impediments to market signals, the common sense neo-liberal representation of contemporary financial crises effectively rests on the assumption that market disciplines are produced by world credit practices. Preventing further crises is viewed as hinging on the adoption of market-conforming macroeconomic policies and the extension of the rational market mode of behaviour from world credit practices to local credit practices.

What the orthodoxy fails to recognise, however, is the inherently subjective nature of all credit practices that was made plain by Keynes. As a range of recent research into contemporary financial crises has stressed, crises are the immediate outcome of shifts in collective market sentiment. Such sentiment informs world credit practices and has the potential to become largely self-fulfilling (Soros 1998; Eatwell and Taylor 2000). Contemporary financial crises do not deviate significantly from the phases of speculative excess, distress, panic and crash that have characterised crises throughout modern world finance (cf. Kindleberger 1978). Fickle shifts in the opinions of those at the apex of contemporary market hierarchies manifest themselves in a speculative rush of often leveraged and typically short-term portfolio investment and inter-bank lending that, as sentiment shifts, heads into a distressed reverse. Given that 'separate national currencies themselves are increasingly inextricably locked into wider financial trends and structures' (Cerny 1994a: 591), sharp fluctuations in capital movements also wreak havoc with exchange rates.[9]

Contrary to the neo-liberal orthodoxy, then, the major crises of contemporary world finance are an expression of structural tendencies and not simply the result of the 'wrong' domestic policy decisions and/or institutional arrangements. Recognition of the inherent subjective and collective nature of credit practices highlights that the immediate source of successive major financial crises has been sudden shifts in the shared meanings and expectations framing world credit practices. Our inquiry suggests two further related conjuncturally specific features of recent systemic financial crises, both of which arise from the generalised financialisation of contemporary credit practices. First, the high incidence of crises in the contemporary financial order can be accounted for in terms of financialisation. Financialisation has involved the speculative accumulation of capital through credit practices themselves becoming a structural feature of contemporary world finance. Such accumulation hinges on the subjective identification of investment opportunities in one type of asset or another, especially in the situation of intensified competition between market institutions. On a daily basis, contemporary speculation focuses on the rapid and on-going opening and closing of opportunities for accumulation that arise in the course of foreign exchange, securities and derivatives trading practices in particular. At the same time, investment and the creation of credit in support of investment have generated a pattern of largely discrete speculative waves in the contemporary financial order – sovereign lending to underdeveloped state-societies in the 1970s, disintermediated and securitised practices in support of developed world corporate restructuring during the 1980s, a focus on so-called emerging markets in the 1990s, and the 'tech stocks' fad at the turn of the millennium. Each speculative wave has been followed by a backwash, that is, a distressed withdrawal of capital and credit, and in some instances by panic and crash.

Second, reference to financialisation also reveals an important contradiction in contemporary world credit practices that comes to the surface in the course of crises. The speculative practices of world finance are not completely separate from the real economy of world production and trade. Claims and obligations arising from investment and credit creation are often directly and indirectly claims and obligations on the real economy. The current situation of financialisation 'expresses itself not only quantitatively as the ascendance of financial contracts over real economic turnover, but also as a qualitative effect of a subordination of real economic and social relations to the financial system' (Altvater 1997: 59). For instance, while the major corporations and states have increasingly funded the majority of their investment from retained earnings or taxation since the late 1990s, the 'tail' of their obligations arising from world credit practices continues to 'wag the dog' of their corporate and state policy objectives (Cutler and Waine 2001; Grahl 2001). Secondary trading strategies focused on short-term returns prevent 'back sliding' by sovereign and corporate borrowers alike from the economistic criteria of embedded financial orthodoxy or shareholder value.[10] All promises to pay generated by credit practices carry with them assumptions that contribute to shaping the context for the undertakings of those to whom debt obligations apply. When world credit practices are subject to financialisation, promises to pay carry with them the assumption that socio-economic relations are commodified. However, as Polanyi's (1944) inspirational analysis serves to remind us, the adjustment of social relations in the face of pressures for commodification encounters significant social, political and embedded institutional forces. It follows that a contradiction is present between credit practices that are subject or respond to speculative motivations on the one hand, and the tensions generated by credit obligations that assume the commodification of real socio-economic relations on the other. Taking subtly different forms in specific instances, financial crises break out as the real economy is not able to consistently meet the obligations and expectations arising from speculative credit practices. The major crises of contemporary world finance share their roots in this structural contradiction that, at different instances, rears its head and finds expression in the distress and panic of financial market sentiment.

By way of brief illustration, this structural contradiction was clearly apparent in the wave of speculation that embraced the so-called emerging markets during the 1990s. For the first years of the decade, the attention of New York and London-centred credit practices in particular was guided by a perception of opportunities for accumulation in Latin America. Underlying the focus of world credit practices on Latin America were the limited returns available from assets in North America and Europe, as securities markets entered a period of slow growth and real interest rates remained comparatively low. This was supplemented by the general air of optimism in the future of the world economy that was generated by the collapse of the Soviet bloc, and a seeming commitment throughout the region to the main planks of the Washington consensus that served to inspire confidence among financiers and investors (Krugman 1995). Mexico was the eye of the storm of speculative excess, receiving net capital inflows of $91 billion between 1990 and 1994 that were equivalent to around one-fifth of all net capital inflows to underdeveloped state-societies during this period (Strange 1998b: 102–5; Bello *et al.* 2000: 10). The Mexican Brady bonds agreement of 1989 to further reschedule the debts outstanding from the crisis of the early 1980s had placed sovereign finances on a firm footing, Mexican capital controls had been all but eliminated, and Mexican production was increasingly intertwined with the neighbouring US economy under the auspices of NAFTA. Borrowing in New York at rates of interest of around 5–6 per cent in order to invest in Mexico where it seemed reasonable to expect a rate of return of at least 12–14 per cent was attractive to US pension and mutual funds in particular (Porter 1997: 183–5; Öniş and Aysan 2000: 126–8). While focusing on Mexican securities broadly and realising a stock market boom that saw a 436 per cent rise over a three year period (Strange 1998b: 97), speculative short-term investment and trading concentrated on *tesebonos* (dollar-denominated sovereign credit instruments).

While Mexico was the star attraction of emerging markets in the early 1990s, the real economy showed little prospect of living up to the wildly optimistic shared assumptions that informed world credit practices (Cameron and Aggarwal 1996). The average economic growth rate in Mexico between 1990 and 1994 was only 2.5 per cent, less than population growth and below the 3.1 per cent average for Latin America as a whole (Krugman 1995: 40–1). A contradiction was present, then, between 'the rosy view of investors' and 'the sorry prospects of the real economy' (Bello *et al.* 2000: 11). This remained obscured for some time, hidden beneath the euphoria surrounding emerging markets in general and disguised by a Mexican balance of payments equilibrium in which net capital inflows offset deficit indicators. However, as Mexican exports slowed further and the government sought to increase fiscal spending rather than devalue the peso, the contradiction surfaced. Distress became panic as speculative foreign investments and lines of credit were rapidly withdrawn, placing the value of the peso under extreme pressure. Interest rate hikes by the Mexican authorities to encourage investors to hold out proved useless, as the real economy was depressed further leading to market expectations that devaluation was unavoidable. The Mexican crisis was, then, 'due to a rapid inflow and even quicker outflow of short-term capital (mainly from United States mutual funds)' (Picciotto and Haines 1999: 352). The peso was devalued and floated on the foreign exchanges in December 1994, unleashing the so-called 'Tequila effect' of similar downward pressures on the other currencies in Latin America. While the governments of Brazil and Argentina were successful in resisting these pressures by increasing interest rates and cutting fiscal expenditure in order to remain attractive to world credit practices, the price was economic stagnation (Strange 1998b: 100–1). Meanwhile, in February 1995 the US Federal Reserve, in conjunction with the IMF and World Bank, put together a rescue package for Mexico of in excess of $50 billion.

The Mexican crisis did not spell the end of the emerging markets fever. Asian economies, most notably the so-called 'Asian five' of Indonesia, Malaysia, Philippines, Thailand and South Korea, were the focal point for a 'credit boom' (Goldstein 1998: 7) that dated from 1993–4. The creation of credit exceeded the already rapid growth of GDP across the Asian five, increasing steadily from 1992 through to 1996 (Bevacqua 1998: 414). While feeding somewhat distinct patterns of investment across the Asian five and ultimately leading to differential experiences of crisis (cf. Henderson 1999), the expectations that underpinned the boom were commonly and dramatically overly-optimistic. World-scale speculative practices were again to the fore, as the foreign financing of the Asian five more than doubled from $45.2 billion in 1994 to $95.2 billion by 1996.[11]

The Asian crisis of 1997 was not, however, simply a repeat of the Mexican crisis. The contradiction between world credit practices that are subject or respond to speculative motivations on the one hand and the tensions generated by obligations that assume the commodification of real socio-economic relations on the other took a specific form in Asia. There were, of course, similarities with the Mexican crisis. For instance, the series of currency crises that spread from Thailand across the Philippines, Indonesia, Malaysia and South Korea were largely a consequence of movements of credit and capital. The exchange rates of the Asian five were pegged to the dollar, stimulating large volumes of short-term, unhedged foreign-currency denominated borrowing that, when it was reversed, wreaked havoc with currency values (IMF 1998a: 4; Corbett and Vines 1999: 157). Furthermore, like Mexico, capital controls across the region had been recently liberalised.

Two key related differences distinguished the Asian crisis from the earlier Mexican crisis. First, the world-scale speculative practices of credit creation and trading that in Mexico had taken the form of portfolio investment in sovereign instruments in particular contrasted with the dominant form of practices in the Asian case. Short-term inter-bank loans were to the fore in stoking and bursting Asia's credit boom, accounting for $55.7 billion of the $95.2 billion of the foreign financing that poured into the region in 1996.[12] Second, speculative short-term inter-bank lending was both primarily Tokyo-centred and Japanese banks were the principal players in the organisation of these practices. This contrasted with the largely New York-centred practices of US institutional investors and investment banks that had characterised the Mexican crisis. The short-term, dollar-denominated inter-bank lending practices of Japanese and non-Japanese commercial banks were undertaken in the offshore space that incorporated Hong Kong, Singapore and, at its hub, the TOM (Bernard 1999: 191–2). By the end of 1997, Japanese banks had an exposure to the Asian five totalling $76 billion, well in excess of German ($29 billion), French ($26 billion), US ($23 billion) and UK ($17 billion) banks (IMF 1998a: 116).

During the early 1990s, Japanese banks had re-established the practices of foreign borrowing that had been important to their position in the bubble years of the late 1980s. Alongside the capital generated by comparatively very high rates of domestic saving and massive current account surpluses, dollar-denominated borrowing by Japanese banks was significant in fuelling the bubble economy (Nakao 1995). The latter tended to be organised by the branches of Japanese banking networks in London, New York, Hong Kong and Singapore, in the main taking the form of short-term inter-bank borrowing. The outstanding net short-term liabilities of Japanese banks increased from $–44 billion in 1985 to reach a peak of $265.9 billion by 1989. When the bubble economy burst, some $190 billion worth of these liabilities were repaid over the next three years as borrowing was seriously curtailed. By 1994, however, the outstanding net short-term overseas liabilities of

Japanese banks had once again climbed to $216 billion (Lapavitsas 1997: 31). In Bevacqua's (1998) terms, such an expansion in support of the Asian credit boom can be read as the effective expansion of the bubble economy throughout the region. By borrowing from the world inter-bank market, the practices of Japanese commercial banks were subject to credit relations that assumed commodification. Simultaneously and given that in large part the credit practices of the Asian five's banks remained embedded in their respective economies, Japanese re-lending to these banks created obligations that could not match the assumption of commodification. Caught between a rock and a hard place, Japanese banks withdrew their inter-bank lines of credit to the Asian five. This volte-face by Japanese banks served as the initial prick that deflated Asia's credit boom. Japanese banks' exposures to the rest of Asia fell from $210 billion in the middle of 1997 to $190 billion by the end of the year, while the exposures to Asia (excluding Japan) of German, French, US and UK banks remained relatively unchanged throughout 1997 (IMF 1998a: 134–5). The volte-face by Japanese banks effectively precipitated the shift in market sentiment, the withdrawals of credit and capital, and the vicious circle of financial and currency crises that followed. The crisis-laden contradiction of speculative world credit practices played itself out in Asia in the first instance, then, within Japanese commercial banking networks.

Formal governance: towards transnational multilateralism

Across successive world financial orders, the formal authority exercised through market, civil and state institutions in the management of credit practices has waxed and waned. For instance, during the Dutch financial order, the widespread acceptance of the cosmopolitan values of Amsterdam's social forces provided the basis for the exercise of authority through market and civil institutions relatively free from state involvement. During the American financial order meanwhile, the forging of relative stability around the principles of embedded liberalism legitimated an organisation of credit practices that was formally managed through a largely state-based structure of governance in which New York's market institutions played a subordinate but supportive role. Two commonalties have, however, been shared by modern world financial orders in terms of formal authority. First, relationships between market, civil and state institutions in the organisation of credit practices have been interdependent in each order, the balance between them reflecting the respective organisational principles of governance. Second, pivotal to the interdependent governance roles of state, market and civil institutions has been their centralisation in the dominant WFC of the day. Even in the American financial order in which the Washington–New York axis and not simply New York stood as the key complex of governance, the centralisation of albeit circumscribed market authority in New York was a significant feature of the structure of governance. It is these comparative historical insights that frame our account of formal governance and the reproduction of the contemporary financial order.

From states to markets

By comparison with the American financial order, a significant shift in the balance of authority between state and market has taken place in contemporary world finance (Porter 1993; Germain 1997; Underhill 1997b). Given the forging of relative stability in the contemporary financial order around the organisational principles of neo-liberalism, it is not surprising that formal governance has and continues to be characterised by increased market authority. Contrary to the neo-liberal discourse of governance, however, financial governance by the 'invisible hand' of the market mechanism is not a natural or apolitical development. Market authority rests not with the cumulative rational decisions of individuals that comprise the market mechanism but, in view of the subjective, hierarchical and collective nature of financial markets, with the principal market institutions that play a role in the organisation of credit practices. It is the political undertaking of financial liberalisation and deregulation and its legitimation that enables a shift of responsibility and authority from state to market.

In comparative historical terms, the formal authority wielded through market institutions in the organisation of credit practices is suggestive of several parallels with the Dutch and British financial orders. In general terms and in contrast with the American financial order, both the Dutch and British orders were also characterised by a largely market-based structure of governance. More specifically and reminiscent of the position of the great merchant houses in the Dutch and British orders, disintermediated credit practices in the contemporary order have been organised largely through the institutional networks of the major investment banks. However, there are several important conjunctural features in the market-based governance of the contemporary financial order, as the institutionalisation of credit practices has a distinctive pattern. The removal of regulations that previously compartmentalised credit practices according to institution type and the associated shift towards the universal banking model has ensured that market institutions in general, and commercial banks in particular, play a broad role in the organisation of practices. More specifically, institutional investors now legitimately play a key role in the organisation of practices of capital investment and secondary trading. Furthermore, the tendency towards consolidation in the financial markets, carried forward in the main by mergers and acquisitions between the major commercial and investment banks, constitutes 'a new departure in the historical balance of power between public and private authority' (Germain 1997: 106). So-called 'global banks' enjoy the lion's share of authority in the organisation of credit practices.

While the design capacity of state institutions has been central to the contemporary marketisation of credit practices and enabling the attendant governance role of market institutions, the operational capacity of state institutions in the structure of governance has been simultaneously and consequently eroded. As Dyson *et al.* (1998: 174) assert, 'a crisis of effectiveness of traditional monetary and exchange rate policy instruments' has become apparent. Such has been the declining authority of central banks that some neo-liberal commentators have suggested that the time is ripe for their monopoly privileges in the issuing of money to be taken away (e.g. Dowd and Timberlake 1998). Direct credit controls have become fruitless in the face of offshore practices, target indicators of the national money supply have been called into question by the massive volume of credit created by world-scale practices, and the sheer value of daily foreign exchange trading practices severely circumscribes efforts to manipulate exchange rates (Dyson *et al.* 1998: 178–81).[13] The operational capacity that does remain at a world-scale is, at one and the same time, more evenly distributed than in previous financial orders and yet continues to be asymmetrical. For instance, as Germain's (1997: 137–61) account of the authority of central banks illustrates, the capacity of US Federal Reserve to decisively manipulate the organisation of credit practices through interest rate changes has been partially circumscribed throughout the contemporary financial order. In the context of a more multi-polar world economy and a decentralised financial order, the Bundesbank and Bank of Japan charted independent interest rate policies throughout the 1990s. With the advent of the European Central Bank and single currency, euro and dollar interest rate policies have continued to diverge (Grahl 2001). At the same time, however, the continued dollar-denomination of the majority of world credit practices, the large volume of outstanding US sovereign debt, the importance of the US economy to world consumption, and the depth of New York's capital and equity markets have all ensured that the Federal Reserve retains the capacity to authoritatively influence credit creation in the short-term through open market operations.[14]

Unlike, for example, the position of the Bank of England in the British financial order, the central banking institutions of any single state lack the necessary reach throughout the contemporary order to contribute significantly to the control of world credit practices. In previous centralised financial orders, the cohesive relationships between the principal central bank and those contiguous market institutions that institutionalised world credit practices ensured that so called 'moral suasion' and personal relationships could contribute to the manipulation of practices. Local and national money management was world management. In the contemporary decentralised order, no individual central bank enjoys such reach and influence throughout the organisation of credit practices. This is compounded by offshore which weakens the governance role of central banks broadly. Strategic attempts to exercise operational capacity by the principal central banks have involved limited co-operative action under the auspices of the G-7 forum of finance ministers, most notably realising the Plaza Accord of 1985 that sought to devalue the US dollar against the Japanese yen (Webb 1995).[15] The circumscribed asymmetries that characterise the authority of the principal central banks in the contemporary financial order are, then, a reflection of the spatiality of credit practices.

Given the declining authority of state institutions, it would seem tempting to represent the structure of governance in the contemporary financial order as a victory for the market over states. Such a 'states against markets' (Boyer and Drache 1996) or 'governance without government' (Rosenau 1992) approach would, however, be misleading. To follow Taylor's (1995) representation of contemporary governance as the transcendence of city-centred market networks over territorially-based state institutions would be similarly erroneous. The decentralisation of the contemporary financial order has indeed led to something of a disjuncture in the structure of governance between the world-scale reach of market institutional networks and the more limited reach of state institutions (cf. Gill 1992). Authority is fragmented and overlapping (Underhill 1997d: 315; Strange 1998a: 171), exercised through a complex array of institutions anchored across the principal financial centres. Yet decentralisation has not destroyed the interdependence of state and market institutions in the governance of the contemporary order. As Underhill (2000: 129) observes, contemporary financial governance is not characterised by a 'tug-of-war' between state and market institutions. Rather, state and market remain interdependent as part of 'the same essential ensemble of governance' (Underhill 2000: 118). The formal reproduction of the decentralised contemporary financial order has hinged upon a structure of governance in which interdependent market and state authority is coming to take an unprecedented form.

Transnational multilateralism

While decentralisation has not proved to be a serious structural impediment to the forging of emerging relative stability around neo-liberal organisational principles, it has been of far greater consequence for formal governance. Interdependent market and state institutions are undergoing unparalleled transformations that, taken together, constitute what can be termed 'transnational multilateralism'. Both market and state authority is increasingly transnationalised. Governance through transnational market networks is being furthered and reinforced by state-based regulatory, supervisory and crisis management programmes that are undertaken multilaterally. While this 'complex multilateralism' (O'Brien *et al.* 2000) often focuses on inter-state co-operation through institutional forums such as the G-7, BIS and IMF and is guided by neo-liberal principles, it also incorporates a transnational financial network of ministers, bureaucrats, financiers and, to a limited extent, other forces of civil society.[16] By comparison with the *ad hoc* inter-state crisis management initiatives of the Dutch and British financial orders, contemporary multilateralism differs in terms of its greater scope, institutionalisation and transnationalisation. At the same time, the transnational and market-reinforcing nature of contemporary multilateralism also distinguishes it from the inter-state arrangements of the Bretton Woods era.

In the Dutch and British financial orders, those market institutions that performed a legitimate governance role at a world-scale were anchored in Amsterdam and London respectively as complexes of governance. By contrast, the market institutions of New York, London and Tokyo each lack the necessary reach throughout the contemporary financial order to comprehensively manage credit practices. For example, New York investment banking networks such as J.P. Morgan, Merrill Lynch and Goldman Sachs enjoy considerable authority in the organisation of capital and equity market practices that provide sovereign and corporate credit. Alongside their market shares, the governance role of these institutions is evidenced in qualitative terms by the rise to prominence of the portfolio selection models they pioneered to mathematically calculate risk and return (cf. Saber 1999). The governance role of New York's investment banks is supplemented by the authority in capital market and equity investment and secondary trading enjoyed by American institutional investors, the governance role of New York's credit rating agencies, and the supervisory and regulatory capacities of the NYSE and SEC. Yet a New York-centred structure of governance in the organisation of capital and equity market practices remains nascent while the majority of these practices are undertaken offshore and centred primarily in London. Furthermore, commercial banking practices are decentralised to an even greater extent, organised primarily through Japanese, European and American market networks. However, as Germain (1997: 103–4) suggests, the absence of a single complex of governance has not realised the complete fragmentation in the management of credit practices that might have been expected. The fragmentary tendencies of decentralisation have been offset by the development of the transnational market networks of so-called global banks. Such networks are facilitated by information and communications technologies that enable co-ordination and control through an infrastructure of monitors and modems. Functional as opposed to national divisions within market networks and intra-institutional movements of capital and credit are representative of genuinely transnational management strategies.

The unique transnationalisation of market authority in the governance of contemporary credit practices would not have been feasible without accompanying multilateral initiatives. State-based governance that performs regulatory and crisis management roles has also come to take an unprecedented form. Such multilateral initiatives have not been a functional inevitability that has followed necessarily from the transnationalisation of market networks, but have reflected two developments. First, the major crises and high-profile failures of market institutions that have punctuated contemporary world finance have generated expedient collective responses from politicians, bureaucrats and financiers. Alongside immediate management initiatives to prevent crises from descending into world financial collapse, these responses have also entailed regulatory initiatives aimed at forestalling future crises (Helleiner 1994: 169–71). Second, multilateral initiatives in the wake of crises have reflected a key structural change in the wider world order, that is, the internationalisation of the state (Cox 1987: 253–67; Baker 1999). While part and parcel of the contemporary de-territorialisation of inter-state rivalry in the sense of adjusting state policies and institutions to perceived competitive imperatives, the newly internationalised state has, as the counterpart to transnational production and financial networks, also become drawn into multilateral agreements and institutions to a greater extent.

The management of financial crises during the Dutch and British financial orders hinged on the lender of last resort facilities provided by the Exchange Bank and Bank of England respectively, in conjunction with their contiguous market networks and *ad hoc* co-operation from the other principal central banks. While similar *ad hoc* co-operative crisis management by central banks has also marked the contemporary financial order, this has been accompanied by multilateralism undertaken under the auspices of the IMF. To date and by virtue of disproportionately placing the burden of post-crisis obligations on debtors rather than lenders, these unparalleled arrangements have ensured that superficial fluctuations to credit practices emanating from successive crises have not led to the structural dislocation and disruption of world finance. The position of the IMF in crisis management was established following its role in the debt crisis of the early 1980s. This constituted 'a profound transformation' (Pauly 1997: 99) from the role of providing short-term offsetting finance that the IMF had previously played in the American financial order. Such a transformation was enabled by the expansion of the IMF's mandate throughout the 1970s to include the surveillance of obligations arising from world credit practices (Pauly 1997: 116–17). Contrary to the view of Strange (1998a: 163–9), the IMF in itself has not simply become the world's lender of last resort. Responses to the debt crisis, the Mexican peso crisis of 1994–5, and most recently the Asian, Russian and Brazilian crises have tended to follow a similar pattern. The IMF, backed by the resources of the principal central banks, provides short-term bridging loans to forestall default, prescribes the policies of the 'Washington consensus' as the *quid pro quo* for assistance, and organises the rescheduling of outstanding obligations. As Pauly (1997: 100) recognises, the IMF has been transformed into a 'ready-made apparatus' for institutionalised multilateral crisis management.

Multilateral initiatives in world financial regulation and supervision began following the panic created by the losses sustained in the Eurocurrency markets by the Franklin National Bank and Bank I.D Herstatt in 1974 (Frieden 1987: 117–19). Under the auspices of the BIS, the Basle Committee on Banking Supervision was formed, comprising officials from the relevant state and civil institutions of the G-10 states (Porter 1993: 56–7; Underhill 1997b: 23). The result was the Basle Concordat of 1975. This established the responsibilities of 'home' and 'host' national regulatory and supervisory institutions with regard to the world credit practices organised through commercial banking networks (Porter 1993: 58–9; Underhill 1997b: 25–6). The Concordat was subsequently revised in 1983, following the Banco D'Ambrosiano affair, placing greater responsibility with 'home' regulatory and supervisory institutions (Porter 1993: 59–60; Underhill 1997b: 26–7). Multilateral co-operation regarding world-scale banking practices was furthered through the 1988 Basle Capital Adequacy Accord which established minimum capital base requirements for commercial banks (Porter 1993: 61–5; Underhill 1997b: 28–30). Kapstein (1996: 6) interprets the 1988 Accord as 'the cornerstone of international financial regulation', accepted by regulators and banks well beyond the G-7. However, more recent BIS-centred initiatives cast doubt on the continued centrality of the Accord. In April 1997 the BIS issued a directive entitled *25 Core Principles of Effective Banking Supervision* (known as the Basle Core Principles). Developed by the Basle Committee in conjunction with regulatory and supervisory bodies from fifteen of the so-called emerging markets, the Core Principles revealed that the BIS has 'virtually thrown in the towel on capital adequacy reserves' (Strange 1998a: 161). With the Core Principles, the emphasis has shifted from regulation to the supervision of self-regulation. Capital adequacy is now complemented by the monitoring of the risk management procedures of banks themselves that have increasingly gained credence among regulators during the 1990s (Underhill 1997b: 37–8; Roberts 1998: 120).

> Current procedures reflect the fundamental proposition that financial risk is most effectively managed by those who are exposed to it, and consequently exposed to failure. It is not the task of the financial regulator to coach firms in the management of risk, still less to dictate or even run the firm's risk management function. Instead, the role of the regulator is constantly to examine the firm's risk management procedures, to pronounce on their broad adequacy, and encourage development of the best practices within firms.
>
> (Eatwell and Taylor 2000: 41)

In sum, BIS-centred multilateralism has not led to legally binding international agreements, but to the establishment of minimum standards or codes of conduct for self-regulation and supervision designed to ensure the soundness of credit practices institutionalised in market networks.

In the wake of the 1987 world stock market crash and through the forum provided by the International Organisation of Securities Commissions (IOSCO), national regulatory and supervisory institutions framing world capital and equity market practices came together (Helleiner 1994: 186). Led by the US SEC through bilateral agreements called 'Memoranda of Understanding' (MOUs), regulatory and supervisory institutions have developed information sharing agreements to assist their activities (Porter 1993: 112–17; Underhill 1997b: 32–3). At the same time, efforts were made to establish minimum standards for capital adequacy for securities firms. Agreement proved more difficult to achieve than in banking, compounded by the complexities of measuring market risk and the resulting discord surrounding the appropriate formula for calculating an adequate capital base (Porter 1993: 118–19; Underhill 1997a: 33–5).[17] However, in 1997 the IOSCO published its *Principles and Objectives of Financial Regulation.* Endorsed by its world-wide membership in 1998, the IOSCO's Principles mirrored the Core Principles for banking practices developed by the BIS. Meanwhile and similarly, during the latter half of the 1990s a grouping of the regulatory institutions responsible for the world's main futures exchanges have committed themselves to information sharing and developed standards of 'best practice' for futures contracts and their supervision (Picciotto and Haines 1999: 367).

The market-reinforcing nature of IOSCO-centred multilateral initiatives has involved a restructuring of national regulatory institutions themselves.[18] Diverse national institutions are less likely to display command and control regulatory relations with their 'home' market networks in the first instance, concentrating instead on supervision. Rooted in the world-wide diffusion of the 'investor-orientated' practices of the US SEC, this change in emphasis has also been associated with the 'codification, institutionalisation and juridification' (Moran 1991) of previous arrangements.[19] For instance, the MOUs signed by securities regulators are widely recognised to have encouraged state regulatory institutions to take up some of the responsibilities for regulation (e.g. disclosure, insider trading, issuing) which in many cases previously resided with stock exchanges as civil institutions (Vogel 1996; Lütz 1997). Such change in the regulation of securities practices has also been engendered by the shift from trading floors to electronic trading platforms and the intensified competition between stock exchanges (cf. Budd 1995). This, in turn, does raise questions as to whether the traditional governance role of stock exchanges is undergoing transformation. The move from membership organisation to publicly listed company is currently either being carried out or considered by the TSE, NYSE and LSE. Mergers between exchanges, such as the high profile failure of the LSE and Deutsche Börse to come together to create the strangely named 'iX – international exchanges', are also being considered. These developments suggest a 'squeeze' on the modern governance remit stock of exchanges from state-based supervision of market-reinforcing regulation on the one hand and market authority on the other. There may be a sense in which, under the influence of neo-liberal organisational principles of governance, stock exchanges are becoming less like civil institutions and more like co-ordination services firms.[20] However, even as publicly listed companies, the principal exchanges still hold discrete competencies which, by their nature, distinguish exchanges from investment banks and institutional investors in the formal governance of world credit practices.

New international financial architecture

The largely unpredicted financial bankruptcies and currency de-valuations of the Asian crisis, quickly followed by the Russian and Brazilian debacles, acted as a wake up call to the transnational financial community. Politicians, bureaucrats and the popular press at the time all voiced the opinion that, without a response, the crises could develop into a world economic crisis reminiscent of the Great Depression. The sharp downturn in New York and London's securities markets in October 1998 seemed to give even greater credence to their pessimism. The response to the crises of the late 1990s entailed not just another round of management and rescue packages organised through the IMF, but also a broad range of initiatives that have taken complex multilateralism in financial governance further. Not surprisingly given the forging of relative stability around neo-liberal organisational principles, the key assumption binding together the initiatives has been that 'global finance' will benefit the world economy as a whole once the frequency and scale of financial crises is reduced. The initiatives have collectively been referred to by those involved as the process of building a 'new international financial architecture'. The use of the 'architecture' metaphor engenders strategic and planned overtones that are somewhat misleading, while the claim to newness also obscures the extent to which change has been incremental. Four main related planks of these recent multilateral initiatives are, however, discernible. The first three planks – strengthening national financial systems, advancing transparency in order to enable market discipline, and responsibility for and the management of crises – correspond to the G-22 (latterly G-20) working groups formed in April

1998.[21] The fourth main plank is the overarching effort to bring a greater level of co-ordination to the various aspects of financial multilateralism.

Multilateral initiatives to strengthen national financial systems under the guise of the new international financial architecture have followed directly from the focus on domestic institutional factors by the neo-liberal explanation of the Asian crisis. Two sets of actions are perceived to be necessary to address institutional deficiencies. First, the market institutions of the G-20 economies should implement common self-regulatory standards and codes of conduct that establish the benchmark for 'best practice'. In addition to the *Principles* for banking and securities practices already developed by the BIS and IOSCO respectively, these standards include data dissemination, fiscal and monetary policy transparency, payments and settlement, accounting and auditing, corporate governance, and insolvency regimes (IMF and World Bank 2000). At the same time, the development of new standards has been accompanied by the updating of existing standards. For instance, in January 2001 the BIS began the process of revising the 1988 Capital Accord. While retaining the overall capital adequacy target of 8 per cent set in the original Accord, revision is focusing upon the use of banks' own internal control and risk management procedures to calculate capital levels (BIS 2001). In short, the new Accord due at the end of 2001 reinforces the shift to self-regulation signalled by the 1997 Core Principles. Second, the IMF, World Bank and regional development banks are taking on a supervisory role to monitor the implementation of self-regulatory standards (Key 1999: 71–2). Particularly as a result of the expansion of the surveillance remit of the IMF's Article IV, recent years have seen the Fund conduct a series of case study reports on members' observance of standards. More broadly and in co-operation with the World Bank, the IMF has undertaken experimental Reports on the Observance of Standards and Codes (ROSCs) (IMF and World Bank 2000). Such supervisory initiatives effectively involve not the direct monitoring of adherence to standards by financial market and corporate institutions, but monitoring national supervisory institutions, that is, supervising the supervisors.

The second main plank of the multilateral initiatives undertaken under the auspices of the new international financial architecture process – that is, furthering transparency – has also followed from the neo-liberal discourse of governance and associated explanations of major crises. Underpinning the call for enhanced transparency is the neo-liberal belief that uncertainties surrounding the availability, reliability and comparability of market information distort financial market participants' decision-making, leading to deficiencies and volatility (cf. IMF 2001: 5). In short, governance by the market mechanism is reliant upon as perfect as possible information. The call for greater transparency has combined a desire for the increased disclosure of data by financial market institutions and corporations according to recognised accounting standards and procedures; improved openness of state fiscal and monetary policy-making; and less secrecy concerning the operations of the IMF and World Bank (IMF 1998b).

The third main plank of the new international financial architecture process has been the bolstering of the capacity of existing international institutions, most notably the IMF, to act as forums for crisis-management. This initiative has focused not on the transformation of the IMF into a world-scale lender of last resort, but on reinforcing the legitimacy of the IMF's policy prescriptions while at the same time making further resources available. Buttressing the role of the IMF in the contemporary structure of financial governance became a particularly pressing task against a backdrop of some considerable debate about its standing (cf. Leaver and Seabrooke 2000). In a speech delivered to the NYSE in September 1998, British Prime Minister Tony Blair gave an indication of the direction of change:

> The banking systems of individual countries are typically supported by a lender of last resort. The IMF does not and cannot play this role – the finance it provides is strictly limited and is usually provided in return for specific policy demands negotiated over a period of time. But it is vital that the international financial community has the means to respond effectively to acute short-term liquidity crises, particularly those caused by a generalised loss of market confidence rather than economic policy failures in the countries concerned. This may require us to look imaginatively at the funding needed to support IMF programmes, without in any way undermining the incentive countries have to pursue sound policies.[22]

Enhancing the legitimacy of the IMF has hinged on the replacement of its long-standing Interim Committee with a new International Monetary and Financial Committee that, unlike its predecessor, allows all member state governments to raise issues concerning the operations of the Fund that they see fit (Germain 2000). Meanwhile, the IMF has gained new resources in the form of Contingent Credit Lines. These are designed to provide the Fund with resources ahead of a crisis, rather than waiting for co-operative central bank action and political agreement in the wake of crises. The Contingent Credit Lines are to be used to lend pre-emptively to help prevent crises, particularly the spread of an existing crisis to a state-society that is adjudged to have sound 'macroeconomic fundamentals'.

The final plank of the new international financial architecture has been the creation of the Financial Stability Forum (FSF) in February 1999. The FSF evolved from proposals made by British Chancellor of the Exchequer Gordon Brown in the autumn of 1998, carried forward under the leadership of Bundesbank President Hans Tietmeyer. Based at the BIS, the FSF is not so much another inter-state financial governance forum, but an attempt to bring some overarching strategic co-ordination to the existing multilateral initiatives (Eatwell and Taylor 2000: xiii). The membership of the Forum includes the regulators, treasury officials and central bankers of the G-7 states, their peers from other states deemed to be structurally significant in the contemporary financial order (the Netherlands, Hong Kong, Singapore, and Australia), and representatives from the other existing international institutions. The Forum provides a mechanism for planning co-operative ventures. These include, for instance, those involving BIS, IMF and World Bank personnel in an institute to train and provide technical assistance to national supervisory authorities, and the efforts to further the standards setting process.[23]

Tensions of transnational multilateralism

Despite the further entrenchment of transnational multilateralism under the banner of the new international financial architecture and in contrast to the view of IPE scholars such as Kapstein (1996) who cast contemporary world finance as 'shockproof', serious question marks remain as to the adequacy of the current structure of governance. To begin with, the capacity of the structure of governance to reproduce the contemporary financial order is not simply assured in a functional manner. While there may be neo-liberal agreement as to the appropriate organisation of credit practices among the principal state and social forces that constitute the transnational financial community, complex multilateralism continues to rest upon on-going co-operation. The principal institutional forums such as the BIS, IMF and FSA cannot operate independently of negotiations among the coalition of forces. For instance, Andrew Crocket, BIS General Manager since 1994, describes the BIS as 'less an organisation than a process'.[24] Similarly, the IMF lacks autonomy from the major states in decision-making (Strange 1996: 167–8; Pauly 1997: 99). Particularistic interests cut across the transnational financial community, ensuring that 'conflict over regulatory and supervisory issues remains endemic even where there are well-developed institutions to deal with these matters' (Underhill 1997d: 314).

Furthermore and related, recent efforts to advance the so-called new international financial architecture have also highlighted tensions in the structure of governance engendered by the narrowness of the coalition of forces involved. Contemporary credit practices have come to entail an uneven yet expanding spatial scale. A legitimate and functioning structure of governance therefore increasingly rests upon co-operation that is more inclusive, incorporating the financiers, market institutions and relevant state agencies from the so-called emerging markets. The creation of the G-20 working groups, including representatives from Argentina, Brazil, China, India, Indonesia, Mexico, Russia and Turkey, and the replacement of the IMF's Interim Committee with the new International Monetary and Financial Committee may both go some way to enabling a more inclusive form of co-operation (Germain 2000). This may further the legitimacy of the structure of governance. However, considerable barriers to inclusive forms of co-operation remain whilst the discourse of neo-liberal governance holds sway. Most notably and reflecting the depression experiences of those already subject to IMF conditionality (cf. Krugman 1999), the adjustment of socio-economic relations and state policies in the emerging markets to the perceived economistic exigencies of world credit practices in line with the neo-liberal Washington consensus is likely to perpetuate underdevelopment. The forging of relative stability and acceptance of the contemporary organisation of credit practices as legitimate among a broad coalition of state and societal forces would, then, appear likely to necessitate a reconstitution of the structure of governance based upon organisational principles other than those of neo-liberalism.

The capacity of the structure of governance to reproduce the contemporary financial order is also undermined by significant gaps between the rhetoric and reality of complex multilateralism. In a simple sense, such 'reality gaps' are largely a consequence of shortfalls and snags in the implementation of multilateral initiatives. Many commentators have complained that regulatory and supervisory provisions still lag behind the pace of innovation in credit practices institutionalised in transnational market networks (e.g. Picciotto and Haines 1999). Similarly and despite the renovation of the IMF as part of the new international financial architecture process, 'the institutions and mechanisms of crisis management . . . do not yet match the increased systemic risk inherent in the unwieldy financial order' (Underhill 1997d: 315). Major financial crises increasingly demand larger rescue packages and more rapid management responses and, as Pauly (1997: 141) observes, the IMF remains 'a coping mechanism, not a solving mechanism'. Meanwhile, the implementation of already established standards of 'best practice' is far from assured. The strengthening of the national financial arrangements of the emerging markets continues to be a key task of the new international architecture process. Perhaps more importantly, the regulators of many of the world's offshore centres and tax havens remain outside complex multilateral initiatives and, as a consequence, are in many instances exempt from the implementation of standards of 'best practice'. The shortfall in implementation is not, however, confined to the financial institutions of the emerging markets or offshore centres. For instance, the current revision of the Basle Capital Accord looks rather hollow while the up-take of existing standards by Japanese banks remains in question. Japanese banks continue to take advantage of a concession included in the 1988 Accord that permitted them to include securities valued at cost of acquisition rather than current market price in their capital adequacy calculations (Lapavitsas 1997: 36). Given the massive downturn in the Nikkei 225 index since the collapse of the bubble economy, very grave doubts are cast on the solvency of some of the world's largest financial market institutions.

The gaps between the rhetoric and reality of the structure of governance also go to the very heart of the contemporary financial order. Informed by the neo-liberal discourse of governance, complex multilateralism initiatives have reinforced the role of the principal transnational market institutions in the organisation of credit practices and increasingly limited state institutions to supervisory and crisis-management roles. As such, the management and administration of credit practices is de-politicised and largely reduced to a purely technical question to be determined by the market mechanism. Yet, as we have shown, inherent to the contemporary marketisation of credit practices has been securitisation and financialisation. Multilateral initiatives currently place great faith in the capacity of securitisation, and particularly derivatives practices, to manage risks arising from price fluctuations. As Strange (1986: 116–19) makes plain, however, risk-adverse derivatives practices have, far from reducing perceived risks, collectively increased systemic uncertainty and price volatility. Meanwhile, financialisation entails a contradiction between speculative credit practices and the real economy that, taking different forms in specific instances, lies at the roots of contemporary systemic financial crises. The reality of the market-reinforcing multilateralism is that it serves only to perpetuate a highly speculative, uncertain and contradictory order that, like a punch-drunk boxer, necessarily lurches from one major crisis to another.

Conclusions

Framed by an Historical IPE approach and informed by comparative inquiry across previous modern world financial orders, we have sought to ask whether the contemporary order is characterised by relative stability, to account for the major crises that have marked the order, and to analyse the formal institutions of governance that contribute the order's reproduction through the management of credit practices. Decentralisation between New York, London and Tokyo has not proved to be a structural impediment to the forging of emerging relative stability in the contemporary financial order. While no single WFC stands as a complex of governance as had been the case in previous world financial orders, the power relations and credit practices of contemporary world finance are accepted as legitimate. The social forces of both New York and London have been to the fore in the forging of relative stability, based upon neo-liberal organisational principles of governance and grounded in epistemic authority itself derived from the competitive success of Anglo-American market institutions. Important in this respect has been the manner in which dominant explanations of the Asian crisis have served to dispel any remaining doubts as to the competitive weakness of Japanese finance, thereby undermining potential and actual objections to the neo-liberal organisation of credit practices. In terms of the interweaving of the coalition of state and social forces involved, relative stability does, however, remain narrow and somewhat fragile. The neo-liberal acceptance of the contemporary financial order is limited, in the main, to the transnational financial community that share a rather minimal perceived interest in preventing its collapse. Contestation as to the appropriate organisation of credit practices in any elemental sense becomes marginalised by a governance discourse that, through the reification of the market mechanism as the rational and natural institutional loci for governance, obscures the subjective, collective, hierarchical and speculative nature of contemporary practices.

Given their importance as moments in the reproduction or otherwise of world financial orders, it is not surprising that the orthodox explanation of the major crises that have dogged contemporary world finance concurs with the forging of relative stability around neo-liberal organisational principles. Misguided domestic policies and/or institutional arrangements are held to have been the principal causal factors in all major crises, viewed as hampering the capacity of marketised world credit practices to rationally determine exchange rates and recycle capital. Yet contrary to this orthodoxy, contemporary crises can be understood as the immediate outcome of shifts in the collective market sentiment that frames world credit practices. As such, contemporary crises do not essentially depart from the pattern of speculative excess, distress, panic and crash that, driven by changes to shared meanings, have marked financial crises throughout modern world finance. The conjunctural distinctiveness of current crises is grounded in the financialisation of contemporary credit practices. The high frequency of crises reflects financialisation, as the speculative accumulation of capital through credit practices themselves rests upon perceptions of on-going and successive opportunities presented by one type of asset or another. Meanwhile, financialisation also entails a highly significant structural contradiction that lies at the roots of major financial crises. Social, political and institutional embedded forces ensure that the real economy is not able to consistently meet those obligations, arising from speculative world credit practices, which assume the commodification of socio-economic relations. Appearing differently in specific crises, the contradiction surfaces and becomes realised in the distress and panic of collective market sentiment.

In the absence of a single WFC as a complex of governance, the current formal reproduction of world finance has no single fulcrum but takes largely unprecedented institutional forms. The present growth of market authority reflects and rests upon neo-liberal organisational principles of governance. It also contrasts sharply with the state-based governance of the American financial order and is suggestive of several parallels with the Dutch and British orders. What differentiates the current formal governance arrangements in world finance are the unparalleled developments that we have termed transnational multilateralism. A fragmentation in the management of credit practices that might have been expected to accompany decentralisation has failed to materialise, compensated for by the transnationalisation of the hierarchical market institutional networks that are anchored across the world's financial centres. Interdependent with this transnationalisation are complex multilateral initiatives in regulation and crisis management. Such initiatives, often taken in the wake of major crises and the high-profile failures of market institutions, are broader in scope and institutionalised to a greater degree than the *ad hoc* inter-state co-operation that contributed to the structure of governance in the Dutch and British financial orders. The market-reinforcing standards for self-regulation and supervision and the IMF-centred crisis-management arrangements that have emerged from complex multilateral initiatives have been further entrenched recently with the construction of the so-called new international financial architecture.

The foregoing understanding of relative stability, crises and authority in contemporary world finance illustrates the utility of the notion of a structure of governance for facilitating consideration of the propensity for financial orders to be reproduced. Attention is drawn to the intersection of the informal and formal or epistemic and institutional aspects of social relationships of authority, the standing of WFCs as complexes of governance, and the manner in which authority relationships relate to the underlying structure of power and the organisation of credit practices. Four significant differences mark out our analysis from current IPE inquiry.

First and as with our inquiry across previous social orders, relative stability has been used not to mean the absence of volatility in price and capital movements, but in social and political terms as indicating acceptance of power relations and the organisation of credit practices in which they are manifest. The effect is to offer a diachronic as opposed to synchronic understanding of stability. Such an understanding enables us to account for the reproduction of contemporary world finance in political as well as technical-functional terms.

Second, much of the current IPE inquiry represents contemporary world financial governance as a victory for the authority of market institutions over state institutions. While not denying this shift in the governance responsibilities of state and market, we have suggested that new forms of transnational market authority have been interdependent with complex multilateral initiatives in regulation and crisis management.

Third, our incorporation of WFCs as complexes of governance in the analysis of the reproduction of world finance has realised some important insights into the contemporary financial order. Grounded in the perceived competitive success of their market institutions, the epistemic authority of the social forces of New York and London can be seen to have placed them at the fore in the forging of relative stability. At the same time, the historically unparalleled absence of a single complex of governance in the relatively stable contemporary financial order provides the principal conjunctural structural conditions that have framed the emergence of the institutions of transnational multilateralism.

Finally, our account suggests that, as it is currently constituted, the contemporary financial order is fragile and beset with significant contradictions and tensions. Contrary to the interpretations offered by mainstream economists and orthodox IPE scholars in particular, increased multilateral co-operation perpetuates rather than alleviates the volatility and inherent crisis-tendencies of contemporary world finance.

Notes

1 This is not to say that relative stability has emerged throughout the wider world order on the basis of neo-liberal principles of governance. For instance, in terms of the environment, there is extensive contestation as to the appropriate organisation of social practices. Considerable disagreement continues over the merits or otherwise of a neo-liberal structure of environmental governance, with proponents of an alternative liberal internationalist discourse offering a coherent alternative (Langley 2001). On the contemporary juxtaposition of neo-liberal and liberal internationalist visions of global governance, see Murphy (1994).

2 The main principles of the consensus have not gone unchallenged or remained static in recent years. For instance, the tenets of the consensus arguably expanded during the 1990s with the World Bank's prescriptions of so-called 'good governance' which includes the promotion of western-style democracy, judiciary, accountability, transparency and, most ambitiously, civil society (Weiss 2000: 801). Despite these challenges and changes, neo-liberal organisational principles of financial governance remain at the heart of the consensus (Broad and Cavanagh 2000).

3 'According to market fundamentalism, all social activities should be looked at as transactional, contract-based relationships and valued in terms of a single common denominator, money' (Soros 1998: xxvi).

4 An opposing view has been put forward by Higgott and Phillips (2000: 360) who argue that 'the recent financial crises, and responses to them in Asia and Latin America, represent less the final triumph of liberalism in a post-Cold War era than a further spur to rethinking significant aspects of the neoliberal project'. However, such an interpretation would seem misleading in two important respects. First, it overstates the extent to which acceptance of the organisation of world credit practices based upon neo-liberal principles of governance included the state and societal forces of Latin America and newly-industrialising Asia in the first place. Second, as Higgott and Phillips (2000: 361) themselves note, any 'transition is evolving rather than settled . . . contested in a range

of quarters' and, as such, may ultimately lead in the further entrenchment of a neo-liberal structure of governance.

5 The 'new economy' represented a (misguided) belief that the defeat of inflationary pressures, the liberalisation and globalisation of the world economy, corporate restructuring and, most importantly, the wave of growth brought about by the information technology revolution had combined to render a cyclical economic downturn impossible. While particularly prevalent in the US in the latter half of the 1990s, reflected in the booming price levels of 'tech-stocks' listed on NASDAQ, the belief did spread to Europe and Japan, finding expression in the so-called 'dot.com' bubble. The bubble burst in mid-2000, leaving the various gurus of the new economy looking rather foolish. On the similarities between the new economy and the 'new era ideology' of 1920s America, see Chancellor (2000: 229–32).

6 On the relationship between everyday saving and borrowing practices and contemporary world credit practices more broadly, see Amoore and Langley (forthcoming).

7 'While the hyperliberal model reasserts the separation of state and economy, the alternative state form that some see as capable of renewed capitalist development promotes a fusion of state and economy. The state-capitalist path may take several forms all according to different national positions within the world economy and different institutional structures and ideologies. The common thread lies in a recognition of the indispensable guiding role of the state in the development of the nation's productive forces' (Cox 1991/1996: 201).

8 <www.nyse.com/speech/NT00019962.html>

9 Not surprisingly, the response from orthodox circles to such an understanding has been to reassert the rationality of the market mechanism. For instance, this was apparent in the comments made by US Federal Reserve Chairman Alan Greenspan to the US House of Representatives in the wake of the 1998 failure and bailout of LTCM (de Goede 2001: 161–2). Greenspan voiced the belief that arbitrage practices were not subjective speculation, but the rational pursuit of asset prices that temporarily did not reflect 'fundamental values' and, therefore, contributed to the determination of prices and make it possible for the market to clear.

10 On the role of secondary trading practices in preventing 'back sliding', that is, a deviation by states or corporations from economistic criteria, I am indebted to the insights provided by a former IMF economist, confidential interview, London, 3 June 1998.

11 Figures from Institute for International Finance, reprinted in *Financial Times*, Survey: World Economy and Finance, 2 October 1998, p. vi.

12 Figures from Institute for International Finance, reprinted in *Financial Times*, Survey: World Economy and Finance, 2 October 1998, p. vi.

13 An important caveat must be added to the view that the authority of central banks has declined in the contemporary financial order. The loss of authority *vis-à-vis* market institutions has been partially offset by the new found 'independence' of central banks from state finance ministries, a unique position from which they legitimately seek to guarantee sound money and price stability (Maxfield 1997b; Dyson *et al.* 1998).

14 Open market operations are concerned with the manipulation of liquidity in response to monetary policy targets. As Germain (1997: 153) summarises, 'If a central bank is concerned with an over hasty expansion of the money supply, it sells government bonds from within its own portfolio, thereby reducing the immediately available funds which banks and other financial sector firms have to lend to their clients. To pump liquidity into the system, a central bank need only to buy discounted bonds offered on the market (or encourage them to be put up for sale), thereby increasing the availability of cash to monetary agents for lending and other uses'.

15 Since 1975, the annual meetings of the G-7 heads of state have been an important mechanism for efforts to strategically manage the world economy, especially through the co-ordination of macroeconomic policies. The G-7 state-societies are America, UK, Japan, Germany, France, Canada and Italy. They were joined by Russia in 1998 to form

the G-8. Since the early 1980s and alongside the annual meetings, central bank and treasury officials have met regularly to address financial and monetary issues.

16 'Multilateralism' has been used in a state-centric manner by orthodox IPE scholars that favour a liberal institutionalist approach to refer to 'the practice of co-ordinating national policies in groups of three or more states, through *ad hoc* arrangements or by means of institutions' (Keohane 1990, in Cox 1997: xvii). Although adding a concern with norms and organisational principles, this state-centricism is maintained by constructivist approaches. For instance, Ruggie (1993: 11 [my emphasis]) casts multilateralism as 'an institutional form that co-ordinates relations among three or more states *on the basis on generalized principles of conduct*'. Such state-centric notions are inadequate in the current era of transnational relations (cf. Risse-Kappen 1995), where civil associations such as the International Primary Market Association, the International Securities Markets Association, and the International Federation of Stock Exchanges occupy governance roles (Filipović 1997). The notion of complex multilateralism is clearly an attempt to capture the distinctive practices of contemporary global governance. Furthermore, my notion of 'transnational multilateralism' reflects a concern not simply with the changing practices of multilateralism, but with the interdependent relationships between these and changes to market institutions in the structure of financial governance.

17 'Capital adequacy for securities firms is similar in principle to capital reserves for international banks, but there are important differences. For banks, the main concern is with the creditworthiness of their loan portfolios and clients, and off-balance sheet activities are converted into the equivalent of loan risks according to the Basle Accord. In contrast, for the most part risk in the securities sector is related to the firm's *position* in the market, called "position" or "market risk"' (Underhill 1997b: 33). Such 'positions' in the market result from securities firms holding their own portfolio of equities that are subject to price fluctuations.

18 On this point I am indebted to the insights provided by a representative of the British Bankers' Association, confidential interview, London, 3 June 1998.

19 Despite restructuring, national regulatory institutions remain remarkably diverse. For instance, after several periods of reform in the contemporary era, the UK arrived at the creation of a single regulatory body in 2000, the Financial Services Authority (FSA). This contrasts with the tendency in Europe for a separate institution to regulate capital and equity market practices, such as the French Commission des Bourses (COB).

20 For more on this distinction, see Chapter 2, note 3.

21 Organised under the auspices of the regular meetings of the G-7 finance ministers, the G-20 brings together finance ministers and central bankers from Argentina, Australia, Brazil, China, India, Indonesia, Mexico, Russia, Saudi Arabia, South Africa, South Korea and Turkey, together with their G-7 counterparts and a peer from the European Union. The reports produced by the G-20 are available from the IMF website.

22 <www.nyse.com/speech/NT00019962.html>

23 <www.fsforum.org>

24 See *The Economist*, 'Lenses of last resort', 6 June 1998, p. 104.

Conclusion

> An option for change rather than preservation of the status quo is dictated more by dissatisfaction with the prevailing order and hope for improvement than by any blueprint for an alternative society. It may arise from scepticism that prevailing political and economic mechanisms will satisfy human needs in a manner that is safe for both individuals and the fabric of society as a whole. It is likely to be driven by a sense of injustice and a hope for greater equity in the distribution of physical necessities and the diffusion of social power. In the minds of those who opt for change, the solution will most likely be seen as lying not so much in the enactment of a specific policy program as in the building of new means of collective action informed by a new understanding of society and polity.
>
> (Cox 1987: 393–4)

At the outset of this book, I indicated that my purpose was principally three-fold. First, to confront the dual problematic that emerges as we seek to apprehend contemporary world finance, that is, the uncertain structural transformation of 'global finance' and the predominance of the neo-liberal mode of knowledge of transformation. The common sense, neo-liberal knowledge of world finance is de-politicised, teleological and exclusionary in nature. It forestalls attempts to consider the social and political bases and consequences of change, and possible alternatives. Second, to look to the field of IPE as an avenue from which to construct an alternative mode of knowledge that (re)socialises and (re)politicises world finance. I have sought to support the efforts of new IPE scholars to delineate their inquiries from those of their orthodox peers who continue to maintain a close affiliation to the main tenets of neo-liberal political economy. In particular, I have argued for and developed an Historical IPE approach that, by disputing the claims of orthodox IPE as to its focus for inquiry and the knowledge that it accepts as legitimate, provides a robust alternative to neo-liberal political economy. Third and underpinning the first two, to offer, in Cox's terms, 'a new understanding' of contemporary world finance that could inform present and future political action to at least forestall its worst consequences. In these terms, an Historical IPE approach would appear particularly apposite. By explicitly recognising the connection between human action, knowledge and reflection, an Historical IPE holds the potential of a transformative form of knowledge that reflects an emancipatory commitment to challenge a dominant mode of knowledge.

It would seem tempting here to 'close out' inquiry by offering a simple restatement of the arguments already made, returning to the conclusions reached in the preceding chapters. Based on the Historical IPE knowledge of contemporary world finance that has been developed, however, the purpose of this conclusion is to briefly reflect upon the 'opening up' of possibilities for progressive change. Reference to our historical understanding of contemporary world finance will ensure that these reflections are not utopian in nature. Our interest does not lie in the technical merits or otherwise of competing blueprints for progressive change, but in the political possibilities of the collective action that is necessary to achieve change.

On political possibilities

By virtue of constructing an alternative to the prevailing neo-liberal mode of knowledge of the contemporary restructuring of world finance, understanding continuity and change has been to the forefront of our inquiry. Indeed, the Historical IPE approach taken has developed and utilised the categories of social change and social time for this very reason. Modern world finance has been shown to have been subject to three principal and related sets of qualitative structural change. Not only does the identification of these sets of change contrast with the teleological and naturalised reading put forward by neo-liberal political economy but, at the same time, an Historical IPE approach leads to significant innovation in terms of the conceptions of world financial restructuring present in IPE inquiry.

First, world credit practices, both across and within successive world financial orders, have been shown to take different synchronic forms. Despite modern assumptions of rationality and reason, the credit instruments employed and patterns of institutionalisation vary considerably throughout modern world finance. In each world financial order, the conjuncturally predominant forms of credit practices have been centralised in successive WFCs as key social spaces. Such identification of change in terms of credit practices contrasts with the tendency in orthodox IPE in particular to focus, *à la* neo-liberalism, on international capital flows. International capital flows are deemed to function largely automatically as a result of the autonomous logic of the market. The concern of an Historical IPE with credit practices brings international flows into relief as arising from the intersection of human agents and mutable social structures.

Second, the diachronic making and unravelling of successive world financial orders has been shown to lead to discrete and qualitatively different orders. Difference has been accounted for in terms of conjunctural configurations of power relations, tensions and contradictions, and conditions in the wider world order which, taken together, frame the possible organisation of credit practices. While the social forces of the primary WFCs have tended to be to the fore in shaping the contours of world financial orders, the American financial order illustrated that this is not always and necessarily the case. The conceptualisation of diachronic change offered contrasts with the inclination present in much existing IPE scholarship to focus on the rise and fall of states' wealth and power. It has been argued throughout that state power is not the sole explanatory factor, but a significant part of what is to be understood as part and parcel of an account of hierarchical social orders. As a result and by way of illustration, both the Dutch and British financial orders were shown to have retained their broad structural distinctiveness for several decades after the predominance of the Dutch and British states had reached their respective zeniths. Meanwhile, the restructuring of credit practices in the contemporary order has been traced to unprecedented change in the nature of power in modern world finance.

Third, relative stability and the reproduction of successive financial orders has been shown to entail considerable variation in terms of the epistemic and institutionalised authority that constitutes successive structures of governance. Periods of relative stability have been a matter for social and political construction, forged around distinct organisational principles or discourses of governance. At the same time, the governance role of market, civil and state institutions has waxed and waned and taken various forms. While WFCs have tended to stand as key complexes of governance, the experience of the American financial order shows that structures of governance in which WFCs occupy a subordinated role are possible. The understanding developed of change in world financial governance contrasts quite markedly with that offered by current IPE research which tends to concentrate somewhat narrowly on the shifting balance between state and market authority. By virtue of accounting for their development in the context of successive financial orders, structures of governance are grasped in diachronic and political as well as synchronic and functional terms by an Historical IPE. Furthermore, state and market authority is viewed as interdependent rather than necessarily opposed. An Historical IPE also draws attention to the manner in which epistemic and institutionalised authority comes together in successive WFCs, and the extent to which changeable structures of governance may contain contradictions that are important to the unravelling of financial orders.

It is in the light of our historical understanding of change in modern world finance, then, that we can begin to reflect upon the political possibilities for progressive change in the contemporary financial order. It is worth noting before we proceed that, as Chin and Mittelman (2000) stress, an assessment of actual and potential action for change is necessarily influenced by the manner in which resistance in an existing order is conceptualised. We seek here to move in support of collective political actions that, sharing our emancipatory commitment to address the malign consequences of the contemporary financial order, seek to open up alternatives in all their forms. Therefore, and following Chin and Mittelman's (2000) insightful work, we employ a broad conceptualisation of resistance that does not lead us to omit political possibilities according to the form or strategy taken by collective action, the agents involved, or the levels and sites of resistance. Such a broad and open approach is particularly pertinent given the tendency for resistance within the contemporary financial order to be relatively embryonic by comparison with oppositions to free trade and multinational corporations (cf. Roberts 1998: 129–31). So, are the conditions ripe for progressive change in the contemporary financial order? We consider political possibilities here in terms of each of the three principal and related sets of change that we have identified across modern world finance.

Transforming credit practices

As the neo-liberal representation of contemporary world credit practices as 'global finance' implies, the present restructuring of credit practices has been characterised by marketisation. 'Global finance' remains, however, a misleading representation of restructuring in many important respects. As Chapter 5 made clear, part and parcel of marketisation has been important qualitative changes to credit practices that include disintermediation, financialisation and the emergence of unprecedented spatial forms. While disintermediated practices undertaken primarily in offshore space may be predominant, credit practices that take the form of loan practices institutionalised within commercial banks also persist. The incomplete process of disintermediation has been revealed during the contemporary financial order by the changing position of London as the world's principal centre for loan practices. While London has retained its position at the apex of the hierarchy, its overall share of world-scale loan practices has fallen over the past two decades. The synchronic variation in contemporary practices revealed by the uneven nature of disintermediation is important in that it illustrates that alternatives to the prevailing form of practices remain politically possible (cf. Pollin 1995).

At the same time, the generalised financialisation of world credit practices, that is, the manner in which practices are subject or respond to speculative motivations to varying degrees but to almost universal extent, is perhaps of even greater political significance. Recognition of the financialisation of credit practices provides a basis for the discursive contestation of neo-liberal explanations of contemporary world finance. Such contestation is given particular political impetus in the course of major financial crises, as the contradictions of financialisation surface amid the distress and panic of subjective and volatile market sentiment. Popular awareness of the speculative nature of contemporary world credit practices and the detrimental implications for both long-term productive investment and exchange rate stability has become widespread (Helleiner 1996). This is especially the case in the so-called emerging market state-societies that have borne the brunt of the crisis-tendencies of contemporary world finance.

Given the propensity for practices to defy competitive pressures for convergence around a predominant form, but also in the light of awareness of the speculative character of current world credit practices, collective political action has either sought to reconfigure current practices or to consciously develop alternatives. The former has focused primarily on so-called 'ethical investment', while the latter has concentrated on constructing sub-national credit practices. Following Chin and Mittelman (2000: 35–6), this type of resistance within the contemporary financial order can be represented as the politics of 'submerged networks', that is, collective action that seeks to build upon everyday consumption practices in order to further values that challenge the economism of neo-liberal political economy. In broad normative terms, investment and credit creation are viewed as prioritising social and environmental concerns over narrow economic considerations.

As a course of collective action, ethical investment emerges dialectically from disintermediation. While at a world-scale we have associated disintermediation with the growing importance of institutional investors, their rising profile has rested on the restructuring of the everyday saving practices of individuals and families. Everyday saving in Anglo-American political economies in particular is now much less likely to take the form of deposits held with commercial banks, while public 'pay-as-you-go' pension provision has become increasingly supplemented by contributions to private and occupational pension schemes. In terms of the growth of private and occupational pensions and with reference to the traditional socialist commitment to the ownership of the means of production by workers, Drucker (1976) describes this shift in everyday saving practices and the broader social ownership of assets that ensues as the 'unseen revolution'. Collective action under the banner of ethical investment seeks, then, to exploit the opportunity offered by this change in ownership in order to reconfigure capital investment practices. In Pollin's (1995: 29) terms, broad-based social ownership could provide a starting point from which to replace an 'elite-voice' with a 'democratic-voice' in investment decision-making.

Ethical investment is that which avoids funding activities that are deemed socially and environmentally unacceptable (Minns 1996b: 56). It draws upon the legacy of many civic associations, most notably churches and universities, that have sought for much of modern world finance to avoid investments in, for example, the production of alcohol (cf. Visser and MacIntosh 1998). Over the last three decades or so, ethical investment practices have grown in significance. While initially carried forward through separate ethical investment institutions, most major institutional investors, fund managers and banks now have specific ethical investment schemes. Such schemes claim to 'screen' investments according to various ethical criteria without necessarily sacrificing returns on investment over the medium and long term. At the same time, ethical stock market indices, such as FTSE4Good that was launched in London in July 2001, are coming to support ethical investment practices.[1]

Several drawbacks mark the political potential of ethical investment as it is currently constituted. First, by its nature, ethical investment is only open to those individuals and families in the developed world that are either able to save significant amounts or enjoy the security of an occupational pension. As such it does little to address the exclusionary nature of many contemporary financial arrangements (cf. Leyshon and Thrift 1995). Second, the extent to which the major market institutional networks are coming to dominate ethical investment clearly undercuts its efficacy as a form of collective action. For instance, while a fund management institution such as the London-centred Jupiter Tyndall may offer a specialist ethical fund, this does not mean that all its investment practices are necessarily subject to ethical screening. Ethical investment services become a financial service like any other, one that is taken up by a relatively small number of customers. Third and related, as the major market institutional networks come to dominate, they also come to occupy a pivotal position in determining the criteria that define what practices are regarded as 'ethical'. As I have argued elsewhere, such marketisation of authority in relation to understandings of the environment tends to further a neo-liberal explanation that seeks solutions in further commodification (i.e. the 'internalising' of environmental 'externalities' in neo-classical terms) (Langley 2001). Such commodification is a key part of the problem of environmental degradation, not part of the solution (Bernard 1997: 84–5). Finally and underpinning the previous two, a highly significant drawback arises from the yawning gap that currently stands between collective social ownership on the one hand, and control over investment decisions on the other. As Minns (1996b: 43) notes in relation to occupational pensions, so-called 'policy holders' generally have little or no control over investment 'policy'. This leads Minns (1996b) to put together a range of state-based regulatory proposals for UK occupational pensions including legally enforceable investment guidelines, employee control through the creation of investment committees, and a single national fund for public sector employees. Taken together, such proposals undertaken multilaterally would be necessary if ethical investment as a means of collective action is to advance democratic-voice and successfully reconfigure contemporary credit practices.

Sub-national credit practices have generated considerable interest among social scientists and activists as a means of collective action that establishes alternatives to world credit practices. While it may be fair to say that in some instances the establishment of local credit practices has been undertaken by people who are excluded from formal financial market structures, the majority of action has been taken by those who consciously seek social change amid the tensions engendered by financialisation (Pacione 1997). Promises to pay arising from contemporary world credit practices indirectly reach into the nooks and crannies of socio-economic life in developed state-societies in particular, carrying with them financialised assumptions of commodification (Lee 1999: 213). Socio-economic practices embedded in social and environmental concerns require, then, alternative credit practices that 'short circuit' pressures for commodification (Douthwaite 1996). Informed not so much by Marxist, economic nationalist or social democratic thought but by and large by ecological political economy, such alternative practices are deemed to be best undertaken at a local scale (Helleiner 1998). This follows from the emphasis placed by ecological political economy on the inherent social and environmental sustainability of local socio-economic relations (cf. Schumacher 1973). National level strategies are held as unable to be genuinely democratic and responsive to local needs. The suggested sub-national focus for contemporary collective action to create alternative credit practices is given further credence by the extent to which national currencies have become enmeshed in world credit practices.

Collective action to undertake sub-national credit practices in contemporary times has led to a wide range of initiatives. These have included various associational savings and loans schemes for low status groups such as micro-credits (Yunis's Grameenbank system), credit unions, local currencies and the 'scriptual' or 'book money' – that is, bookkeeping entries of debits and credits (Braudel 1984: 470) – that underpin Local Economic Trading Systems (LETS). In some rare instances, such as the Ithaca Hours used by businesses, farmers and consumers in upstate New York, sub-national practices have led to the creation of a physical paper currency. More commonly, local book monies are denominated in their respective national currencies or notional currencies (e.g. 'Readies' in Reading, 'Bricks' in Brixton) but are not convertible and are solely for local investment and exchange. The names given to alternative credit practices and their notional currencies often seek to symbolise the 'alternative morality' (Thrift and Leyshon 1999) upon which they are based. For instance, Edgar Khan's 'Time Dollars' scheme avoids the value of labour altogether by facilitating the exchange of services purely on a time basis (cf. Boyle 2000). All sub-national credit practices tend to be accompanied by information networks that comprise regular newsletters and meetings.

It seems clear that in numerous (admittedly small-scale) instances, sub-national credit practices have proved successful in facilitating local socio-economic relations that stand against the pressures of commodification. Sub-national credit practices have also tended to disproportionately involve the unemployed and low-income families (Seyfang 2000; Lee 1999). Arguably, such inclusion goes beyond a simple alternative to financial exclusion in the sense that people's worth is re-cast amid the communitarian morality that underpins sub-national credit practices. The caring and household work that is often represented as 'women's work' has also been given value, placed on a par with 'men's work' that is already valued by the formal market (Hutchinson *et al.* forthcoming). Furthermore, as a counter-movement in the contemporary financial order, the rather disparate and somewhat disjointed submerged networks are bound together by a shared consciousness, summarised in the popular admonition to 'think globally, act locally', that challenges the neo-liberal mode of knowledge (Helleiner 1998). Yet there remains the danger that rather than providing an alternative that facilitates sustainable local socio-economic relations, sub-national credit practices simply facilitate relations that are currently not supported by formal financial market practices. Advocates of sub-national credit practices have recognised this, referring, for instance, to the 'complementary' and 'supplementary' currencies in which practices are denominated (Seyfang 2000). Only a small share of the socio-economic relations of participants in sub-national credit practices are enabled by these alternative arrangements, around 10 per cent according to one UK study (Williams 1996). Meanwhile, LETS and other local arrangements can become merely a 'policy tool' for those state managers seeking to address pockets of social exclusion. As one form of collective action that seeks to address the detrimental consequences of contemporary world credit practices, then, the creation of sub-national credit practices needs, in the first instance, to address its own shortcomings in order to further its undoubted potential.

Transforming financial regulation

In addition to change within and across credit practices, modern world finance has been marked by shifting patterns of power relations, tensions and contradictions, and conditions in the wider world order that have framed the diachronic making and unravelling of qualitatively different world financial orders. As Chapter 6 stressed, the contemporary financial order has been marked by an unprecedented structure of power. Given the transformation of material power relations associated with the emergence of offshore space and also the multi-polarity of the current world economy, the tendency for the state and societal forces of an ascendant WFC to frame the making of world financial orders has been displaced. The social forces of the long-established WFCs of New York and London, rather than those of recently ascendant Tokyo, have been to the fore in shaping the possible organisation of contemporary credit practices. Crucial to carrying forward the marketisation, disintermediation and changing institutionalisation of current practices has been a US-initiated and London-supported competitive liberalisation and de-regulation dynamic. This dynamic has been reinforced by conditions in the wider world order that intensify competitive pressures.

It is perhaps not surprising, then, that actual and prospective collective political action to address the worst eventualities of contemporary world finance often tend to focus on the prospects of re-regulation. Regulation stands as the totem pole for many who seek the controlled unravelling of the contemporary financial order and the making of a new order. Such collective action is united by a growing awareness that highly marketised world credit practices severely constrain national policy-making in terms of monetary, fiscal, tax and regulatory policies and, for underdeveloped state-societies in particular, punish development strategies that back-slide from those prescribed by the Washington consensus (Helleiner 1996; Bello *et al.* 2000). Such discursive contestation of the neo-liberal mode of knowledge of contemporary finance is given particular normative weight by the common perception that the bond market rather than the ballot box now determines state governments' policy preferences, institutionally manifest in the new-found 'independence' of central banks. As Eatwell and Taylor (2000: xiii) observe, 'Without regulatory structures in place, democratic authorities lose all control of the financial side of the economy.' There is a contradiction, then, between liberal democracy on the one hand, and the neo-liberal reading of contemporary world finance as an objective and natural reality to which national policy-makers must rationally respond on the other.

Collective action in terms of re-regulation seeks to take advantage of the political space offered by this contradiction. Three broad variations are prescribed. First, collective action seeks to work towards the regulation of speculative short-term foreign exchange trading in particular. This has followed largely in the wake of the proposals made by Tobin (1978). Tobin sought to 'throw sand in the wheels' of contemporary world finance by putting in place a 0.05 per cent tax on all foreign exchange transactions. Proponents of a 'Tobin tax' or similar proposals based on Tobin's initial foray argue that such regulation would, in addition to reducing exchange rate volatility, minimise the extent to which national monetary policies are based upon defending the value of the national currency. It would also generate revenues for progressive social investment at a world-scale (Jetin and de Brunhof 2000: 199–201). The political possibilities of achieving a 'Tobin tax' or similar proposals may not be as far-fetched as they first sound. Alongside considerable support in civil society from academics and non-governmental organisations (NGOs),

French, Australian and Canadian governments have at different times expressed interest in the Tobin-style regulation of speculation (Helleiner 1996). Implementation is clearly feasible. Supporters cogently argue that a Tobin tax could be enforced through the expansion of either the existing electronic arrangements for the surveillance of money laundering (Malhotra 2000: 56–7) or the electronic settlements systems (Schmidt 2000).

Second, collective action in terms of re-regulation focuses upon what might be termed 'global Keynesianism' (Bello *et al.* 2000: 19), that is, building co-operative capital controls reminiscent of those proposed by Keynes at the Bretton Woods negotiations. Rather than a Tobin-style tax to throw sand in the wheels, the global Keynesian approach seeks to reverse the structural transformation of contemporary world finance with large regulatory boulders. The starting assumption here is that, given the liberalisation and deregulation dynamic and the conditions in the wider world order that intensify competitive pressures, 'any effort to reverse financial liberalisation must be co-operative' (Helleiner 1996: 202). Unilateral restrictions on capital alone are unlikely to be sufficient (Griffith-Jones 1999: 420). The problems inherent to inter-state co-operation and the capacity of market institutions to move credit practices to offshore space(s) ensures that global Keynesianism often entails proposals for some kind of new supranational body or calls for the reform and extension of existing multilateral institutions. For instance, high-profile supporters of global Keynesianism Eatwell and Taylor (2000) offer the ideal-type blueprint of a 'World Financial Authority' to implement re-regulation. Commonly, multilateral institutions tend to be seen as needing to be beyond the control of any one state or group of states. In Eatwell's (1999) terms, what is needed is not simply the co-operation and co-ordination of existing multilateral initiatives, but public institutions capable of exercising some control.

Finally, collective action in terms of re-regulation is orientated toward installing a raft of unilateral regulations that will enable a state-society to withdraw from the world financial order (cf. Bello *et al.* 2000; Bienefeld 2000). The focus is primarily upon those underdeveloped state-societies that, while only partially integrated into the contemporary financial order, find that the current organisation of world credit practices severely constrains their socio-economic options. Essentially there is a recognition that financialisation encourages the qualitative ascendancy of economistic criteria and the prioritising of export sectors and policies to attract foreign capital. While the extensive use of unilateral capital controls in support of a more domestic-orientated approach to development is likely to lead to significant socio-economic hardship in the short-term, it is held to be a necessary feature of putting notions of sustainable development into practice.

Taken together, the various means of collective action that focus on re-regulation can be understood as 'territorialist' (Scholte 2000: 287) resistance in that it seeks to build on the potential authority of the territorial state in the institutionalisation of financial orders. The agenda here is the strengthening of the national political economy in the name of social democracy. Concentrating collective action on the regulatory potential of states, as the principal aggregations of political power and authority, clearly represents a viable option for the making of a new world financial order in both practical and discursive terms. Yet several drawbacks remain in terms of the political potential of collective action that focuses on re-regulation. The transnational financial community's response to the Asian crisis has effectively dissipated the calls for re-regulation that, at the time of the crisis, received considerable media attention. There currently appears little prospect that debates as to the potential use of Tobin-style taxes and capital controls will re-emerge in the popular consciousness, at least until the next major financial crisis. Neo-liberal representations of capital controls as technical devices that should be carefully dismantled in sequence with the strengthening of national financial arrangements continue to predominate. For those forces seeking to make a new financial order through the institutions of the territorial state, then, a future major crisis is once again likely to offer an opportunity to mobilise around an agenda that recognises the social and political significance of capital controls.

Territorialist calls for re-regulation often appear to hark back to the 'golden age' of the American financial order as the example of how world-scale credit practices institutionalised within market networks can be restricted in favour of national economic development. Talk among global Keynesians in particular is often of the need for 'a new Bretton Woods' that will address the balance between state and market authority in favour of the former. Throughout our account here we have stressed that the social and political foundations of world finance extend through and beyond the interdependent intersection of states and markets. What marked the American financial order in our terms was not simply increased state authority. Rather, a state-based structure of governance that sought to ensure that market networks played a subordinate but supportive role rested upon a specific configuration of state and societal forces in which the principal financiers were largely isolated. It was the unilateral maintenance of war time controls and US capital outflows, not a Keynesian system of co-operative capital controls and state-based creation of credit, that characterised the American financial order. Furthermore, as a regulatory and imaginary construct that emerged and became consolidated during the British and American financial orders, the national political economy has been partially eroded during the contemporary financial order. By implication, then, global Keynesian collective action to make a new financial order will clearly need to do far more than simply encourage co-operation based around the re-regulatory potential of states. The extensive re-regulation of contemporary world finance would also entail fundamental change in the wider world order if the edifice of the national political economy is to be rebuilt.

Transforming financial governance

Alongside qualitative change in both the forms taken by credit practices and the making of discrete world financial orders, throughout our account of modern world finance we have also stressed change in the bases of relative stability in, and reproduction of, successive orders. Chapter 7 showed that relative stability and the reproduction of the contemporary financial order has entailed a distinctive structure of epistemic and institutionalised authority. Acceptance of power relations and the organisation of credit practices in which they are manifest has been forged through the neo-liberal discourse of governance, itself grounded in the perceived competitive success of New York-centred and London-centred market networks. Dominant explanations of the major financial crises endemic to the contemporary order have buttressed the neo-liberal stability, viewing domestic policies and institutions, not world credit practices themselves, as the key causal factors. Relative stability only extends, however, to a narrow coalition of state and societal forces that comprises the transnational financial community. Meanwhile, and in the absence of a WFC as a single complex of governance, the formal reproduction of contemporary world finance has taken the largely unprecedented institutional forms that we have termed transnational multilateralism. This combines the authority of decentralised transnational market networks on the one hand with complex multilateral initiatives in regulation and crisis management on the other. As it is currently constituted, the structure of financial governance perpetuates a situation that might be termed 'turbulent stasis' (Cox 1999: 3): that is, the volatility and crisis-laden contradictions of world credit practices remain while there appears little prospect of a transformation of the contours of the world finance.

Potential and actual collective political action for transformation emerges dialectically from the structure of world financial governance. While the contemporary financial order is characterised by the relative stability that has been forged among the forces of the transnational financial community, the vast majority of people's experiences of world finance are in terms of marginalisation, coercion and disciplinary competitive pressures for commodification. There is a widespread awareness that the current structure of governance in general, and the complex multilateralism furthered through the IMF in particular, does little to alleviate and much to further the socially detrimental consequences of world finance (cf. Bond 2000). This provides the basis for contestation of the market-reinforcing qualities of complex multilateralism, combining critiques of the legitimacy of existing institutions and their policies and popular protests. Examples of the latter include anti-IMF riots in Venezuela in 1989, leaving over 300 people dead, and more recently in Argentina during July 2001. In short, as the institutions of complex multilateralism have come to play an increased role in world financial governance and consequently impact on the life chances of people to a much greater extent, the institutions themselves have become the focus for conscious political action.

As a course of collective action for transformation, that which focuses on the institutions of complex multilateralism can be conceptualised as the politics of a 'new multilateralism' (Cox 1997; O'Brien *et al.* 2000). 'New multilateralism' is the attempt to 'reconstitute civil societies and political authorities on a global scale, building a system of global governance from the bottom up' (Cox 1997: xxvii). Unlike those who have focused their collective action on the prospects of state-led re-regulation, proponents of new multilateralism hold that the democratic deficit present in existing governance arrangements cannot be adequately addressed by simply reinvigorating liberal democracy (cf. Held 1995). The neo-liberal policies of the principal states have been to the fore in carrying forward world economic and financial restructuring, institutionalised state-societal relationships have been re-articulated as part and parcel of the politics of economic slowdown so that there is considerable public cynicism with regard to politicians and state managers, and the national political economy has become interpenetrated by transnational financial and production networks with the result that the sovereignty of state institutions is undermined. In the light of such structural change, and despite the spread of liberal democracy throughout much of Africa, Latin America, Asia and Eastern Europe over the last few decades, liberal democracy is rendered somewhat hollow and largely unsubstantive (Gills 1996). It follows that the democratisation of world finance and the wider world order requires creating and strengthening participative linkages between civil society and formal institutions of governance, thereby addressing transnational issues and appealing to solidarities that cross state-societal borders (cf. Cox 1999; Scholte 2000: 277–80). In the complex multilateralism that prevails at present, a relative narrow group of financial interests and their civic associations dominate the linkages between civil society and the institutions of governance. Key to the democratisation of world finance for new multilateralism is collective action in the realm of civil society by social movements that will ultimately transform both the epistemic and formal governance of the contemporary financial order.

The Jubilee 2000 campaign arguably provides an example of the potential for substantive influence on the contours of world finance that resides within civil society. Jubilee 2000 campaigned for a one-off cancellation of the debts of the world's poorest state-societies as a fitting act to mark the turn of the millennium. Drawing together NGOs including charities, churches, trade unions, and business associations, the campaign enjoyed some albeit limited success in convincing the G-7 governments to provide debt relief for the so-called heavily indebted poor countries (HIPCs). By the end of 2000, 22 HIPCs were receiving relief on around a third of their outstanding debts. Despite the high profile achievement of Jubilee 2000, however, even those seeking to invigorate civil society recognise that, to date and in the main, increased encounters between multilateral institutions and social movements have only realised limited progressive change (O'Brien *et al.* 2000). While social movements may now enjoy greater official channels of pluralistic access to multilateral institutions, this has not tended to be accompanied by significant policy change. For instance, the growing remit of the IMF in the governance of the contemporary financial order has stimulated considerable opposition from labour, environmental and feminist social movements. Direct lobbying by these movements and indirect pressure through other multilateral institutions, governments and the mass media has also been accompanied by increased interaction between NGO representatives and the Fund's various departments. Only limited shifts in policy have followed, most notably in terms of the inclusion of some environmental and 'good governance' prescriptions within IMF conditionality, 'in part because the Fund has received constant countervailing endorsements from other civic circles' (O'Brien *et al.* 2000: 177). It remains revealing, by way of illustration, that HIPCs obligations to the IMF have remained largely untouched by Jubilee 2000 and its successor campaign Drop the Debt. As Scholte (2000: 279) as observed more generally, 'Much of the promise of global civil society is . . . yet unproven'. The challenge remains to bring together disparate civic associations that often hold contending particularistic interests into movements capable of transforming world financial governance.

Closing remarks

While our account of world finance suggests that the most powerful tendencies framing the future of the contemporary financial order favour the continuation of the status quo, this should not lead to defeatist pessimism. Armed with alternative modes of knowledge of contemporary world finance to that provided by neo-liberal political economy, we can begin to consider opportunities for, and move in support of collective action towards, a progressive transformation. The utility of an Historical IPE approach that builds in an innovative manner on the existing work of new IPE scholars is in this regard, I would contend, considerable. An Historical IPE challenges neo-liberalism head on in terms of its principal assumptions and common-sense knowledge claims. It offers a set of categories for reflection that, when employed, yield a robust understanding of contemporary world finance that brings into view its distinctive social and political bases. Furthermore, such an understanding reveals the dialectical possibilities for progressive transformation that arise from the contradictions and tensions present in contemporary world financial restructuring. Informed by an Historical IPE and carried forward through a wide range of collective action, then, transformation is not only desirable, but feasible. All forms of collective action do, of course, contain drawbacks, confront structural constraints, and encounter an unfavourable configuration of power relations at present. However, the reconfiguration of, or construction of alternatives to, current world credit practices, the reorientation of contemporary multilateralism through movements in civil society, and, most ambitiously, the controlled unravelling and making of a new financial order through state-led re-regulation are all possible. In particular, the major financial crises that will undoubtedly emerge over the coming years hold out the potential of disrupting the current configuration of forces and bringing fresh impetus to collective action. Contrary to the teleology of neo-liberal political economy, the future history of world finance is yet to be made.

Notes

1 *Observer*, 'Footsie takes a walk on the ethical side', Business and Society Supplement, 8 July 2001.

Bibliography

Aglietta, M. (2000) 'Shareholder value and corporate governance: a comment and some tricky questions', *Economy and Society* 29, 1: 146–59.

Agnew, J. (1994) 'The territorial trap: the geographical assumptions of International Relations Theory', *Review of International Political Economy* 1, 1: 53–80.

Agnew, J. and Corbridge, S. (1995) *Mastering Space: Hegemony, Territory and International Political Economy*, London: Routledge.

Albert, M. (1993) *Capitalism against Capitalism*, London: Whurr.

Allen, R.E. (1994) *Financial Crises and Recession in the Global Economy*, Aldershot: Elgar.

Altvater, E. (1997) 'Financial crises on the threshold of the 21st century', in L. Panitch (ed.) *Socialist Register – Ruthless Criticism of All That Exists*, Suffolk: Merlin.

Amin, A. and Palan, R. (1996) Theme: 'Historizing International Political Economy', editorial: 'The need to historicize International Political Economy', *Review of International Political Economy* 3, 2: 209–15.

Amin, S. (1996) 'The challenge of globalization', *Review of International Political Economy* 3, 2: 216–59.

Amoore, L. and Langley, P. (forthcoming) 'Process, project, practice: the politics of globalisation', in J. Abbott (ed.) *Critical Perspectives on International Political Economy*, Basingstoke and New York: Palgrave.

Amoore, L., Dodgson, R., Gills, B.K., Langley, P., Marshall, D. and Watson, I. (1997) 'Overturning "globalisation": resisting the teleological, reclaiming the "political"', *New Political Economy* 2, 1: 179–95.

Amoore, L., Dodgson, R., Germain, R.D., Gills, B.K., Langley, P. and Watson, I. (2000) 'Paths to a historicized International Political Economy', *Review of International Political Economy* 7, 1: 53–72.

Anderson, P. (1987) 'The figures of descent', *New Left Review* 161: 20–77.

Andrews, D.M. (1994) 'Capital mobility and state autonomy: toward a structural theory of International Monetary Relations', *International Studies Quarterly* 38, 1: 193–218.

Ankersmit, F.R. (1995) 'Historicism: an attempt at synthesis, forum: the meaning of historicism and its relevance for contemporary theory', *History and Theory* 34, 2: 143–61.

Arrighi, G. (1994) *The Long Twentieth Century: Money, Power and the Origins of Our Times*, London: Verso.

Augelli, E. and Murphy, C.N. (1993) 'Gramsci and International Relations: a general perspective and example from recent US policy toward the Third World', in S. Gill (ed.) *Gramsci, Historical Materialism and International Relations*, Cambridge: Cambridge University Press.

Bagehot, W. (1873/1991) *Lombard Street: A Description of the Money Market*, Philadelphia, PA: Orion Editions (first published New York: Scriber, Armstrong and Co.).

Baker, A. (1999) '*Nébuleuse* and the "internationalization of the state" in the UK? The case of HM Treasury and the Bank of England', *Review of International Political Economy* 6, 1: 79–100.

Bank of International Settlements (1996) *Central Bank Survey of Foreign Exchange and Derivatives Market Activity 1995*, Basel: Bank of International Settlements.

—— (1999a) *Central Bank Survey of Foreign Exchange and Derivatives Market Activity 1998*, Basel: Bank of International Settlements.

—— (1999b) *Comments on the Reports on the International Financial Architecture*, August, Bank of International Settlements website.

—— (2001) *The New Basel Capital Accord: An Explanatory Note*, Secretariat of the Basel Committee on Banking Supervision, Basel: Bank of International Settlements.

Barbour, V. (1963) *Capitalism in Amsterdam in the Seventeenth Century*, Michigan: Ann Arbour.

Bareau, P. (1979) 'International money and capital markets', in E. Victor Morgan, R.A. Brealey, B.S. Yamey and P. Bareau (eds) *City Lights: Essays on Financial Institutions and Markets in the City of London*, London: IEA.

Bello, W. (1998) 'East Asia: on the eve of the great transformation?', *Review of International Political Economy* 5, 3: 424–44.

Bello, W., Malhotra, K., Bullard, N. and Mezzera, M. (2000) 'Notes on the ascendancy and regulation of speculative capital', in W. Bello, N. Bullard and K. Malhotra (eds) *Global Finance: New Thinking on Regulating Speculative Capital Markets*, London and New York: Zed Books.

Bernard, M. (1997) 'Ecology, Political Economy and the Counter-Movement: Karl Polanyi and the Second Great Transformation', in S. Gill and J.H. Mittelman (eds) *Innovation and Transformation in International Studies*, Cambridge: Cambridge University Press.

—— (1999) 'East Asia's tumbling dominoes: financial crises and the myth of the regional model', in L. Panitch and C. Leys (eds) *Socialist Register – Global Capitalism Versus Democracy*, Suffolk: Merlin.

Bernard, M. and Ravenhill, J. (1995) 'Beyond product cycles and flying geese: regionalization, hierarchy, and the industrialization of East Asia', *World Politics* 47, 2: 171–209.

Bernstein, P.L. (1992) *Capital Ideas: The Improbable Origins of Modern Wall Street*, New York: The Free Press.

Bevacqua, R. (1998) 'Whither the Japanese model? The Asian economic crisis and the continuation of Cold War politics in the Pacific Rim', *Review of International Political Economy* 5, 3: 410–23.

Bienefeld, M. (2000) 'Can global finance be regulated?', in W. Bello, N. Bullard and K. Malhotra (eds) *Global Finance: New Thinking on Regulating Speculative Capital Markets*, London and New York: Zed Books.

Biersteker, T.J. (1992) 'The "triumph" of neoclassical economics in the developing world: policy convergence and bases of governance in the international economic order', in J.N. Rosenau and E.-O. Czempiel (eds) *Governance Without Government: Order and Change in World Politics*, Cambridge: Cambridge University Press.

Block, F.L. (1977) *The Origins of International Economic Disorder*, Berkeley, CA: University of California Press.

Bond, P. (2000) 'Their reforms and ours: balance of forces and economic analysis in a new global financial architecture', in W. Bello, N. Bullard and K. Malhotra (eds) *Global Finance: New Thinking on Regulating Speculative Capital Markets*, London and New York: Zed Books.

Born, K.E. (1977) *International Banking in the 19th and 20th Centuries*, Warwickshire: Berg Publishers.

Boyer, R. (2000) 'Is a finance-led growth regime a viable alternative to Fordism? A preliminary analysis', *Economy and Society* 29, 1: 111–45.

Boyer, R. and Drache, D. (eds) (1996) *States Against Markets: The Limits of Globalization*, London and New York: Routledge.

Boyle, D. (2000) *Funny Money: In Search of Alternative Cash*, Second Edition, London: Flamingo.

Braudel, F. (1977) *Afterthoughts on Material Civilization and Capitalism*, London: Johns Hopkins University Press.

—— (1980) 'History and the social sciences: the *longue durée*', in F. Braudel (ed.) *On History*, trans. S. Matthews, Chicago, IL: University of Chicago Press.

—— (1982) *Civilization and Capitalism 15th–18th Century, Vol. II: The Wheels of Commerce*, trans. S. Reynolds, New York: Harper & Row.

—— (1984) *Civilization and Capitalism 15th–18th Century, Vol. III: The Perspective of the World*, trans. S. Reynolds, London: Collins.

Brenner, R. (2001) 'The world economy at the turn of the millennium: toward boom or crisis?' *Review of International Political Economy* 8, 1: 6–44.

Brett, E.A. (1983) *International Money and Capitalist Crisis: The Anatomy of Global Disintegration*, London: Heinemann Educational.

Brewer, J. (1989) *The Sinews of Power: War, Money and the English State, 1688–1783*, Cambridge, MA: Harvard University Press.

Broad, R. and Cavanagh, J. (2000) 'The death of the Washington consensus?', in W. Bello, N. Bullard and K. Malhotra (eds) *Global Finance: New Thinking on Regulating Speculative Capital Markets*, London: Zed Books.

Bröker, G. (1993) 'World banking and securities markets after 1992', in H. Genberg and A.K. Swoboda (eds) *World Financial Markets After 1992*, London: Kegan Paul International.

Brown, J.R. Jr (1999) *The Ministry of Finance: Bureaucratic Practices and Transformation of the Japanese Economy*, Westport, CT and London: Quorum Books.

Brown, W.A. (1940) *The International Gold Standard Reinterpreted, 1914–34*, 2 Vols, New York: National Bureau of Economic Research Inc.

Buck, J.E. (1992) *The New York Stock Exchange: The First 200 Years*, Connecticut, CT: Greenwich Publishing Group.

Budd, L. (1995) 'Globalisation, territory and strategic alliances in different financial centres', *Urban Studies* 32, 2: 329–44.

Burch, K. and Denemark, R.A. (eds) (1997) *Constituting International Political Economy*, International Political Economy Yearbook, Vol. 10, Boulder, CO: Lynne Rienner.

Burk, K. (1992) 'Money and power: the shift from Great Britain to the United States', in Y. Cassis (ed.) *Finance and Financiers in European History, 1880–1960*, Cambridge: Cambridge University Press.

Burn, G. (1997) 'The state, the city and the Euromarkets', paper presented at the British International Studies Association Annual Conference, December, University of Leeds.

Buzan, B. and Jones, R.J.B. (eds) (1981) *Change and the Study of International Relations: The Evaded Dimension*, London: Pinter.

Calleo, D. (1982) *The Imperious Economy*, Cambridge, MA: Harvard University Press.

Cameron, A. and Palan, R. (1999) 'The imagined economy: mapping transformations in the contemporary state', *Millennium: Journal of International Studies* 28, 2: 267–88.

Cameron, M. and Aggarwal, V. (1996) 'Mexican meltdown: markets and post-NAFTA financial turmoil', *Third World Quarterly* 17, 5: 975–88.

Canals, J. (1993) *Competitive Strategies in European Banking*, Oxford: Clarendon Press.

Caporaso, J.A. (1987) 'International Political Economy: fad or field?' *International Studies Notes* 13, 1: 1–8.

Carnoy, M., Castells, M., Cohen, S.S. and Cardoso, F.H. (1993) *The New Global Economy in the Information Age: Reflections on Our Changing World*, Pennsylvania, PA: Pennsylvania State University Press.

Carr, E.H. (1964) *What is History?*, Harmondsworth: Penguin Books.

Cassis, Y. (1991) 'Financial élites in three European financial centres: London, Paris, Berlin, 1880s–1930s', *Business History* 33, 3: 53–71.

—— (1994) *City Bankers, 1890–1914*, Cambridge: Cambridge University Press.

Castells, M. (1989) *The Information City: Information Technology, Economic Restructuring, and the Urban Regional Process*, Oxford: Blackwell.

—— (1996) *The Information Age: Economy, Society and Culture, Vol. I: The Rise of the Network Society*, Cambridge, MA and Oxford: Blackwell.

de Cecco, M. (1974) *Money and Empire: The International Gold Standard, 1890–1914*, Oxford: Blackwell.

Cerny, P.G. (1989) 'The "little big bang" in Paris: financial market deregulation in a *dirigiste* system', *European Journal of Political Research* 17, 2: 169–92.

—— (1990) *The Changing Architecture of Politics: Structure, Agency and the Future of the State*, London: Sage.

—— (1993a) 'The Political Economy of international finance', in P.G. Cerny (ed.) *Finance and World Politics: Markets, Regimes and States in the Post-Hegemonic Era*, Aldershot: Elgar.

—— (1993b) 'The deregulation and re-regulation of financial markets in a more open world', in P.G. Cerny (ed.) *Finance and World Politics: Markets, Regimes and States in the Post-Hegemonic Era*, Aldershot: Elgar.

—— (1993c) 'American decline and the emergence of embedded financial orthodoxy', in P.G. Cerny (ed.) *Finance and World Politics: Markets, Regimes and States in the Post-Hegemonic Era*, Aldershot: Elgar.

—— (1994a) 'Money and finance in International Political Economy: structural change and paradigmatic muddle', *Review of International Political Economy* 1, 3: 587–92.

—— (1994b) 'The infrastructure of the infrastructure? Towards "embedded financial orthodoxy" in the International Political Economy', in R. Palan and B. Gills (eds) *Transcending the State-Global Divide: A Neostructuralist Agenda in International Relations*, Boulder, CO.: Lynne Rienner.

—— (2000) 'The big bang in Tokyo, financial globalisation, and the unravelling of the Japanese model', paper presented to the British International Studies Annual Conference, December, University of Bradford.

Chancellor, E. (2000) *Devil Take the Hindmost: A History of Financial Speculation*, New York: Penguin Putnam Inc.

Chapman, S. (1984) *The Rise of Merchant Banking*, London: Allen & Unwin.

Chase-Dunn, C. (1989) *Global Formation: Structures of the World Economy*, Oxford: Blackwell.

Chin, C.B.N. and Mittelman, J.H. (2000) 'Conceptualizing resistance to globalization', in B. Gills (ed.) *Globalization and the Politics of Resistance*, Basingstoke and New York: Macmillan and St Martins Press.

City Research Project (1995) *The Competitive Position of London's Financial Services: Final Report*, London: Corporation of London.

Clark, G.L. (1999) 'The retreat of the state and the rise of pension fund capitalism', in R. Martin (ed.) *Money and the Space Economy*, Chichester: John Wiley & Sons.

Clarke, S. (1987) 'Capitalist crisis and the rise of monetarism', in R. Miliband, L. Panitch and J. Saville (eds) *Socialist Register*, London: The Merlin Press.

Coakley, J. (1992) 'London as an international financial centre', in L. Budd and S. Whimster (eds) *Global Finance and Urban Living: A Study of Metropolitan Change*, London: Routledge.

Cohen, B.J. (1977) *Organizing the World's Money: The Political Economy of International Monetary Relations*, New York: Basic Books.

——(1990) 'The Political Economy of international trade', *International Organization* 44, 2: 261–81.

——(1996) 'Phoenix risen: the resurrection of global finance', *World Politics* 48, 1: 268–96.

Coleman, W.D. (1997) 'The French state, *dirigisme*, and the changing global financial environment', in G.R.D. Underhill (ed.) *The New World Order in International Finance*, Basingstoke: Macmillan.

Collingwood, R.G. (1946) *The Idea of History*, Oxford: Clarendon Press.

COM (1999) 134, European Commission Communication, *Towards a Single Market for Supplementary Pensions*, 11 May 1999.

Cooper, R.N. (1968) *The Economics of Interdependence: Economic Policy in the Atlantic Community*, New York: Columbia University Press.

Corbett, J. and Vines, D. (1999) 'Asian currency and financial crises: lessons from vulnerability, crisis and collapse', *The World Economy* 22, 2: 155–78.

Corporation of London (2000) *London–New York Study: The Economies of Two Great Cities at the Millennium*, London: Corporation of London.

Costigliola, F. (1977) 'Anglo-American financial rivalry in the 1920s', *Journal of Economic History* 37, 4: 911–35.

Cottrell, P.L. (1995) 'The Bank of England in its international setting', in R. Roberts and D. Kynaston (eds) *The Bank of England: Money, Power and Influence 1694–1994*, Oxford: Clarendon Press.

Cox, R.W. (1976/1996) 'On thinking about the future of world order', *World Politics* 28, 2: 175–96, reprinted in R.W. Cox with T.J. Sinclair, *Approaches to World Order*, Cambridge: Cambridge University Press.

——(1981) 'In search of International Political Economy: a review essay', *New Political Science* 5, 6: 59–78.

——(1981/1996) 'Social forces, states and world orders: beyond International Relations theory', *Millennium: Journal of International Studies* 10, 2: 126–55, reprinted in R.W. Cox with T.J. Sinclair, *Approaches to World Order*, Cambridge: Cambridge University Press.

——(1985/1996) 'Postscript 1985: realism, positivism, and historicism', in R.O. Keohane (ed.) *Neorealism and Its Critics*, New York: Columbia University Press, reprinted in R.W. Cox with T.J. Sinclair, *Approaches to World Order*, Cambridge: Cambridge University Press.

——(1987) *Production, Power and World Order: Social Forces and the Making of History*, New York: Columbia University Press.

——(1989/1996) 'Middlepowermanship, Japan, and the future world order', *International Journal* (Canadian Institute of International Affairs) 44, 4: 823–62, reprinted in R.W. Cox with T.J. Sinclair, *Approaches to World Order*, Cambridge: Cambridge University Press.

——(1991/1996) 'The global political economy and social choice', in D. Drache and M.S. Gertler (eds) *The New Era of Global Competition: State Policy and Market Power*, Montreal: McGill-Queens University Press, reprinted in R.W. Cox with T.J. Sinclair, *Approaches to World Order*, Cambridge: Cambridge University Press.

——(1992a/1996) '"Take six eggs": theory, finance and the real economy in the work of Susan Strange', paper presented to the International Studies Association Annual Conference, March–April, reprinted in P.W. Cox with T.J.Sinclair, *Approaches to World Order*, Cambridge University Press.

——(1992b/1996) 'Towards a post-hegemonic conceptualisation of world order: reflections of the relevancy of Ibn Khaldun', in J.N. Rosenau and E.-O. Czempiel (eds) *Governance Without Government: Order and Change in World Politics*, Cambridge: Cambridge University

Press, reprinted in R.W. Cox with T.J. Sinclair, *Approaches to World Order*, Cambridge: Cambridge University Press.

—— (1996a) 'Civilizations in world political economy', *New Political Economy* 1, 2: 141–56.

—— (1996b) 'A perspective on globalization', in J.H. Mittelman (ed.) *Globalization: Critical Reflections*, Boulder, CO: Lynne Rienner.

—— (1997) 'Introduction', in R.W. Cox (ed.) *The New Realism: Perspectives on Multilateralism and World Order*, Tokyo: United Nations University Press and Basingstoke and New York: Macmillan and St Martin's Press.

—— (1999) 'Civil society at the turn of the millennium: prospects for an alternative world order', *Review of International Studies* 25, 1: 3–28.

Cox, M., Booth, K. and Dunne, T. (1999) 'Introduction', *Review of International Studies* 25, Special Issue: *The Interregnum: Controversies in World Politics 1989–1999*: 3–20.

Crawford, D. (2001) 'Globalisation and *Guanxi*: the ethos of Hong Kong finance', *New Political Economy* 6, 1: 45–65.

Cutler, A.C., Haufler, V. and Porter, T. (1999) 'Private authority and international affairs', in A.C. Cutler, V. Haufler and T. Porter (eds) *Private Authority and International Affairs*, New York: SUNY.

Cutler, T. and Waine, B. (2001) 'Social insecurity and the retreat from social democracy: occupational welfare in the long boom and financialization', *Review of International Political Economy* 8, 1: 96–117.

Daniels, P.W. (1993) *Service Industries in the World Economy*, Oxford: Blackwell.

Davis, E.P. (1990) 'International financial centres: an industrial analysis', *Bank of England Discussion Paper*, 51.

Davis, E.P. and Latter, A.R. (1989) 'London as an international financial centre', *Bank of England Quarterly Bulletin* 29, 4: 516–28.

Deane, P. (1978) *The Evolution of Economic Ideas*, Cambridge, London and New York: Cambridge University Press.

Dickson, P.G.M. (1967) *The Financial Revolution in England: A Study in the Development of Public Credit, 1688–1756*, London: Macmillan.

Dodd, N. (1994) *The Sociology of Money: Economics, Reason and Contemporary Society*, Cambridge: Polity Press.

Dombrowski, P. (1998) 'Haute finance and high theory: recent scholarship on global financial relations', *Mershon International Studies Review* 42: 1–28.

Doremus, P.N., Keller, W.W., Pauly, L.W. and Reich, S. (1998) *The Myth of the Global Corporation*, Princeton, NJ: Princeton University Press.

Douthwaite, R. (1996) *Short Circuit: Strengthening Local Economies for Security in an Unstable World*, London: Lilliput Press.

Dowd, K. and Timberlake, R.H. (eds) (1998) *Money and the Nation State: The Financial Revolution, Government and the World Monetary System*, New Brunswick, NJ: Transaction Publishers.

Drainville, A.C. (1994) 'International Political Economy in an age of open Marxism', *Review of International Political Economy* 1, 1: 105–32.

—— (1995) 'Of social spaces, citizenship, and the nature of power in the world economy', *Alternatives* 20, 1: 51–79.

Drennan, M.P. (1996) 'The dominance of international finance by London, New York and Tokyo', in P.W. Daniels and W.F. Lever (eds) *The Global Economy in Transition*, Harlow: Addison Wesley Longman Ltd.

Drucker, P.F. (1976) *Unseen Revolution: How Pension Fund Socialism Came to America*, New York: Harper & Row.

—— (1986) 'The changed world economy', *Foreign Affairs* 64, 4: 768–91.

Dyson, K., Featherstone, K. and Michalopoulos, G. (1998) 'Strapped to the mast: EU central bankers between global financial markets and regional integration', in W.D. Coleman and G.R.D. Underhill (eds) *Regionalism and Global Economic Integration: Europe, Asia and the Americas*, London and New York: Routledge.

Eatwell, J. (1999) 'From cooperation to coordination to control?', *New Political Economy* 4, 3: 410–14.

Eatwell, J. and Taylor, L. (2000) *Global Finance at Risk: The Case for International Regulation*, New York: The New Press.

The Economist (1994) 'A survey of international banking: recalled to life', 30 April.

—— (1998) 'A survey of financial centres: capitals of capital', 7 May.

Eichengreen, B. (1990) *Elusive Stability: Essays in the History of International Finance, 1919–1939*, Cambridge: Cambridge University Press.

—— (1999) *Toward a New International Financial Architecture: A Practical Post-Asia Agenda*, Washington, DC: Institute for International Economics.

Eichengreen, B. and Flandreau, M. (1997) 'Editor's introduction', in B. Eichengreen and M. Flandreau (eds) *The Gold Standard in Theory and History*, 2nd Edition, London: Routledge.

Eichengreen, B. and Portes, R. (1987) 'The anatomy of financial crisis', in R. Portes and A.K. Swoboda (eds) *Threats to International Financial Stability*, Cambridge: Cambridge University Press.

Eken, S. (1984/1994) 'Integration of domestic and international financial markets: the Japanese experience', *International Monetary Fund Staff Papers* 31, 3: 499–548, reprinted in R. Roberts (ed.) *Global Financial Centres: London, New York, Tokyo*, Aldershot: Edward Elgar Reference Collection.

Emmott, B. (1993) *Japan's Global Reach: The Influences, Strategies and Weaknesses of Japan's Multinational Companies*, London: Arrow Books.

Epstein, G. (1996) 'International capital mobility and the scope for national economic management', in R. Boyer and D. Drache (eds) *States Against Markets: The Limits of Globalisation*, London: Routledge.

Feis, H. (1930/1964) *Europe, The World's Banker, 1870–1914*, New York: Augustus M. Kelley.

Filipovic, M. (1997) *Governments, Banks and Global Capital: Securities Markets in Global Politics*, Aldershot: Ashgate.

Financial Times, various issues.

Fine, B. (1999) 'A question of economics: is it colonizing the social sciences?', *Economy and Society* 28, 3: 403–25.

Frankel, J.A. (1995) 'Still the lingua franca', *Foreign Affairs* 74, 4: 9–16.

Frieden, J. (1987) *Banking on the World: The Politics of International Finance*, London: Hutchinson Review.

Friedman, R.B. (1990) 'On the concept of authority in political philosophy', in J. Raz (ed.) *Authority*, Oxford: Blackwell.

Galbraith, J.K. (1975) *Money: Whence it Came, Where it Went*, London: Andre Deutsch Ltd.

—— (1993) *A Short History of Financial Euphoria*, New York: Penguin Books.

Germain, R.D. (1996a) 'The worlds of finance: a Braudelian perspective on IPE', *European Journal of International Relations* 2, 2: 201–30.

—— (1996b) 'Free trade and finance in North America: a Braudelian view', *New Political Economy* 1, 2: 157–84.

—— (1996c) 'Regionalism and finance: a conceptual approach', *Competition and Change: The Journal of Global Business and Political Economy* 1, 3: 357–78.

—— (1997) *The International Organization of Credit: States and Global Finance in the World-Economy*, Cambridge: Cambridge University Press.

—— (2000) 'Reforming the international financial architecture: the new political agenda', paper presented at the British International Studies Association Annual Conference, December, University of Bradford.

Ghosh, D.K. and Ortiz, E. (eds) (1997) *The Global Structure of Financial Markets: An Overview*, London: Routledge.

Giddens, A. (1979) *Central Problems in Social Theory: Action, Structure and Contradiction in Social Analysis*, London: Macmillan.

—— (1985) *The Nation State and Violence*, Cambridge: Polity Press.

—— (1990) *The Consequences of Modernity*, Cambridge: Polity Press.

Gilbert, E. and Helleiner, E. (1999) 'Introduction – nation-states and money: historical contexts, interdisciplinary perspectives', in E. Gilbert and E. Helleiner (eds) *Nation-States and Money: The Past, Present and Future of National Currencies*, London and New York: Routledge/RIPE Series in Global Political Economy.

Gill, S. (1991) 'Reflections on global order and sociohistorical time', *Alternatives* 16: 275–314.

—— (1992) 'Economic globalisation and the internationalisation of authority: limits and contradictions', *Geoforum* 23, 3: 269–83.

—— (1995) 'Globalization, market civilization, and disciplinary neoliberalism', *Millennium* 24, 3: 399–423.

—— (1997) 'Transformation and innovation in the study of world order', in S. Gill and J.H. Mittelman (eds) *Innovation and Transformation in International Studies*, Cambridge: Cambridge University Press.

—— (1999) 'The geopolitics of the Asian crisis', *Monthly Review* 50, 10: 1–9.

Gill, S. and Law, D. (1988) *The Global Political Economy*, Hertfordshire: Harvester Wheatsheaf.

Gill, S. and Mittelman, J.H. (eds) (1997) *Innovation and Transformation in International Studies*, Cambridge: Cambridge University Press.

Gills, B. (1994) 'The international origins of South Korea's export orientation', in R. Palan and B. Gills (eds) *Transcending the State-Global Divide: A Neostructuralist Agenda in International Relations*, Boulder, CO: Lynne Rienner.

—— (1996) 'Whither democracy? Globalization and the "new Hellenism"', in C. Thomas and P. Wilkin (eds) *Globalization and the South*, Basingstoke: Macmillan.

Gills, B. and Palan, R. (1994) 'The neostructuralist agenda in international relations', in R. Palan and B. Gills (eds) *Transcending the State-Global Divide: A Neostructuralist Agenda in International Relations*, Boulder, CO: Lynne Rienner.

Gilpin, R. (1987) *The Political Economy of International Relations*, Princeton, NJ: Princeton University Press.

de Goede, M. (1998) 'Virtue, fortune and faith: a social history of credit networks', paper presented at the 38th International Studies Association Annual Conference, March, Toronto.

—— (2001) 'Discourses of scientific finance and the failure of long-term capital management', *New Political Economy* 6, 2: 149–70.

Goldsmith, R.W. (1987) *Premodern Financial Systems: A Historical Comparative Study*, Cambridge: Cambridge University Press.

Goldstein, M. (1998) *The Asian Financial Crisis: Causes, Cures, and Systemic Implications*, Washington, DC: Institute for International Economics.

Goodman, J.B. (1992) *Monetary Sovereignty: The Politics of Central Banking in Western Europe*, Ithaca, NY: Cornell University Press.

Goodman, J.B. and Pauly, L.W. (1993) 'The obsolescence of capital controls? Economic management in an age of global markets', *World Politics* 46, 1: 50–82.

Gordon, D. (1988) 'The global economy: new edifice or crumbling foundations?', *New Left Review* 168: 24–65.

Graham, S.D.N. (1992) 'The role of cities in telecommunications development', *Telecommunications Policy* 16, 3: 187–93.

Grahl, J. (2001) 'Globalized finance: the challenge to the euro', *New Left Review* 8, Second Series, March/April: 23–47.

Granville, B. (1999) 'Bingo or fiasco? the global financial situation is not guaranteed', *International Affairs* 75, 4: 713–28.

Griffith-Jones, S. (1999) 'Identifying needs and filling gaps', *New Political Economy* 4, 3: 419–24.

Grilli, V. (1989) 'Europe 1992: issues and prospects for the financial markets', *Economic Policy*, October: 387–421.

Guardian, various issues.

Guttmann, R. (1994) *How Credit-Money Shapes the Economy: The United States in a Global System*, New York: M.E. Sharpe.

Haley, K.H.D. (1988) *The British and the Dutch: Political and Cultural Relations Through the Ages*, London: George Philip.

Hall, J.A. (1996) *International Orders*, Cambridge: Polity Press.

Hamilton, A. (1986) *The Financial Revolution: The 'Big Bang' and the Explosion of the World's Money Markets*, Middlesex: Viking.

Harmes, A. (1998) 'Institutional investors and the reproduction of neoliberalism', *Review of International Political Economy* 5, 1: 92–121.

Harvey, D. (1982) *The Limits to Capital*, Oxford: Blackwell.

Hawley, J.P. (1987) *Dollars and Borders: US Government Attempts to Restrict Capital Flows, 1960–1980*, New York: M.E. Sharpe.

Hay, C. and Marsh, D. (1999) 'Introduction: towards a new (International) Political Economy', *New Political Economy* 4, 1: 5–22.

Healey, N.M. (2000) 'European Monetary Union: one money, one Europe?, in P. Lynch, N. Neuwahl and W. Rees (eds) *Reforming the European Union: From Maastricht to Amsterdam*, Harlow: Pearson Education Ltd.

Heisler, J. (1994) 'Recent research in behavioral finance', *Financial Markets, Institutions and Instruments* 3, 5: 76–104.

Held, D. (1995) *Democracy and the Global Order: From the Modern State to Cosmopolitan Governance*, Cambridge: Polity Press.

Held, D., McGrew, A., Goldblatt, D. and Perraton, J. (1999) *Global Transformations: Politics, Economics, Culture*, Cambridge: Polity Press.

Helleiner, E. (1992) 'States and the future of global finance', *Review of International Studies* 18, 1: 31–49.

—— (1993a) 'When finance was the servant: international capital movements in the Bretton Woods order', in P.G. Cerny (ed.) *Finance and World Politics: Markets, Regimes and States in the Post-Hegemonic Era*, Aldershot: Edward Elgar.

—— (1993b) 'The challenge from the East: Japan's financial rise and the changing global order', in P.G. Cerny (ed.) *Finance and World Politics: Markets, Regimes and States in the Post-Hegemonic Era*, Aldershot: Edward Elgar.

—— (1994) *States and the Re-emergence of Global Finance*, Ithaca, NY: Cornell University Press.

—— (1996) 'Post-globalization: is the financial liberalization trend likely to be reversed?', in R. Boyer and D. Drache (eds) *States Against Markets: The Limits of Globalization*, London and New York: Routledge.

—— (1998) 'Think globally, transact locally: green Political Economy and the local currency movement', paper presented at the 39th International Studies Association Annual Convention, February, Washington, DC.

—— (1999) 'Denationalising money? Economic liberalisation and the "national question" in currency affairs', in E. Gilbert and E. Helleiner (eds) *Nation-States and Money: The Past, Present and Future of National Currencies*, London and New York: Routledge/RIPE Series in Global Political Economy.

—— (2000) 'Still an extraordinary power, but for how much longer? The United States in world finance', in T.C. Lawton, J.N. Rosenau and A.C. Verdun (eds) *Strange Power: Shaping the Parameters of International Relations and International Political Economy*, Aldershot and Vermont, VT: Ashgate.

Henderson, J. (1999) 'Uneven crises: institutional foundations of East Asian economic turmoil', *Economy and Society* 28, 3: 327–68.

Henwood, D. (1997) *Wall Street: How it Works and for Whom*, New York: Verso.

Hettne, B. (1997) 'The double movement: global market versus regionalism', in R.W. Cox (ed.) *The New Realism: Perspectives on Multilateralism and World Order*, Basingstoke and New York: Macmillan and St Martin's Press.

Hewson, M. and Sinclair, T.J. (1999) 'The emergence of global governance theory', in M. Hewson and T.J. Sinclair (eds) *Approaches to Global Governance Theory*, New York: SUNY.

Higgott, R. (1998) 'The Asian economic crisis: a study in the politics of resentment', *New Political Economy* 3, 3: 333–56.

Higgott, R. and Phillips, N. (2000) 'Challenging triumphalism and convergence: the limits of global liberalization in Asia and Latin America', *Review of International Studies* 26, 3: 359–79.

Hirst, P. and Thompson, G. (1996) *Globalization in Question*, Cambridge: Polity Press.

HMSO (1991) *London: World City*, London: HMSO.

Hobsbawm, E. (1968) *Industry and Empire: An Economic History of Britain Since 1750*, London: Weidenfeld & Nicolson.

—— (1994) *Age of Extremes: The Short Twentieth Century, 1914–1991*, London: Penguin Books.

—— (1997) *On History*, London: Weidenfeld & Nicolson.

Hobson, J.M. (1997) *The Wealth of States: A Comparative Sociology of International Economic and Political Change*, Cambridge: Cambridge University Press.

Hodgson, G. (1994) 'Some remarks on "economic imperialism" and International Political Economy', *Review of International Political Economy* 1, 1: 21–8.

Hollis, M. and Smith, S. (1990) *Explaining and Understanding International Relations*, Oxford: Clarendon Press.

Honeygold, D. (1989) *International Financial Markets*, New York: Woodhead-Faulkner.

Hoogvelt, A. (2001) *Globalization and the Postcolonial World: The New Political Economy of Development*, Second Edition, Basingstoke: Palgrave.

Hudson, A.C. (1998) 'Reshaping the regulatory landscape: border skirmishes around the Bahamas and Cayman offshore financial centres', *Review of International Political Economy* 5, 3: 534–64.

Hutchinson, F., Mellor, M. and Olsen, W. (forthcoming) *The Political Economy of Money*, Pluto Press: London.

Imlah, A.H. (1958) *Economic Elements of the* Pax Britannica: *Studies in British Foreign Trade in the Nineteenth Century*, New York: Russell & Russell.

Ingham, G. (1984) *Capitalism Divided: The City and Industry in British Social Development*, London: Macmillan.

—— (1994) 'States and markets in the production of world money: sterling and the dollar', in S. Corbridge, R. Martin and N. Thrift (eds) *Money, Power and Space*, Oxford: Blackwell.

—— (1996) 'Money is a social relation', *Review of Social Economy* 54, 4: 507–29.

International Monetary Fund (1986) 'External debt, savings and growth in Latin America', papers presented to an IMF seminar, Instituto Torcuato di Tella, Buenos Aires, October, Washington, DC: IMF.

—— (1995) *International Capital Markets: Developments, Prospects and Key Policy Issues*, World Economic and Financial Surveys, Washington, DC: IMF.

—— (1997) *International Capital Markets: Developments, Prospects and Key Policy Issues*, World Economic and Financial Surveys, Washington, DC: IMF.

—— (1998a) *International Capital Markets: Developments, Prospects and Key Policy Issues*, World Economic and Financial Surveys, Washington, DC: IMF.

—— (1998b) *Report of the Working Group on Transparency and Accountability*, October, Washington, DC: IMF.

—— (2000) *International Capital Markets: Developments, Prospects and Key Policy Issues*, World Economic and Financial Surveys, Washington, DC: IMF.

—— (2001) *Reforming the International Financial Architecture: Progress Through 2000*, 9 March, Washington, DC: IMF.

International Monetary Fund and World Bank (2000) *Reports on the Observance of Standards and Codes (ROSCs): An Update*, 30 March, Washington, DC: IMF.

Israel, J.I. (1995) 'Innovation in Dutch cities', *History Today* 45, 3: 14–20.

Jacobs, J. (1963) *Cities and the Wealth of Nations*, Harmondsworth: Penguin.

Jenkins, K. (1991) *Re-Thinking History*, London: Routledge.

Jetin, B. and de Brunhof, S. (2000) 'The Tobin Tax and the regulation of capital movements', in W. Bello, N. Bullard and K. Malhotra (eds) *Global Finance: New Thinking on Regulating Speculative Capital Markets*, London and New York: Zed Books.

Johnson, C. (1982) *MITI and the Japanese Miracle: The Growth of Industrial Policy, 1925–1975*, Stanford, CA: Stanford University Press.

Jones, R.J.B. (1995) *Globalisation and Interdependence in the International Political Economy: Rhetoric and Reality*, London: Pinter.

—— (1999) 'Overview: globalization and change in the International Political Economy', *International Affairs* 75, 2: 357–67.

Kalder, K.E. (1997) 'Assault on the banker's kingdom: politics, markets, and the liberalization of Japanese industrial finance', in M. Loriaux, M. Woo-Cumings, K.E. Calder, S. Maxfield and S. Perez, *Capital Ungoverned: Liberalizing Finance in Interventionist States*, Ithaca, NY: Cornell University Press.

Kapstein, E.B. (1994) *Governing the Global Economy: International Finance and the State*, Cambridge, MA: Harvard University Press.

—— (1996) 'Shockproof: the end of the financial crisis', *Foreign Affairs* 75, 1: 2–8.

Kennedy, P. (1989) *The Rise and Fall of the Great Powers: Economic Change and Military Conflict from 1500 to 2000*, London: Fontana Press.

Keohane, R.O. (1984) *After Hegemony: Co-operation and Discord in the World Political Economy*, Princeton, NJ: Princeton University Press.

Key, S.J. (1999) 'Trade liberalization and prudential regulation: the international framework for financial services', *International Affairs* 75, 1: 61–75.

Kindleberger, C.P. (1973) *The World in Depression, 1929–39*, London: Allen Lane.

—— (1974/1978) 'The formation of financial centers', *Princeton Studies in International Finance* 36: 1–78, reprinted in C.P. Kindleberger (ed.) *Economic Response: Comparative Studies in Trade, Finance and Growth*, London: Harvard University Press.

—— (1978) *Manias, Panics and Crashes: A History of Financial Crises*, London: Macmillan.

—— (1983) 'Key currencies and financial centres', in F. Machlup, G. Fels and H. Muller-Groeling (eds) *Reflections on a Troubled World Economy: Essays in Honour of Herbert Giersch*, London: Macmillan.

—— (1984/1993) *A Financial History of Western Europe*, 2nd Edition, Oxford: Oxford University Press.

—— (1987) *Marshall Plan Days*, Boston, MA: Allen & Unwin.

—— (1996) *World Economic Primacy 1500–1990*, New York: Oxford University Press.

King, A.D. (1990) *Global Cities: Post-Imperialism and the Internationalization of London*, London: Routledge.

Klopstock, F.H. (1973/1994) 'Foreign banks in the United States: scope and growth of operations', *Federal Reserve Bank of New York Monthly Review* 55, 6: 140–54, reprinted in R. Roberts (ed.) *Global Financial Centres: London, New York, Tokyo*, Aldershot: Edward Elgar Reference Collection.

Knox, P.L. (1995) 'World cities in a world-system', in P.L. Knox and P.J. Taylor (eds) *World Cities in a World-System*, Cambridge: Cambridge University Press.

Krasner, S.D. (1976) 'State power and the structure of international trade', *World Politics* 28, 2: 317–47.

—— (1994) 'International Political Economy: abiding discord', *Review of International Political Economy* 1, 1: 13–20.

—— (1996) 'The accomplishments of International Political Economy', in S. Smith, K. Booth and M. Zalewski (eds) *International Theory: Positivism and Beyond*, Cambridge: Cambridge University Press.

Krugman, P. (1993) *Geography and Trade*, Cambridge, MA: MIT Press.

—— (1994) 'The myth of Asia's miracle', *Foreign Affairs* 73, 6: 62–78.

—— (1995) 'Dutch tulips and emerging markets', *Foreign Affairs* 74, 4: 28–44.

—— (1999) *The Return of Depression Economics*, London: Allen Lane.

Kuhn, T. (1962/1970) 'The structure of scientific revolutions', *International Encyclopedia of United Science* 2, 2, 2nd Edition, Chicago, IL: University of Chicago Press.

Kynaston, D. (1994) *The City of London, Vol. I: A World of its Own, 1815–1890*, London: Random House.

—— (1995) *The City of London, Vol. II: Golden Years, 1890–1914*, London: Random House.

Langley, P. (2001) 'Transparency in the making of global environmental governance', *Global Society: Journal of Interdisciplinary International Relations* 15, 1: 73–92.

Langley, P. and Mellor, M. (2002) '"Economy", sustainability, and sites of transformative space', *New Political Economy*, 7, 1: 49–70.

Lapavitsas, C. (1997) 'Transition and crisis in the Japanese financial system: an analytical overview', *Capital and Class* 62: 21–48.

Latham, R. (1999) 'Politics in a floating world: toward a critique of global governance', in M. Hewson and T.J. Sinclair (eds) *Approaches to Global Governance Theory*, New York: SUNY.

Leaver, R. and Seabrooke, L. (2000) 'Can the IMF be reformed?', in W. Bello, N. Bullard and K. Malhotra (eds) *Global Finance: New Thinking on Regulating Speculative Capital Markets*, London and New York: Zed Books.

Lee, R. (1999) 'Local money: geographies of autonomy and resistance', in R. Martin (ed.) *Money and the Space Economy*, Chichester: John Wiley & Sons.

Lefebvre, H. (1991) *The Production of Space*, Oxford: Blackwell.

Lewis, M.K. (1999) 'International banking and offshore finance: London and the major centres', in M.P. Hampton and J.P. Abbott (eds) *Offshore Finance Centres and Tax Havens: The Rise of Global Capital*, London: Macmillan.

Leyshon, A. and Thrift, N. (1995) 'Geographies of financial exclusion: financial abandonment in Britain and the United States', *Transactions of the Institute of British Geographers* 20: 312–41.

—— (1997) *Money/Space: Geographies of Monetary Transformation*, London: Routledge.

Lindgren, C.-J., Garcia, G. and Saal, M.I. (1996) *Bank Soundness and Macroeconomic Policy*, Washington, DC: IMF.

Linklater, A. (1996) 'The achievements of critical theory', in S. Smith, K. Booth and M. Zalewski (eds) *International Theory: Positivism and Beyond*, Cambridge: Cambridge University Press.

Little, R. (1994) 'International relations and large-scale historical change', in A.J.R. Groom and M. Light (eds) *Contemporary International Relations: A Guide to Theory*, London: Pinter.

Loriaux, M., Woo-Cumings, M., Calder, K.E., Maxfield, S. and Pérez, S. (1997) *Capital Ungoverned: Liberalizing Finance in Interventionist States*, Ithaca, NY and London: Cornell University Press.

Lütz, S. (1997) 'Bringing the state back in? Stock exchange regulation in an era of internationalized financial markets', paper presented at the ECPR Joint Sessions of Workshops, Bern-Unitobler, February–March.

McGahey, R., Malloy, M., Kazanas, K. and Jacobs, M.P. (1990) *Financial Services, Financial Centres: Public Policy and the Competition for Markets, Firms and Jobs*, Boulder, CO: Westview Press.

McKenzie, R.B. and Lee, D.R. (1991) *Quicksilver Capital: How the Rapid Movement of Wealth has Changed the World*, New York: Free Press.

MacLean, J. (2000) 'Philosophical roots of globalization and philosophical routes to globalization', in R.D. Germain (ed.) *Globalization and its Critics: Perspectives from Political Economy*, Basingstoke: Macmillan.

McNamara, K.R. (1998) *The Currency of Ideas: Monetary Politics in the European Union*, Ithaca, NY and London: Cornell University Press.

Madden, J.T. and Nadler, M. (1935/1994) 'New York as an international financial centre', in J.T. Madden and M. Nadler, *The International Money Markets*, London: Pitman, reprinted in R. Roberts (ed.) *Global Financial Centres: London, New York, Tokyo*, Aldershot: Edward Elgar Reference Collection.

Maier, C.S. (1987) *In Search of Stability: Explorations in Historical Political Economy*, Cambridge: Cambridge University Press.

Malhotra, K. (2000) 'Renewing the governance of the global economy', in W. Bello, N. Bullard and K. Malhotra (eds) *Global Finance: New Thinking on Regulating Speculative Capital Markets*, London and New York: Zed Books.

Martin, R. (1994) 'Stateless monies, global financial integration and national economic autonomy: the "end of geography"?', in S. Corbridge, R. Martin and N. Thrift (eds) *Money, Power and Space*, Oxford: Blackwell.

—— (1999a) 'The new "geographical turn" in economics: some critical reflections', *Cambridge Journal of Economics* 23: 65–91.

—— (1999b) 'Selling off the state: privatisation, the equity market and the geographies of shareholder capitalism', in R. Martin (ed.) *Money and the Space Economy*, Chichester: John Wiley & Sons.

Marwick, A. (1970) *The Nature of History*, London: Macmillan.

Maxfield, S. (1997a) 'Capital mobility and Mexican financial liberalisation', in M. Loriaux, M. Woo-Cumings, K.E. Calder, S. Maxfield and S. Pérez (eds) *Capital Ungoverned: Liberalizing Finance in Interventionist States*, Ithaca, NY and London: Cornell University Press.

—— (1997b) *Gatekeepers of Growth: The International Political Economy of Central Banking in Developing Countries*, Princeton, NJ: Princeton University Press.

May, C. (1996) 'Strange fruit: Susan Strange's theory of structural power in the International Political Economy', *Global Society: Journal of Interdisciplinary International Relations* 10, 2: 167–90.

Mendelsohn, M.S. (1980) *Money on the Move: The Modern International Capital Market*, New York: McGraw-Hill Book Company.
Meyer, D.R. (1991) 'The formation of a global financial center: London and its intermediaries', in R. Kasaba (ed.) *Cities in the World-System*, New York: Greenwood Press.
Michie, R.C. (1992) *The City of London: Continuity and Change, 1850–1990*, Basingstoke: Macmillan.
Milward, A. (1984) *The Reconstruction of Western Europe, 1945–51*, London: Methuen.
Minns, R. (1996a) 'The political economy of pensions', *New Political Economy* 1, 3: 375–92.
—— (1996b) 'The social ownership of capital', *New Left Review* 219: 42–61.
Mizruchi, M.S. and Brewster Stearns, L. (1994) 'Money, banking and financial markets', in N.J. Smelser and R. Swedberg (eds) *The Handbook of Economic Sociology*, Princeton, NJ: Princeton University Press.
Moore, B. (1987) *Authority and Inequality Under Capitalism and Socialism*, Oxford: Clarendon Press.
Moran, M. (1991) *The Politics of the Financial Services Revolution*, London: Macmillan.
Moss, M.L. (1987) 'Telecommunications and international financial centres', in J. Brotchie, P. Hall and P. Newton (eds) *The Spatial Impact of Technological Change*, London: Croom Helm.
Murphy, C.N. (1994) *International Organisation and Industrial Change: Global Governance Since 1850*, Cambridge: Polity Press.
Murphy, C.N. and Tooze, R. (1991a) 'Introduction', in C.N. Murphy and R. Tooze (eds) *The New International Political Economy*, Boulder, CO: Lynne Rienner.
—— (1991b) 'Getting beyond the "common sense" of the IPE orthodoxy', in C.N. Murphy and R. Tooze (eds) *The New International Political Economy*, Boulder, CO: Lynne Rienner.
Nadler, M., Heller, S. and Shipman, S.S. (1955/1994) 'New York as an international financial centre', in M. Nadler, S. Heller and S.S. Shipman, *The Money Market and its Institutions*, New York: Ronald Press, reprinted in R. Roberts (ed.) *Global Financial Centres: London, New York, Tokyo*, Aldershot: Edward Elgar Reference Collection.
Nakao, S. (1995) *The Political Economy of Japan Money*, Japan: University of Tokyo Press.
Neal, L. (1990) *The Rise of Financial Capitalism: International Capital Markets in the Age of Reason*, Cambridge: Cambridge University Press.
—— (1989) 'New York's competitiveness', in T. Noyelle (ed.) *New York's Financial Markets: The Challenges of Globalization*, Boulder, CO and London: Westview Press.
O'Brien, R. (1992) *Global Financial Integration: The End of Geography*, London: Pinter.
O'Brien, R., Goetz, A.M., Scholte, J.-A. and Williams, M. (2000) *Contesting Global Governance: Multilateral Economic Institutions and Global Social Movements*, Cambridge: Cambridge University Press.
O'Connor, J. (1973) *The Fiscal Crisis of the State*, New York: St Martins Press.
Öniş, Z. and Aysan, A.F. (2000) 'Neoliberal globalisation, the nation-state and financial crises in the semi-periphery: a comparative analysis', *Third World Quarterly* 21, 1: 119–39.
Organisation for Economic Co-operation and Development (1994) *Pension Fund Investment from Ageing to Emerging Markets*, OECD Development Centre, Policy Brief No. 9, Paris: OECD.
Overbeek, H. (1990) *Global Capitalism and National Decline: The Thatcher Decade in Perspective*, London: Unwin Hyman.
Overbeek, H. and van der Pijl, K. (1993) 'Restructuring capital and restructuring hegemony: neo-liberalism and the unmaking of the post-war order', in H. Overbeek (ed.) *Restructuring Hegemony in the Global Political Economy: The Rise of Transnational Neo-liberalism in the 1980s*, London and New York: Routledge.

Pacione, M. (1997) 'Local exchange trading systems as a response to the globalisation of capitalism', *Urban Studies* 34, 8: 1179–99.

Palan, R.P. (1993) 'Underconsumption and widening income inequalities: the dynamics of globalization', *Newcastle Discussion Papers in Politics* No. 4, Department of Politics, University of Newcastle-upon-Tyne.

—— (1998) 'Trying to have your cake and eating it: how and why the state system has created offshore', *International Studies Quarterly* 42, 4: 625–44.

—— (1999) 'Offshore and the structural enablement of sovereignty', in M.P. Hampton and J.P. Abbott (eds) *Offshore Finance Centres and Tax Havens: The Rise of Global Capital*, London: Macmillan.

—— (2000) 'New trends in global political economy', in R.P. Palan (ed.) *Global Political Economy: Contemporary Theories*, London and New York: Routledge/RIPE Series in Global Political Economy.

Panitch, L. (1994) 'Globalisation and the state', in R. Miliband and L. Panitch (eds) *Socialist Register - Between Globalism and Nationalism*, London: The Merlin Pres.

Parboni, R. (1981) *The Dollar and its Rivals*, London: Verso.

Parsons, W. (1989) *The Power of the Financial Press: Journalism and Economic Opinion in Britain and America*, Aldershot: Edward Elgar.

Pauly, L.W. (1994a) 'National financial structures, capital mobility, and international economic rules: the normative consequences of East Asian, European, and American distinctiveness', *Policy Sciences* 27, 4: 343–63.

—— (1994b) 'Promoting a global economy: the normative role of the International Monetary Fund', in R. Stubbs and G.R.D. Underhill (eds) *Political Economy and the Changing Global Order*, Basingstoke: Macmillan.

—— (1997) *Who Elected the Bankers? Surveillance and Control in the World Economy*, Ithaca, NY: Cornell University Press.

Pauly, L.W. and Reich, S. (1997) 'National structures and multinational corporate behavior: enduring differences in the age of globalization', *International Organization* 51, 1: 1–30.

Payne, A. and Gamble, A. (1996) 'Introduction: the political economy of regionalism and world order', in A. Gamble and A. Payne (eds) *Regionalism and World Order*, London: Macmillan.

Perraton, J., Goldblatt, D., Held, D. and McGrew, A. (1997) 'The globalisation of economic activity', *New Political Economy* 2, 2: 257–78.

Petrella, R. (1991) 'World city-states of the future', *New Perspectives Quarterly* 8, 1: 59–64.

Picciotto, S. (1999) 'Offshore: the state as legal fiction', in M.P. Hampton and J.P. Abbott (eds) *Offshore Finance Centres and Tax Havens: The Rise of Global Capital*, London: Macmillan.

Picciotto, S. and Haines, J. (1999) 'Regulating global financial markets', *Journal of Law and Society* 26, 3: 351–68.

van der Pijl, K. (1989) 'Ruling classes, hegemony, and the state system', *International Journal of Political Economy* 19, 3: 7–35.

—— (1998) *Transnational Classes and International Relations*, London and New York: Routledge/RIPE Series in Global Political Economy.

Plender, J. (1987) 'London's big bang in international context', *International Affairs* 63, 1: 39–48.

Pohle, M. (1995) 'Risk, information and noise: risk perception and risk management of French and German banks during the nineteenth century', *Financial History Review* 2, 1: 25–39.

Polanyi, K. (1944) *The Great Transformation*, New York: Rinehart.

Pollin, R. (1995) 'Financial structures and egalitarian economic policy', *New Left Review* 214: 26–61.

Popper, K. (1957/1960) *The Poverty of Historicism*, 2nd Edition, London: Routledge.

Porter, M.E. (1990) *The Competitive Advantage of Nations*, London: Macmillan.

Porter, T. (1993) *States, Markets and Regimes in Global Finance*, Basingstoke: Macmillan.

—— (1997) 'NAFTA, North American financial integration, and regulatory co-operation in banking and securities', in G.R.D. Underhill (ed.) *The New World Order in International Finance*, London: Macmillan.

Power, M. (1997) *The Audit Society: Rituals of Verification*, Oxford: Oxford University Press.

Pryke, M. and Lee, R. (1995) 'Place your bets: towards an understanding of globalisation, socio-financial engineering and competition within a financial centre', *Urban Studies* 32, 2: 329–44.

Radice, H. (1984) 'The national economy: a Keynesian myth?', *Capital and Class* 22: 111–40.

Reed, H.C. (1980) 'The ascent of Tokyo as an international financial center', *Journal of International Business Studies* 9, 3: 19–35.

—— (1981) *The Preeminence of International Financial Centres*, New York: Praeger.

Riley, J.C. (1980) *International Government Finance and the Amsterdam Capital Market, 1740–1815*, Cambridge: Cambridge University Press.

RIPE Editors (1994) Editorial: 'Forum for heterodox International Political Economy', *Review of International Political Economy* 1, 1: 1–12.

Risse-Kappen, T. (ed.) (1995) *Bringing Transnational Relations Back In*, Cambridge: Cambridge University Press.

Roberts, R. (1991) 'The city of London as a financial centre in the era of the depression, the Second World War, and post-war official controls', in A. Gorst, L. Johnman and W. Scott Lucas (eds) *Contemporary British History 1931–1961: Politics and the Limits of Policy*, London: Pinter.

—— (1995) 'The Bank of England and the city', in R. Roberts and D. Kynaston (eds) *The Bank of England: Money, Power and Influence, 1694–1994*, Oxford: Oxford University Press.

Roberts, S.M. (1994) 'Fictitious capital, fictitious spaces: the geography of offshore financial flows', in S. Corbridge, R. Martin and N. Thrift (eds) *Money, Power and Space*, Oxford and Cambridge, MA: Blackwell.

—— (1998) 'Geo-governance in trade and finance and political geographies of dissent', in A. Herod, G. O'Tuathail and S.M. Roberts (eds) *Unruly World? Globalization, Governance and Geography*, London: Routledge.

Rosenau, J.N. (1992) 'Governance, order, and change in world politics', in J.N. Rosenau and E.-O. Czempiel (eds) *Governance Without Government: Order and Change in World Politics*, Cambridge: Cambridge University Press.

Rosow, S.J. (1994) 'On the political theory of political economy: conceptual ambiguity and the global economy', *Review of International Political Economy* 1, 3: 465–88.

Ruggie, J.G. (1982) 'International regimes, transactions, and change: embedded liberalism in the postwar economic order', *International Organisation* 36, 2: 379–416.

—— (1985) 'Continuity and transformation in the world polity: toward a neorealist synthesis', in R.O. Keohane (ed.) *Neorealism and its Critics*, New York: Columbia University Press.

—— (1993) 'Multilateralism: anatomy of an institution', in J.G. Ruggie (ed.) *Multilateralism Matters: The Theory and Praxis of an Institutional Form*, New York: Columbia University Press.

Ruigrok, W. and van Tulder, R. (1995) *The Logic of International Restructuring*, London: Routledge.

Rupert, M.E. (1995) *Producing Hegemony: The Politics of Mass Production and American Global Power*, Cambridge: Cambridge University Press.

Saber, N. (1999) *Speculative Capital: The Invisible Hand of Global Finance*, London: Pearson Education Ltd.

Sally, R. (1994) 'Multinational enterprises, political economy and institutional theory: domestic embeddedness in the context of internationalization', *Review of International Political Economy* 1, 1: 161–92.

Sassen, S. (1991) *The Global City: New York, London, Tokyo*, Princeton, NJ: Princeton University Press.

—— (1999) 'Global financial centres', *Foreign Affairs* 78, 1: 75–87.

Schmidt, R. (2000) 'A feasible foreign exchange transactions tax', in W. Bello, N. Bullard and K. Malhotra (eds) *Global Finance: New Thinking on Regulating Speculative Capital Markets*, London and New York: Zed Books.

Scholte, J.A. (1993) 'From power politics to social change: an alternative focus for international studies', *Review of International Studies* 19, 1: 3–21.

—— (2000) *Globalization: A Critical Introduction*, Basingstoke and New York: Palgrave.

Schumacher, E.F. (1973) *Small is Beautiful: Economics as if People Mattered*, New York: Harper & Row.

Seyfang, G. (2000) 'The euro, the pound and the shell in our pockets', *New Political Economy* 5, 2: 227–46.

Shefter, M. (ed.) (1993) *Capital of the American Century: The National and International Influence of New York City*, New York: Russell Sage Foundation.

Shutt, H. (1998) *The Trouble with Capitalism: An Enquiry into the Causes of Global Economic Failure*, London: Zed Books.

Simonsen, K. (1996) 'What kind of space in what kind of social theory?', *Progress in Human Geography* 20, 4: 494–512.

Sinclair, T.J. (1994a) 'Passing judgement: credit rating processes as regulatory mechanisms of governance in the emerging world order', *Review of International Political Economy* 1, 1: 133–59.

—— (1994b) 'Between state and market: hegemony and institutions of collective action under conditions of international capital mobility', *Policy Sciences* 27, 4: 447–66.

—— (1996) 'Beyond international relations theory: Robert W. Cox and approaches to world order', in R.W. Cox with T.J. Sinclair (eds) *Approaches to World Order*, Cambridge: Cambridge University Press.

—— (1999) 'Synchronic global governance and the international political economy of the commonplace', in M. Hewson and T.J. Sinclair (eds) *Approaches to Global Governance Theory*, New York: SUNY.

Smith, A.D. (1992) *International Financial Markets: The Performance of Britain and its Rivals*, Cambridge: Cambridge University Press.

Smith, R.C. (1989) 'International stock market transactions', in T. Noyelle (ed.) *New York's Financial Markets: The Challenges of Globalization*, Boulder, CO and London: Westview Press.

Smith, S. (1996) 'Positivism and beyond', in S. Smith, K. Booth and M. Zalewski (eds) *International Theory: Positivism and Beyond*, Cambridge: Cambridge University Press.

Smith, W.D. (1984) 'The function of commercial centres in the modernization of European capitalism: Amsterdam as an information exchange in the seventeenth century', *Journal of Economic History* 44: 985–1005.

Snidal, D. (1985) 'The limits of hegemonic stability theory', *International Organization* 39, 3: 579–614.

Soros, G. (1998) *The Crisis of Global Capitalism: Open Society Endangered*, London: Little, Brown and Company.

Spero, J.E. (1977) *The Politics of International Economic Relations*, London: Allen & Unwin.

Stafford, L. (1992) 'London's financial markets: perspectives and prospects', in L. Budd and S. Whimster (eds) *Global Finance and Urban Living: A Study of Metropolitan Change*, London: Routledge.

Stanford, M. (1994) *A Companion to the Study of History*, Oxford: Blackwell.

Storper, M. and Walker, R. (1989) *The Capitalist Imperative: Territory, Technology, and Industrial Growth*, Oxford: Blackwell.

Story, J. (1997) 'Globalisation, the European Union and German financial reform: the political economy of "Finanzplatz Deutschland"', in G.R.D. Underhill (ed.) *The New World Order in International Finance*, Basingstoke: Macmillan.

Story, J. and Walter, I. (1997) *Political Economy of Financial Integration in Europe. The Battle of the Systems*, Manchester: Manchester University Press.

Strange, S. (1970) 'International economics and international relations: a case of mutual neglect', *International Affairs* 46, 2: 304–15.

—— (1976) *International Economic Relations of the Western World 1959–1971, Vol. 2: International Monetary Relations*, London: Oxford University Press.

—— (1982) 'Still an extraordinary power: America's role in the global monetary system', in R. Lomra and B. Witte (eds) *The Political Economy of International and Domestic Monetary Relations*, Ames, IA: Iowa State University Press.

—— (ed.) (1984) *Paths to International Political Economy*, London: George Allen & Unwin.

—— (1986) *Casino Capitalism*, Oxford: Blackwell.

—— (1988) *States and Markets*, London: Pinter.

—— (1990) 'Finance, information and power', *Review of International Studies* 16, 2: 259–74.

—— (1994) 'From Bretton Woods to the casino economy', in S. Corbridge, R. Martin and N. Thrift (eds) *Money, Power and Space*, Oxford: Blackwell.

—— (1996) *The Retreat of the State: The Diffusion of Power in the World Economy*, Cambridge: Cambridge University Press.

—— (1998a) *Mad Money*, Manchester: Manchester University Press.

—— (1998b) 'The new world of debt', *New Left Review* 230: 91–114.

Suzuki, Y. (1992) 'Japan's growing role as an international financial centre', in C. McKenzie and M. Stutchbury (eds) *Japanese Financial Markets and the Role of the Yen*, Sydney: Allen & Unwin.

Taggart Murphy, R. (1996) *The Real Price of Japanese Money*, London: Weidenfeld & Nicolson.

Talani, L. (2000) 'Who wins and who loses in the city of London from the establishment of European Monetary Union', in C. Crouch (ed.) *After the Euro: Shaping Institutions of Governance in the Wake of European Monetary Union*, Oxford: Oxford University Press.

Taylor, P.J. (1995) 'World cities and territorial states: the rise and fall of their mutuality', in P.L. Knox and P.J. Taylor (eds) *World Cities in a World-System*, Cambridge: Cambridge University Press.

Thrift, N. (1994) 'On the social and cultural determinants of international financial centres: the case of the city of London', in S. Corbridge, R. Martin and N. Thrift (eds) *Money, Power and Space*, Oxford: Blackwell.

—— (1999) 'Moral geographies of money', in E. Gilbert and E. Helleiner (eds) *Nation-States and Money: The Past, Present and Future of National Currencies*, London and New York: Routledge/RIPE Series in Global Political Economy.

Thurow, L. (1992) *Head to Head: The Coming Economic Battle Among Japan, Europe and America*, New York: Morrow.

Tickner, J.A. (1991) 'On the fringes of the world economy: a feminist perspective', in C.N. Murphy and R. Tooze (eds) *The New International Political Economy*, Boulder, CO: Lynne Rienner.

Tilly, C. (1990) *Coercion, Capital, and the European States,* AD *900–1990*, Oxford: Blackwell.

Tobin, J. (1978) 'A proposal for international monetary reform', *The Eastern Economic Journal* 4, 3–4: 153–9.

Tooze, R. (1984) 'Perspectives and theory: a consumers' guide', in S. Strange (ed.) *Paths to International Political Economy*, London: George Allen & Unwin.

Tooze, R. and Murphy, C.N. (1996) 'The epistemology of poverty and the poverty of epistemology in IPE: mystery, blindness, and invisibility', *Millennium: Journal of International Studies* 25, 3: 681–707.

Triffin, R. (1960) *Gold and the Dollar Crisis: The Future of Convertibility*, New Haven, CT: Yale University Press.

Tsoukalis, L. (1997) *The New European Economy Revisited*, Oxford: Oxford University Press.

Underhill, G.R.D. (1991) 'Markets beyond politics? The state and the internationalization of financial markets', *European Journal of Political Research* 19, 2: 197–225.

—— (1993) 'Negotiating financial openness: the Uruguay Round and trade in financial services', in P.G. Cerny (ed.) *Finance and World Politics: Markets, Regimes and States in the Post-Hegemonic Era*, Aldershot: Edward Elgar.

—— (1997a) 'Introduction', in G.R.D. Underhill (ed.) *The New World Order in International Finance*, Basingstoke: Macmillan.

—— (1997b) 'Private markets and public responsibility in a global system: conflict and co-operation in transnational banking and securities regulation', in G.R.D. Underhill (ed.) *The New World Order in International Finance*, Basingstoke: Macmillan.

—— (1997c) 'The making of the European financial area: global market integration and the EU single market for financial services', in G.R.D. Underhill (ed.) *The New World Order in International Finance*, Basingstoke: Macmillan.

—— (1997d) 'Conclusion', in G.R.D. Underhill (ed.) *The New World Order in International Finance*, Basingstoke: Macmillan.

—— (2000) 'Global money and the decline of state power', in T.C. Lawton, J.N. Rosenau and A.C. Verdun (eds) *Strange Power: Shaping the Parameters of International Relations and International Political Economy*, Aldershot and Vermont, VT: Ashgate.

Vipond, P.A. (1993) 'The European financial area in the 1990s: Europe and the transnationalization of finance', in P.G. Cerny (ed.) *Finance and World Politics: Markets, Regimes and States in the Post-Hegemonic Era*, Aldershot: Elgar.

Visser, W.A.M. and MacIntosh, A. (1998) 'A short review of the historical critique of usury', *Accounting, Business and Financial History* 8, 2: 175–89.

Vogel, D. (1993) 'New York city as a national and global financial center', in M. Shefter (ed.) *Capital of the American Century: The National and International Influence of New York City*, New York: Russell Sage Foundation.

Vogel, E. (1986) 'Pax Nipponica?', *Foreign Affairs* 64, 4: 752–67.

Vogel, S.K. (1996) *Freer Markets, More Rules: Regulatory Reform in Advanced Industrial Countries*, Ithaca, NY: Cornell University Press.

Wachtel, H.M. (1990) *The Money Mandarins: The Making of a Supranational Economic Order*, London: M.E. Sharpe.

Wade, R. and Veneroso, F. (1998) 'The Asian crisis: the high debt model versus the Wall Street-Treasury-IMF complex', *New Left Review* 228: 3–22.

Walker, R.J.B. (1993) *Inside/Outside: International Relations as Political Theory*, Cambridge: Cambridge University Press.

Wallerstein, I. (1974) *The Modern World-System*, New York: Academic.

—— (1980) *The Modern World-System, Part II: Mercantilism and the Consolidation of the European World Economy, 1600–1750*, New York: Academic.

Walter, A. (1993) *World Power and World Money: The Role of Hegemony and International Monetary Order*, Revised Edition, Hertfordshire: Harvester Wheatsheaf.

Waltz, K.N. (1979) *The Theory of International Politics*, Reading, MA: Addison-Wesley.

Warf, B. (1995) 'Telecommunications and the changing geographies of knowledge transmission in the late 20th century', *Urban Studies* 32: 361–78.

Warner, F. (1991) *Anglo-Japanese Financial Relations: A Golden Tide*, Oxford: Blackwell.

Watson, M. (1999) 'Rethinking capital mobility: re-regulating financial markets', *New Political Economy* 4, 1: 55–75.

Webb, M.C. (1995) *The Political Economy of Policy Co-ordination: International Adjustment Since 1945*, Ithaca, NY and London: Cornell University Press.

Weiss, T.G. (2000) 'Governance, good governance and global governance: conceptual and actual challenges', *Third World Quarterly* 21, 5: 795–814.

White, W.R. (2000) 'What have we learned from recent financial crises and policy responses?', *Bank of International Settlements Working Paper* No. 84, January, Basel: Bank of International Settlements.

Williams, C. (1996) 'The new barter economy', *Journal of Public Policy* 16, 1: 85–101.

Williams, D. (1963) 'London and the 1931 financial crisis', *Economic History Review* 15, 3: 513–28.

Williams, D. (1999) 'Constructing the economic space: the World Bank and the making of *Homo Oeconomicus*', *Millennium: Journal of International Studies* 28, 1: 79.

Wriston, W. (1988) 'Technology and sovereignty', *Foreign Affairs* 67, 1: 63–75.

Zuckerman, M. (1998) 'A second American century', *Foreign Affairs* 77, 3: 18–31.

Zysman, J. (1983) *Governments, Markets and Growth: Finance and the Politics of Industrial Change*, Ithaca, NY: Cornell University Press.

—— (1996) 'The myth of a "global" economy: enduring national foundations and emerging regional realities', *New Political Economy* 1, 2: 157–84.

Index